THE SERVICE OF GOD

THE SERVICE OF GOD
Christian Work and Worship

William H. Willimon

Illustrations by Bruce Sayre

ABINGDON PRESS/Nashville

THE SERVICE OF GOD: CHRISTIAN WORK AND WORSHIP

Copyright © 1983 by Abingdon Press

Library of Congress Cataloging in Publication Data

WILLIMON, WILLIAM H.
  The service of God.
  Includes index.
  1. Public worship.   2. Christian ethics—
Methodist authors.   I. Title.
BV15.W537   1983   264   82-16365

ISBN 0-687-38094-4

•

Proceeds from the sale of this book will be given to
ministerial education at Wofford College, Spartanburg,
South Carolina.

MANUFACTURED BY THE PARTHENON PRESS AT
NASHVILLE, TENNESSEE, UNITED STATES OF AMERICA

*For the People of God who worship
and work at Northside Church*

Phrases like Worship Service or Service of Worship are tautologies. To worship God means to serve him. Basically there are two ways to do it. One way is to do things for him that he needs to have done—run errands for him, carry messages for him, fight on his side, feed his lambs, and so on. The other way is to do things for him that you need to do—sing songs for him, create beautiful things for him, give things up for him, tell him what's on your mind and in your heart, in general rejoice in him and make a fool of yourself for him the way lovers have always made fools of themselves for the one they love.

Frederick Buechner

Contents

Preface

ᗡ‖ᘜ

During my seminary days of the late sixties—in those frenetic times of protest and social upheaval—I do not remember being overly concerned about worship. My most vivid memories center more around activities in the streets rather than activities in the seminary chapel.

How many sermons, on those rare occasions when we were in chapel, urged us to "get out there and do something"? How many times were we told, in popular books of the period, that the real life of the church was in the "world"? Theologians of the day heralded a "religionless Christianity" and urged us to let the "world set the agenda" for our Christian work.[1] "Teargas is the incense of real Christians," declared a young minister as he led a protest demonstration on the steps of the New Haven Courthouse.

Despite the "liturgical" character of these public gatherings where we sang hymns of protest, celebrated the symbols of radical change, or denigrated the symbols of the old order, dreamed dreams, and saw visions; the liturgy of the church seemed irrelevant to our activism.

Now nearly two decades later, older if not wiser, I question some of the slogans of my seminary days. In an uncertain time, in which the survival of the status quo takes precedence over involvement in social change, where Narcissus has replaced Prometheus as our idol, where much so-called social action has run out of steam and become little more than a bland parroting of whatever liberal values the culture considers adequate, I ponder what a rather tame, introverted, acculturated church can learn from a reconsideration of its worship. Wherewith can an otherwise bland and unsavory *ecclesia* be salted if not by new encounters with its God? Back to the sanctuary.

On the other hand, even as enrollment rises in my seminary worship courses and we Protestants who once knew not a chasuble from a cassock now wear them, I feel a nagging discomfort at the recent upsurge of interest in liturgical renewal. Is it back to the sanctuary to let the world fend for itself? Some feel that our future, far from being merely secular, may be hyper-religious. If so, the history of the church shows repeatedly that something is fundamentally amiss when *leitourgia* is without *diakonia*. This book asks: How are worship and work, liturgy and ethics, *leitourgia* and *diakonia* related?

A couple of years ago, in *Worship As Pastoral Care*, I examined worship as a significant context for pastoral care in the church. More recently, John Westerhoff and I attempted to delineate some of the practical aspects of looking at the liturgy as an educational experience.[*] Now I find myself invading yet another discipline, ethics; treading on someone else's turf in order to expand my understanding of Christian worship.

Such interdisciplinary work is risky. But my present situation has convinced me even more of its necessity. Over two years ago, I moved from seminary teaching back into the pastoral ministry. Here, in the day-to-day work of a pastor, in week-to-week leadership of this congregation in worship, I am reminded that any liturgical theology worth its salt must be interdisciplinary in order to see liturgy as people actually experience it.

This book was written, not only by engaging two theological disciplines (ethics and liturgics) but also by being a pastor. The book was conceived the only way pastors think about anything: in the day-to-day crush of the myriad of contemporary pastoral concerns—after a counseling session, before the board meeting, while the sermon is germinating, on the way to a hospital visit, while wondering with a teen-ager what he ought to do with his life, in evaluating what went wrong with last Sunday's worship.

This book may therefore be uneven in places, inconsistent at points, but I hope that it is faithful and somewhere breathes with the life of one who is present within the work and worship of a vibrant congregation.

Thanks to my students at Duke Divinity School, the 1981 Iliff Summer School, and the 1982 Wake Forest Pastors' School; to Dr. Stanley Hauerwas, Dr. Harmon Smith, and Dr. Richard Lischer, who reacted to this material while it was in progress; to Mrs. Margaret Ross, my secretary; to my family who makes everything worth risking; to my ministerial friends, especially those in the Greenville District of The United Methodist Church; and to Dr. James Gustafson who taught me ethics at Yale.

And thanks to the good folk of Northside Church who call me preacher and treat me like family. They probably will not read this book. But they helped write it.

William H. Willimon
Pentecost 1982

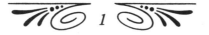

Work and Worship

*L*aborare est orare, "To work is to pray," said medieval monks. But this was not saying enough, for there is a difference between a Christian's prayer and a Christian's work. Both action in the world and worship in the sanctuary may be done by the same person for the same purpose, for "the glory of God," but we rarely do both at the same time.

In recent decades, those allegedly religionless Christians who claimed they need not pray or worship because "work is our prayer" might testify that without prayer one's work quickly falls short of the glory of God. On the other hand, church history is full of evidence that pious folk who think prayer is Christian work enough end with something less than full Christian discipleship.

Laborare est orare implies, not that a Christian ought either to work or to pray, but that worship and work are distinct and inseparable Christian activities.

This book asks: *Does Christian worship make any difference to Christian moral life?*

Many will agree that ethics relates to worship. Massey Shepherd speaks of "the one test by which all worship and prayer is laid under judgment, namely, the sense of mission that they evoke among the faithful."[1] This implies that mission, good works, moral activity are somehow the test, the validation, the critic of the liturgy.

On the other hand, some see worship as the source of our

ethics. The liturgy, according to the Second Vatican Council, is "the summit toward which the activity of the church is directed; at the same time it is the fountain from which all her power flows."[2]

While many have experienced this relationship in their own lives, few have studied the dynamics and shape of the relationship. That is my purpose here.

There are those who doubt a fruitful relationship exists between worship and ethics, all pious talk of *laborare est orare* notwithstanding. Daniel Berrigan flatly declares, "No one has been able to demonstrate that Christian worship leads, in any large or direct sense, to Christian conduct in the world."[3]

Those of us with Puritan roots may suspect that undue concern about sacraments, vestments, lace, and proper behavior inside the sanctuary indicates unconcern for the world outside. Or we expend our energies cultivating good feelings, beautiful surroundings, or noble sentiments in worship only to avoid the hard, grimy, sweaty, Christian work that needs doing in the world.

In a recent discussion in a small church, two women expressed their sentiments. When asked, "Why do you come to worship?" one replied, "I come to worship to be quiet, at peace, alone; to get rest and refuge from the problems that confront me in my everyday life."

"I disagree," said the other woman. "I come to worship only to get motivated to live a better life in the real world."

One saw worship as an escape from the world while the other saw worship as motivation for involvement in the world. Both agreed that, whatever happened in worship, it was not an integral part of life in the *real* "world."

I propose to speak here to both these perspectives in order to reestablish a more integral and fruitful relationship between worship in the sanctuary and ethical work in the world.

Definitions

First let me define what I mean by "worship" and "ethics." (1) By "worship" I mean all those formal and informal, written and unwritten, spontaneous and rigidly prescribed, high-church and low-church words and acts by which Christians meet and are met by God in intentional, corporate gatherings of the church. By defining worship in this manner I make clear that I am not advocating one style or form of public worship as more ethically formative than another. I want to draw from the richness of Christian worship practices—from the gorgeous processions of Eastern Orthodoxy, to the inner directed quiet of a Quaker Meeting, to the toe-tapping jubilation of a black Free Will Baptist hymn-sing—a multifarious, multidimensional, liturgical setting that is the context for all Christian life and work.

Because I am a United Methodist, I intend to do justice to both the catholic and free church traditions when I speak of worship, for we United Methodists have roots in both.

"Liturgy" when used here does not refer exclusively to the worship of so-called liturgical churches. All churches have rituals (i.e., patterned, predictable, public, purposeful worship behavior). All churches have a liturgical life that can be observed, defined, predicted, and that influences the moral life in important ways. There is a shape, a pattern, within every church's worship—even those Pentecostals who claim to be led exclusively by the promptings of the Spirit. There can be no completely informal worship in any human group which values communion, continuity, and cohesion. This is true particularly for the group which calls itself "church."

(2) "Ethics" is as rich a term as "liturgy," because both of these terms refer to a wide array of Christian activity and a multifaceted picture of Christian formation. Liturgics inquires, "What is 'right praise'?" (Greek: *(ortho-doxy)*. Ethics inquires, "What principles lead to right work?" Ethical questions surround all those decisions in which right or wrong is at stake, all those decisions in which the good is envisioned.

At times, ethics inquires into the nature of goodness. At other times it studies imperatives and motivation to do good. American Christian ethicists have generally been preoccupied with practical questions of good decisions and how to arrive at them. In recent years, many have turned their attention to the nature of the moral life; its formation, cultivation, and direction; the "ethos" from which ethics arises. Many of these ethicists say the real question is "Who ought I to be?" rather than "What ought I to do?" This book has drawn from these recent investigations. For example, how are ethically responsible Christians formed, cultivated, and given direction through their participation in worship?

"Ethics" here means a study of conscious and unconscious, subjective and objective, personal and institutional ways that form and re-form a responsible and responding Christian.

Work and Worship

The manner in which I speak of ethics and worship has its precedent in Scripture.

"Worship" not only refers to that which cultically happens at a certain time and place but also to the Christian's whole existence. The Hebrew *'Abad* ("to serve") is used for both work and worship. The life and work of Christ are referred to in the Fourth Gospel in terms of worship and mission (John 6:51, 57). Paul uses formerly cultic terms to apply to the whole Christian life, not merely gathering for the cult. The term *leitourgia* means literally "service" or "work" of "the people." This "work" is applied to everything from the duties of Zechariah in the temple (Luke 1:23), to the worship of Christ (Heb. 8:6), to the collection of money for missions (II Cor. 9:12), to prayer, even to Paul's death (Phil. 2:30).

Even the term *thusia* ("sacrifice") covers a wide array of ethical obedience (Rom. 12:1, Phil. 4:18). *Latreia* ("service") denotes action performed both in the cult and in daily life (Matt. 4:10). The line between liturgy and life is significantly blurred in the New Testament. The whole of a Christian's life is liturgical life.[4]

While warning against any reductionism that simply equates worship with service in the world, or work in the world with cultic work in the sanctuary, we must note at the outset the New Testament's constant linking of these two modes of a Christian's service. *Laborare est orare; orare est laborare.*

Then there is the question of authority. While worship may be a major experience for Christians, how can that experience be said to have an authoritative function in regard to Christian ethics? Protestantism began in a critical theological confrontation with existing liturgy. Protestants agree with Catholics that our doctrine, ethics, and worship should complement each other and express Christian truth; but Protestants have differed with Roman Catholics and among ourselves on which activity—doctrine, ethics, or worship—should be the norm for the rest and which is most prone to fall into error. But to affirm simply that worship, doctrine, and ethics ought to be complementary, reciprocal, mutually enriching is justification enough for their interplay in this book. Worship and ethics have the same Lord. When there is a disparity between them, something has gone wrong. According to I John, anyone who claims to love God (in worship?) and hates his or her neighbor (in the world?) is a liar.

An Overview

Here are some central questions:

What is the difference Christian worship does make, and ought to make, in the moral lives of members of the church?

How can the liturgy be a source for ethical thought?

How does liturgy criticize ethics?

How do ethics criticize liturgy?

How does the liturgy contribute to the development of a Christian's character or to decision-making and action?

How does the liturgy help prepare the church for its ethical role and criticize and support the church in its action?

Our examination will move from general assertions about the relationship between worship and ethics to specific examples of that relationship. In the next two chapters I reflect upon ethics and then worship. These are the most technical parts. Chapter 4 is an attempt to specify some of the ways in which worship does make and ought to make a difference in the moral lives of Christians.

By using Paul as an early example of a pastoral attempt to link liturgy and ethics, chapters 5 and 6 examine baptism and the Lord's Supper, noting how liturgy provides the context for ethics and how ethics is sometimes the chief critic of the liturgy. Another familiar act of worship, the sermon, is examined in chapter 7. Using the tools of philosophical ethics, principally linguistic analysis, the Service of Christian Marriage is discussed in chapter 8 as a source for ethical reflection about matrimony. Theological ethics is enlisted in chapter 9 to consider the place of children as defined in the service of marriage. Finally, we discuss the offering in Sunday worship as an act that summarizes all we have said about Christian worship and work.

I do not intend to be reductionistic about the nature of Christian moral life or worship. Nor do I mean to imply that we ought to *use* worship to make morally sensitive Christians. Whenever worship is *used* for any other purpose, even for our most worthy human purposes, it is being used for some other purpose than the glorification and enjoyment of God, and it is being abused. Worship *is* a moral activity. Like ethics, worship is response to what is good and right.

While Christians are busy serving God, they are also being served by God. While Christians are attempting to pray like God's people, they are being made into God's people. Christian doing and being is therefore a gracious by-product of Christian praying.

Likewise, while we are struggling with the complexities of what it means to act like God's people in the world, we are gathering the vision, the frustration, hope, hopelessness, questions, fatigue, and exhilaration out of which authentic Christian worship arises. *Laborare est orare; orare est laborare.* How this is so is the concern of the following pages.

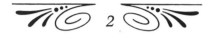

The Work of Ethics

The early fathers were fond of referring to Christian baptism and the Eucharist as "divinization." As we deal with these holy mysteries, the Holy deals with us; as we adore the Holy, we are surprised to find that we become holy.

In recent years there has been talk in liberal theological circles about "humanization" and the church as the context where people "become more human." The specific content of such humanization is often unclear. Albert Outler, in his *Psychotherapy and the Christian Message,* speaks of the ethical "ordering of life" as that which is distinctively human about us.

> Human life has this distinction: it is consciously and deliberately ordered toward its possibilities and ends by men themselves. There are all manner of hindrances and complications to this effort to shape life after a conscious pattern. The springs of action lie below the level of reason and deliberation. But the effort must still be made—because we are human . . . all that is distinctively human about our lives focuses in this mystery of self-involved decision about the right and the good.[1]

According to Outler, ethics is the distinctively human endeavor because it creates the necessary conditions whereby life is "consciously and deliberately ordered toward its possibilities and ends" by disciplined reflection on What ought I to do?

For many contemporary ethicists, human beings are mainly makers, deciders, and performers; those who, in Outler's words, "consciously and deliberately" order their own lives. This view of human beings as Promethean deciders and actors has its appeal. We enjoy thinking of ourselves as godlike creators. Curiously, this view of ethics has arisen during a period when—even as we gained increasing control over our destinies—wars, ecological disasters, famine, exploding population, and other realities remind us of our frightening limitations.

I shall argue for another view, one that sees ethics more concerned with Who ought I to *be?* than with What ought I *do?* Taking its cues from our liturgical life, ethics must not only account for what we do to make life human, but also what the Creator is doing to us and to our world to make us the creatures we are intended to be.

Our task is difficult because American theological ethics (between 1930 and 1965) has been dominated largely by practical, pragmatic, moral concerns of deciding and doing. When substantive issues have emerged, it has been as a result of practical interests, i.e., "What ought I to do in this dilemma?" When theoretical issues are pursued, it has been undertaken with the aid of the social, political, and natural sciences rather than the theological disciplines.[2] Because we have neglected the wider theoretical issues and the theological bases, much contemporary Christian ethics tends to be only vestigially Christian or a cultural commentary on the current consensus of behavior.

We will focus on how Christian worship influences Christian ethics, viewing such influence as a possible by-product of Christian worship rather than its purpose. Worship has an intrinsic value, regardless of any extrinsic effects. Worship is its own reward. Service of God and neighbor is what Christians do upon discovering that they have learned to love God.

The most that such theoretical investigation as this can do is to enlighten us in the nature of the moral life, or perhaps set things in proper perspective. Nevertheless, this is where truly Christian ethics begins: from an understanding of the nature of the moral life in general and a determination of the peculiar orientation of the Christian moral life in particular.[3]

I link worship and ethics because I am convinced (along with a number of contemporary Christian ethicists) there are some fundamental flaws in the way we do ethics. In order to describe the flaws, I will first set aside my specifically liturgical interests and attempt a brief survey of some major contemporary ethicists.

Contemporary Ethics

Christian ethics has tended to concern itself either with laws and principles that could be derived from the Christian faith and then applied to Christian life, or with a rather antinomian interpretation of how, to use Paul's words, "for freedom Christ has set us free" from laws and principles.

Roman Catholic moral law in many of its forms (before Vatican II) is an example of the former; contemporary Situation Ethics is an example of the latter.

Catholic moral theology was based on certain metaphysical and biblical assumptions, such as the adequacy of human reason or the orderliness of nature, from which fixed norms were derived. Casuistic reasoning then attempted to deduce specific implications for Christian morality when applied to difficult cases of conscience.

Moral theology of this sort, in the eyes of most Protestants, was at variance with much of the New Testament. There—barring such notable exceptions as the Epistle of James and perhaps the Gospel of Matthew—morality of code, rules, and principles seems antithetical to Christian freedom and obedience. Natural law, Protestants charged, took reason and nature more seriously than revelation. It domesticated God's will into a simplistic, legalistic system that failed to respect the sovereignty of divine command and the complexity of many ethical dilemmas.

Protestant theologians (except for Calvin) struggled to define a basis for Christian ethics other than natural law. Luther debated the difference between "law" and "gospel," attempting to discern what this meant for the Christian who is "a perfectly free lord of all, subject to none" and "a perfectly dutiful servant of all, subject to all."[4] While Calvin began with anthropology, his *Institutes* bases ethics on an affirmation of the otherness and greatness of God.[5]

Protestants agreed that any Christian ethical stance must be "biblical." But the nature of the Bible made determination of such ethics no simple matter.[6] How are Christians to be true to the concrete, ethical tradition of their Judeo Christian roots, to the radical freedom Christ gives them, and to the radical obedience discipleship demands?

A contemporary attempt to struggle with this radical freedom and obedience is Situation Ethics or contextualism. Joseph Fletcher, a popular spokesman for this viewpoint, stressed the necessity of approaching each moral dilemma, each situation, without prejudice or casuistically derived notions of what ought to be done. The only law to which a Christian must answer is the law of love. Self-giving *agape* is the Christian's only guiding principle. According to Fletcher, the duty of a Christian is not to discern and then to obey some code of behavior but rather to confront the claims of each situation, and decide on the basis of Christian love and freedom alone.[7]

Paul Lehmann agreed that one cannot decide, "What ought I to do?" apart from a consideration of the specific situation out of which the need for decision arises. Lehmann tried to specify a more dynamic base for ethics than Fletcher's reductionistic *agape*, so he spoke of the "humanizing" work of God in the world as the context for a Christian's decisions. When confronted with a decision, the responsible Christian asks, "What is God doing in the world to make and to keep life human?"[8] For Lehmann, Christians must not seek false security by looking for rules and principles, nor by heroically applying the law of love; we must look with "imaginative and behavioral sensitivity," with a "theonomous conscience" at what God is doing to "humanize" creation—then the Christian must act in conformity with God's humanizing activity.

Both Fletcher and Lehmann continue the traditional Protestant emphasis on the necessity of freedom to obey God's freely given commands—even if those commands are given in what appear, to our comprehension, to be ambiguous ways. Fletcher said that right and wrong depend upon the situation. In its extreme form, contextualism seems to deny any continuity between one command of God and the next, any continuity of grace, any real possibility of God's command coming through traditional, institutional, or social means.

The individual Christian is thus at the mercy of each new event, approaching each decision with lone, intentional ignorance. The present moment is everything. Courageous, autonomous (literally "self-law"), independent decision is the main test of morality.

Contextualism oversimplifies the moral life. Any meaningful ethical discussion is terminated since all appeals to tradition, to sacred values, to wider experience, even to biblical data are negated. Kind sensitivity replaces clear thinking. The free individual, acting in the present moment, in a value-neutral universe, is the final arbiter of ethical worth.[9] Questions of truth, right, and good are deferred in favor of a sort of well-intentioned openness. Little wonder that worship, an inherently conserving and conservative activity, a supremely social activity, has no place in the autonomous ethics of Fletcher or Lehmann.

At first glance, Lehmann appears to have the more ecclesial, social base for his ethics. Lehmann says the church is the starting point for ethics: the koinonia ("community") is called the "laboratory," the "bridgehead of maturity" where God's humanizing first, but not exclusively, takes place. By koinonia, Lehmann does not simply mean the empirical reality of the church as an institution. This would be too restrictive. He means that sometimes less-than-visible body of Christians who are the custodians of "the secret of the maturity of humanity." The terms Lehmann uses are abstract, unspecific, and vague enough to include actions done to and by, not only Christians, but also undefined persons in the world who act in accord with God's humanizing work.[10] Because *koinonia* and "humanization" appear to be used with such intentional vagueness, one wonders if the Christian moral life has any discernible pattern or content at all.

Lehmann's context for Christian ethics remains unspecified—to define it more clearly would risk foreclosure of God's free and transcendent power to command anew in each situation. Contextualism thus forecloses rational ethical discourse and transforms the moral life from a continuous, coherent, social experience to a personal, psychological event.

Both the advocates of norms and the advocates of contextualism are amiss in dislocating the moral self from the forces that make it a discernible self in the first place. Both those who advocate rigid adherence to principles[11] and those who advocate rigid attentiveness to the situation polarize the moral life into an either/or matter of simple adherence to norms or to situations when, in reality, the moral enterprise is more complex and dynamic than either the contextualists or the defenders of norms indicate.[12]

The contextualists view the moral self, not as an end-product of a social and historical process, but rather as a generously endowed, amazingly trustworthy, radically free, discontinuous, and autonomous maker of decisions. I am Christian only as I decide anew in each situaion. This view has been shared, in various forms, by many Protestant theologians and ethicists. Since its beginning, Protestantism has been the religion of conversion, fresh beginning, anti-institution and anti-tradition. The sermon was thus the supremely Protestant liturgical activity—the Word spoken afresh, today, bringing the divine imperative to bear on this situation; the word heard afresh by the individual Christian who decides how to respond to the Word in his or her specific context.

Karl Barth saw the Christian as one who is placed in a new position of command-obedience in which God and humanity are in dialogue, a speaking and hearing in which we are to approach each decision in humility and openness, humbly awaiting the command of God rather than presumptuously calculating what course of action is most reasonable or workable. The ethics of reason, Barth believed, is invariably more interested in finding reasons to justify what we think we ought to do than in what God commands. This is why Barth says somewhere, "Ethics is sin."[13]

Other Protestant theologians (e.g., Tillich and Bultmann) drew upon existentialism, accentuating the free individual and the individual's free, heroic, and courageous decisions as the chief concerns of ethics: "The man of faith is free for love, which opens his eyes to what God requires of him in the moment,"[14] says Bultmann.

The value of the Protestant ethics of command is that it stresses the otherness of God and the total freedom of God's grace. In this perspective, the task of ethics is not to determine or to mediate the good—only God is good. If we know the good, it is only by the grace of God who graciously wills that we should hear the divine command and follow.

The principal weakness of the metaphor of command-obedience, in the ethics of theologians like Barth and Bultmann, is that it forecloses an adequate appreciation of the larger framework of ethical experience—the long-term, communal formation of the moral self. In spite of Barth's criticism of Bultmann's "Lutheranism," the same criticism can be leveled at the ethics of Barth. Sanctification is neglected in an over-stress of justification. Any positive assessment of the roles of institutions, socialization, experience, and tradition in the moral life is prevented by the command-obedience metaphor. Its view of the self is one of passivity and autonomy. Its view of divine revelation is occasionalistic, *ad hoc,* and detached. Understandably, Barth distrusted liturgy as much as ethics. Both liturgy and ethics have a way of offering false security. As for Bultmann, he was high on preaching—the Word spoken anew in the decisive present—but he was either apathetic or derisive toward the sacraments. These mystical vestiges obscured the decisive command of God.

By conceiving the moral life around the central homiletical metaphor of divine command and human obedience, Protestant ethics neglected the Christian's growth and sanctification. In this view, the purpose of the moral life was not divinization, maturity, and depth of the moral self but rather an intentional ignorance, a repeated readiness to hear and obey freely each new command in each new situation.

A number of ethicists have attempted to counter this simplistic emphasis on individualistic, intuitive, command-obedience, situations versus principles, and preoccupation with choice and decision. James Gustafson and his student, Stanley Hauerwas, have urged ethics to be more attentive to the long-term formation of the moral self and to the role of the community in that formation. I feel that this concept of ethics provides the best opportunity for viewing worship and ethics as mutually enriching activities.

Community and Character in Ethics

Aristotle first noted that ethics is not simply a matter of correct opinions or philosophical distinctions. People do not become good simply by holding correct opinions. "The soul of the listener must have been conditioned by habits to the right kinds of likes and dislikes, just as land must be cultivated before it is able to foster seed.[15] *Character* is that disposition of the moral self acquired through gradual growth and a host of forces and influences acting upon the self, as well as directions shaped by the self in its affections and actions.

Most people have character—they can be counted upon to act in similar ways in similar circumstances. "That's just what I would have expected her to do," is affirmation that the person is a coherent, identifiable self who can be expected to behave in certain ways because of the nature of the self. Character is our basic moral orientation that gives unity, definition, and direction to our lives by forming our habits and intentions into meaningful and predictable patterns that have been determined by our dominant convictions. Character is the cumulative result of a person's moral environment, history, choices, and affections.

Unlike the relativism of existential, contextual, and situational ethics or the fixed, abstracted ethics of Natural Law, the ethics of character takes seriously the dynamics of the moral formation of a person.[16] While not denying that our principles and our decisions are important, it is impressed that so many of the "ethical" things we do or avoid doing arise, not out of specific moral precepts or out of agonized decisions, but simply out of habit. It sees decisions as important, not only for their origins and results, but also for what they are doing to the person who is deciding and what they tell us about who that person is.[17]

Christian character is formed in a myriad of conscious and unconscious ways.

1. *Character is formed in a social matrix, a community.* In spite of what the situationalists and existentialists say, we do not come to ethical decisions as autonomous, lone, exclusively rational, or exclusively intuitive free agents. We come to our ethical dilemmas with a history that is more social than psychological, out of an ethical community, a *Sittlich keit,* as Hegel called it. Consideration of Christian ethics apart from the Christian community that forms (or malforms!) those ethics artificially abstracts and detaches the moral self. Modern psychology and sociology remind us that our ethics is part and parcel of living within a social framework.[18] We learn ethics as we learn language, as incidental to learning how to live in this place with this people. "Social ethics" is a tautology—all ethics arise out of and occur in some ethos, some interaction between persons that requires ethics in the first place.

John Wesley asserted "Christianity is essentially a social religion . . . to turn it into a solitary religion, is indeed to destroy it."[19] The church is, in James Nelson's words, the "moral nexus" wherein a Christian's moral life is formed for the living of this essentially social religion.

> Moral life is responsive life. It is life lived in response to other beings under God. Because relationships (not ideals or norms)

are the primary "stuff" of ethics, we must inquire into the meaning of a person's moral communities to him, particularly the meaning of the church to the Christian.[20]

Socialization, in the church or anywhere else, insures that a person will grow into society as a functioning member. It is a powerful factor, which—even though we may be unaware of its workings—is often difficult to resist. The activism of the sixties that expressed contempt for the "system" and the do-your-own-thing Narcissism of the seventies were ironic proof that we had been socialized by the American system's values of freedom, individualism, autonomy, and self-reliance. *Homo ethicus* is *homo socius*.

Situationalist and existentialist ethics see socialization as a mostly negative influence on the Christian. They define ethics as that enterprise which helps us rise above, or act in spite of our social, communal context. This negative view of the social matrix has its roots in Kant who sought to raise morality above the level of social convention and particular communities.

Kant failed to see that our moral ideas arise from the shared life within a particular community. The lone individual (if such a creature could really exist) lacks the moral equipment, the skills of discernment, and the coherent convictions to be moral. Our moral lives are cumulative. The "command of God," in which Barth posits so much value, is not always a crisis intrusion into human life. The divine command is more often a divine leading that arises out of quantitative human experience. We do not escape from human experience into some a-social realm where good and right can be known apart from life together. The autonomous character of many modern ethical systems is in part the culmination of a continuing problem throughout the history of Protestant worship and ethics: autonomous, subjectivized, privatized, individualized religion. Where religion is preoccupied with the individual's lonely quest for salvation, its worship will seek private meetings with God, and its ethics will stress autonomy and self-sufficiency as the supreme virtues.

To be sure, we have many examples (Nazism, for instance) of the tyranny of society over individual moral conscience. Substituting "let your community be your guide" for "let your conscience be your guide" does not make morality. Any community that loses the habit of moral self-criticism is in grave danger. But this is true for individuals as well. Perhaps our preoccupation with ethics as autonomous, individualized endeavor is an attempt to avoid the tough task of communal self-criticism. In the Southern church in which I grew up, we always talked about purely personal morality. Talking about morality as a social phenomenon in a segregationist society would be too painful. Allowing others to judge my behavior is too risky. Little wonder that we attempt to make religion "a private affair."

True, one cannot assume that because one is in a community of faith one has that faith. As Barth noted somewhere, "Christians go to church to make their last stand against God." Socialization in the church is not a guarantee of radical confrontation with the faith. But neither are individualism and autonomy tests of obedience to the faith. When our personal faith is tested for its congruence with the Christian faith, it must be tested by criteria that are always ecclesial, historical, and communal rather than individual and private.[21]

The ethics of Barth, for instance, in their attempt to break through the egocentrism of existentialist ethics by a humble listening for the command of God, do not insure that even this listening is not an extension of the ego. While the ethics of character with their stress on a more ecclesial, communal context for a Christian's moral listening and action will not insure the defeat of egocentric, autonomous ethics, they offer a context where such development can begin, an accurate description of day-to-day moral experience, and a means of judging any claim that our choices are based upon specifically Christian convictions.[22]

With my Wesleyan heritage, I affirm the social, communal, relational, ecclesial context of the Christian moral life. The church is, in Gustafson's words, "the community of moral discourse." This affirms the sociological observation that identity and morality are group products and the theological judgment that God can and does work through the mundane groups and structures of life to bless us. It also raises the troubling question of which communities are true and which are not—a question our pluralistic, individualistic society would endlessly defer.

We are in the church because God has called us together. While we are together, the church becomes the primary locus of a Christian's moral formation.[29] No sanctification outside the church. No sustained, long-term, moral growth outside the context of a worshiping, witnessing, serving, biblical People of God and community of faith.

2. *Character is formed by lifelong cultivation of virtues.* Aristotle noted that it was too much to expect ordinary people (which I take to be most of us) to be good. About the most one could hope for in common folk was that we might develop good habits. By "virtue" I mean "habits" in much the way Aquinas uses the word. Those persisting tendencies, that "practical reason" which leads a person to act in a way that may be said to have intention, posture, and direction arising out of certain persisting dispositions. "That's just what I would have expected him to do," is an everyday observation of character. It would be "out of character" for him to do otherwise.

Contrary to certain modern pretensions, we do not arrive on the scene of a moral dilemma *de novo.* We come with dispositions. These dispositions are the stuff of which our character is made. Habits may be correlated with institutional loyalties, convictions, beliefs, perceptions. Observation of my actions will enable you to "characterize" the kind of person I am. If you watch what I do, you can tell whom I worship.

Even my emotions can be formed by habit. Jonathan Edwards said that the quality of one's faith is to be assessed by "the fixedness and strength of habit that is exercised in affection, whereby holy affection is habitual." Our religious affections, for Edwards, must be practiced, out of habit, until they become consistent, deep, and abiding motives for our life—else they are mere fickle, dangerously "enthus-siastic" commotions and little else.[24]

Virtue is an important, if recently neglected, aspect of moral existence. Like moral principles, the main value of virtue is not as a possession, but as a skill, a way of looking at life, a way of living, an instrument in the promotion of the good and in the formation of good people. Virtues are instrumental and relative to the moral functioning of a community and the need of the moral self to grow.[25] Unfortunately in our atomistic, autonomous, situationalist approach to ethics we have neglected these persisting tendencies and skills necessary for any human community to exist and for the moral self to be described as a *self* in the first place.

Habits are those actions a person can be counted on to do habitually, ritualistically. In our day-to-day lives, we do not agonize over most of our decisions. We are predisposed to behave in certain ways, we do things as "second nature," out of habit. These predispositions and habits are no less ethical because they are second nature to us. They are the fruit of the ethical life. They not only form a person in a particular way to be a certain kind of person, but they also continually point to the qualities of life valued and esteemed by the moral community and which members of the community wish to cultivate in themselves.

Most of us do not steal out of habit. We do not approach the issue of theft with great agony and deliberation. We simply react habitually. Most of us participate in the church's worship out of habit. Contrary to some traditional Protestant notions, our participation is no less sincere because it is habitual. We grow, not simply by our decisions, but also by doing something until it becomes part of us. Our everyday habits are as important as our rare heroic decisions.

To speak of habits (dispositions, persisting tendencies) and intentions (deliberately chosen and cultivated) is to speak contrary to the way Protestant situationalists and contextualists have spoken. Virtue implies long-term, habitual, and intentional effort on the part of the moral agent—discipline, ritual, continuity—all of which are suspect in today's church. Contrary to the advocates of principles and norms, an emphasis on virtue gives more attention to the practical problem of the morphology of the moral self. The moral question is not simply the pragmatic and utilitarian, *"What ought I to do?"* but also the more visionary, *"Who ought I to be?"*, the more affective question of Augustine and Edwards, *"With whom am I in love?"*

In the next chapter I hope to show how the discipline and ritual of the liturgy are an integral part of this formation and expression of Christian character and virtue.

3. *Christian character is formed, not only within a community, through habits and virtues formed in that community, but also by sharing the Christian vision. If you will tell me what you see, I can tell you who you are and how you will act.*[26]

Our perspective of reality is a major determinant of our behavior. A perspective helps us literally to "see through" (Latin: *per speco*) the tug and pull of the present and its demands to the future.[27] My moral self not only comes out of my past history or my present decisions but also out of my vision of my future. This vision gives me basic intentions, a purposive orientation, an object for my deepest affections, a fundamental direction for my life journey even though it does not define the specific steps along the way.

To speak of intentions as one of the results of vision is to view my moral self as an active self, a self which decides, moves toward goals, and sets a course of action. My self is not merely a predetermined product of my past or the sum of my institutional and social commitments. I am not merely an automatic reactor to external stimuli. I shape myself through my intentions, which arise out of what I value, out of my convictions about what is and what ought to be.[28] My intentions are, in Gustafson's words, the "beam of light" that marks the way into my future.[29]

The moral life is not merely a matter of deciding on the basis of either rules or situations what ought to be done. The moral life is woven from the way I learn to see and what I want to see in my world. The moralist is as much an artist as a decision-maker. Every time I decide on anything, I shape that particular situation, and I also shape myself. I either reinforce or weaken my habitual orientation and the sustained vision of life that make me who I am.[30]

To be a Christian means to learn to see the world in a certain way until, day by day, I become as I see. Adoration is part of my formation. Of course, insight cannot replace action. Seeing without doing is hardly morality. On the other hand, meaningful action cannot occur without some vision of the world. I cannot decide whether or not it is right to tell a lie in a given situation without some vision of what kind of world I want to live in and what kind of person I want to be. My vision of myself as a trustworthy, dependable, human being determines the appropriateness of my truthfulness.

The ethos[31] of a Christian includes norms and rules. It includes some ability to discern rationally and intuitively the complexities and contours of a given situation. I do not mean to deprecate the role of reason and the value of norms in my effort to highlight the aesthetic and the intuitive. Pure intuitivism is subjective and blind. Pure rationalism can be cold and abstract. Rules, concepts, applied reason are part of the moral matrix. The moral life also includes a more open and dynamic perspective, a posture, an angle of vision of the way things are and ought to be. This vision is never a merely subjective, intuitive matter. Each individual Christian is not forced to invent a new language to meet each new situation, or new symbols and metaphors with which to grasp the nature of reality. These gifts are part of the substantive vision of the Christian community. These gifts are given, to a great extent, within worship.

The ethics of character enables us to overcome some of the inadequacies in Protestant ethics of the past by paying more attention to formation of the moral self in its community and continuity. The moral self is social from start to finish—an inheritor of a past and an envisioner of a future. This view is both truer to moral experience and less presumptuous than the ethics of the contextualists. It is less presumptuous because it admits, at the beginning, that a Christian is shaped in response to his or her beliefs and the moral community that mediates those beliefs. We are finite beings who do not often perceive the will of God immediately and directly. We have habits, intentions, and visions which form our character—a character which is a lifelong human response to our perception of what God is doing and wants us to do and be in the world.

The ethics of character and community imbues the ethical task with a greater objectivity than the situationalists and radical contextualists allow. The moral life must be criticized and judged. Unless the self has overcome its finitude and self-deception, truthful criticism is impossible without the community of moral discourse.[32]

Current debate on ethical questions tends to be abstract and subjective because many ethicists are unwilling to specify the contours and landmarks of the communal context within which one makes decisions or to specify the dispositions and intentions that should be cultivated within the moral person. The images, stories, sacraments, and actions of our liturgical life give specificity to the Christian vision. Without such specificity, it is tempting for us to stop agonizing over what is right and true and settle for well-intentioned kindness, or decency in general, rather than Christian ethics in particular.

This book rests on the assumption that the development of Christian men and women who know the cost of discipleship and are willing to pay the price in their daily lives can come only from within a Christian community (church) that has confidence in the truth of its moral vision, undying affection for the God it worships, and is willing to embody that vision and affection without apology or embarrassment.[33] Life in the wider society can never foster the countercultural vision and virtue discipleship demands. The surrounding culture has its own secular visions that are seductive to those Christians who have neglected the development of Christian character and who are careless about whom they bow before.

The more contemporary Christians rely on the freedom of individual conscience rather than on traditional and institutional codes of behavior, the more important close attention to the formation of that conscience becomes. The more individual Christians immerse themselves in the cultural pluralism of modern American life, the more important it is for the church to see how its particular loyalties and values form Christians who are rightly shaped by specific loyalties and commitment.

In reading Philip Hallie's moving account of how the little village of Le Chambon protected its Jews from the Hallocaust, one is amazed at the courage of the villagers who daily risked death to shield the Jews from the Nazi terror. How could these ordinary, humble people risk everything for these strangers? What led them quietly but firmly to resist? What led them to forsake comfort, safety, patriotism, and legality in order to preserve the life of even one endangered Jew?

In subsequent interviews with survivors, in researching records of this quietly courageous people, Hallie comes to this conclusion: Week-in-week-out, every Sunday, the villagers entered the little Protestant Temple of Le Chambon to hear pastor Trocmé preach. Over the entrance to their church were inscribed the words Love One Another. Ethics, says Hallie, is not a matter of rules, skillful decision-making, heroic acts of choice, "ethics is only a matter of character."[34]

We do not worship God in order to become better people. Christians worship God simply because we are God's beloved ones. Christian worship is an intrinsic activity. But as we worship, something happens to us. The love we return in worship is, in turn, lovingly forming us for the better. The worship of the church—that predictable, patterned, public, purposeful behavior through which the church tells its Story as opposed to other stories, where God is named and praised and let loose in our lives, where the church rehearses and reminds itself of who it is and who it, by God's grace, is becoming—is a major context of moral formation.[35]

The Work of Worship

You park your car and make your way with others to the front door. Joe Smith stops to remind you that you are in charge of the church school lesson next Sunday. You make a note to yourself to start preparing earlier than last time. As you reach the front steps you take a moment to help old Miss Cooper.

The usher greets you with a handshake at the door, makes some remark about the weather today, thrusts a bulletin in your hand, and asks you if you have seen the pastor because he is looking for you.

You move through the narthex into the sanctuary. The organ prelude has begun, a soft background tune which you momentarily recognize as some hymn, but you don't remember the name. The music is accompaniment for the whispers of the gathering congregation.

You take a seat in the fourth pew from the front, the place where you always sit, smiling to Frank and Doris White who sit at the end of the pew where they always sit. You pull the hymnal from the rack in front of you, glancing down today's Order of Service, noting that they are singing a hymn that you do not know and that the creed has been moved to a different place in the service. The Parish Notices on the page opposite the Order of Service remind you that your monthly pledge for

THE WORK OF WORSHIP

the church budget is due, that more clothes are needed for the church's Clothes Closet for the needy, that the church's adopted refugee family needs a washing machine if anyone has one to offer.

A few minutes later the pastor enters, a man in a black robe with a red stole. The organ music ends and the pastor speaks: "But the hour is coming, and now is, when the true worshipers will worship the Father in spirit and truth, for such the Father seeks to worship him. God is spirit, and those who worship him must worship in spirit and truth."

A hymn is sung, "O for a Thousand Tongues to Sing." Then the congregation is enjoined to "confess our sin before God and one another."

The Prayer of Confession refers to those things we have done which we ought not to have done and those things which we ought to have done and have not done, declaring that "there is no health in us," a statement you notice for the first time.

"In the name of Jesus Christ, you are forgiven," declares the pastor, making the sign of the cross over the kneeling congregation. Your knees crack a bit as you struggle to your feet to sing the Gloria Patri.

An anthem is then sung, an arrangement of the hymn, "Breathe on Me, Breath of God," a petition for God's Spirit to work "Until my heart is pure, Until with thee I will one will, To do and to endure."

After the anthem, there is a responsive reading of one of the psalms, the congregation sings a response at the end, and the scripture lessons are then read. The lessons are for the Sunday after Pentecost, each of them treats some aspect of the work of the Holy Spirit, though you can't be sure what the exact point of the Epistle is.

The preacher has about a twenty-minute sermon in which he speaks of the "fruits of the Spirit" in the early church and in the church today. The sermon ends with the congregation being

urged to "look for the workings of the Spirit in your own life
and in the life of this church." You think about that, not
altogether sure what specifically the pastor may be referring to,
but you do believe you have felt something working within you
during this hour, whether it be the Holy Spirit or not, you
can't say for sure.

After the sermon the minister leads the congregation in the
Apostles' Creed and then says, "As a forgiven and reconciled
people let us offer ourselves and our gifts to God." Ushers
come forward and the offering plates are passed down each
aisle. You put in your check. The plates are then brought
forward by the ushers as the congregation sings the Doxology.

The minister offers a short closing prayer, pronounces a
benediction, the congregation sings a closing hymn, and the
minister greets people as they pass out the door. You shake
hands with him and with a dozen or so of your fellow
worshipers. You go out and are soon on your way home.

It is difficult to specify how participation in this
experience affects the character of the participant. Most
Christians hope that participation in Sunday worship has
some beneficial effect, but this would be difficult to prove in
an empirical way. Over the years, segments of the church
have held that worship is edifying in therapeutic, emotional,
moral, aesthetic, and a host of other ways. Pius X opened his
1903 encyclical on worship reform by stating that Christian
worship has a two-dimensional purpose: "the glorification
of God and the sanctification and edification of the
faithful."[1]

Archbishop Temple spoke of the ethical fruits of worship
in glowing terms, "To worship is to quicken the conscience
by the holiness of God, to feed the mind with the truth of
God, to purge the imagination by the beauty of God, to open
the heart to the love of God, to devote the will to the purpose
of God."[2]

After his revival in Kingswood, John Wesley noted a great
reduction in drunkenness, whoring, and other vices. His
cause-effect relationship between religious revival and

public morals is surely possible. But is it probable? Can liturgical participation really affect a person's moral life?

Preliminary Qualifications

There is not a necessary correlation. St. Paul, as well as the author of James, long ago noted that not everyone who cries "Lord, Lord" in the sanctuary does the Lord's will in the world. How often the Old Testament prophets decried the degeneration of worship into an escape from morality.

> What to me is the multitude of your sacrifices?
>   says the Lord, . . .
> Bring no more vain offerings;
>   incense is an abomination to me. . . .
>   I cannot endure iniquity and
>   solemn assembly.
> Wash yourselves; make yourselves clean;
>   remove the evil of your doings
>   from before my eyes!
> cease to do evil,
>   learn to do good!
> seek justice,
>   correct oppression;
> defend the fatherless,
>   plead for the widow.

Isa. 1:11a, 13a, 16, 17 (See also Amos 5:21-24)

Paul Hoon, in speaking of the "frightening gulf between the Church's worship and the ethical witness of her people in the world," laments that "The powerlessness of worship to transform life is appalling."[3]

To be sure, worship can be used as a narcotic trip into another world to escape the ethical responsibilities of living a Christian life in this world. Religious rituals easily lend themselves to corruption. Most biblical scholars agree that the prophetic criticism of the cult was not an attack on sacrificial worship as such, but rather upon sacrificial worship that found no expression in social righteousness.

The prophets remind us that our rituals can become a retreat from reality, crude attempts to compensate for our moral misdeeds through cultic deeds, and a means of avoiding the ethical cost of discipleship through the ersatz discipleship of the cult. The essence of idolatry is the easy certainty that our rituals and cultic institutions are the sole custodians of what is right and righteous.[4] Karl Barth deprecated our "religion" as a culture-bound, sinful attempt at self-salvation through self-appointed means.[5]

But surely this is an abuse rather than an inherent part of worship. *Any* aspect of the church's life—scripture, polity, theology, even our good works, as Paul so aptly noted—can be twisted into the service of human sinfulness. The church's worship is not immune from such abuse.

While worship is not an escape from ethics, neither is worship the mere servant of ethics. Like art *(Ars gratia ars)*, worship is its own reward. To *use* the church's worship for any human purpose other than the glorification of God, is to abuse it. Worship loses its integrity when it is regarded instrumentally as a means to something else—even as a means of achieving the most noble of human purposes, even the noble purpose of moral edification. *Leitourgia* must be celebrated for its own sake, not simply as a means of rallying the faithful for *diakonia*. Worship must not be one more "resource" in our pastoral bag of tricks for getting people to be more just or more loving or more anything else.

Utilitarianism, the persistent temptation in American ethics, remains the greatest temptation in American Christian worship as well. Whether it be the old-time tent revivalist who sees worship as "preliminaries" to soften up hardshell sinners for a walk down the sawdust trail or the new social activist using worship as a pep rally to motivate enculturated racists or sexists to "get out into the world and do something," such worship is a human-centered, human-orchestrated perversion of what is meant to be a divine-centered activity. However, it is true that while we worship God, we are also being formed into God's people. While we are attempting to see God, we are acquiring, as a kind of by-product, a vision of who we are and who we are meant to be. This was what Pius X meant. As we worship for "the glorification of God," we are also receiving and participating in the "sanctification and edification of the faithful."

The Effects of Ritual upon Ethics

Ritual (patterned, purposeful, predictable, public behavior) is an integral part of all public worship. Ritual is a part of worship whether it be a Roman Catholic Pontifical Mass or a Holy Roller meeting. Human beings in groups—particularly groups that deal with potentially threatening aspects of life such as birth, death, sex, and God—do things in prescribed, patterned ways. While the primary purpose of these rituals is to praise, to placate, open oneself to God in the midst of life, rituals also have human consequences. At the risk of violating my own interpretive principle and conceiving of our liturgies in utilitarian fashion, it may be helpful to review their sociological/anthropological function. How might the rites and rituals of Christian worship positively affect Christian moral development?

Anthropologist, Edward Norbeck, has noted two types of rituals in so-called primitive societies that have counterparts in the rites of Christendom.[6] These are *crisis rites* that occur during important times in the community (birth, death, puberty, war, famine) and *cyclic rites* that are periodically repeated for the maintenance of group life (regular cultic gatherings, memorial days, feast days).

(1) Ritual is "a complex act of self-protection from destructive, unintelligible, and immoral forces."[7] *Crisis rites* provide a patterned, predictable way of coping by focusing our attention upon norms, beliefs, and sentiments derived from those visions and values the community holds dear.

Any significant transition in life provokes an identity crisis in the person or group experiencing the transition. When faced with the limits of life, the "limnal" situations (death, birth, sickness, marriage),[8] we are required to move from one state of existence to another, shedding one identity for another. The crisis of transition threatens to overwhelm us. Crisis rites help us cope by giving us the knowledge, skills, and vision needed to negotiate the journey from one state of being to another.

For instance, marriage is the crisis in which two people make the passage from being single to being married. The wedding itself is the rite in which the couple says to each other, in the presence of "God and these witnesses," that their love for each other is appropriate in the sight of God and this company, that the values they affirm are shared by this community, that their marriage is sanctioned and confirmed by the community of faith. All that talk about fidelity, "forsaking all others," "for better or worse," and "until death us do part" is an attempt by the Christian community to say what it believes at the time of marriage. The Service of Holy Matrimony is the church saying, "These are the things we want you to say and do in order to be married."

Similar observations could be made about other Christian crisis rites such as the funeral, baptism, penance, or ordination. If you want to know what a given community officially believes about these changes and crises in peoples' lives, you must look at what is said and done in these rites. The content of such rites—both verbal and symbolic—is an ethical statement about what the community considers appropriate behavior for those going through this change in status. In this way liturgy is a source for ethics. It tells us how we are expected to behave.

Rites of crisis not only provide ethical clues for those individuals who are currently experiencing the acute crisis of death or marriage or birth or other role changes; they are important for everyone in the community. Every time I attend a wedding, even though it is not my own wedding, I continue to live out the significance of my own marriage. Witnessing someone else's marital commitments may lead me to renewed commitment in my own marriage. The educational, formative value of these rituals continue long after the immediate, acute crisis of my own change has passed. Thus the church insists that a service of worship like a funeral or a wedding is not a private affair for the grieving family or the bride and groom. Every service of worship is for the whole church—those who are preparing for, or who are continuing to struggle with, the long-term implications of such transitions.

(2) *Cyclic rites* are periodically repeated for the maintenance of the group. They provide both the sustenance for and the judgment of the group's myth upon itself. Christmas, Easter, and Pentecost are examples of cyclic rites within the church. At such times we tell the Story again, passing it on to our young, confirming who we are by telling where we have been, rehearsing and reenacting the truth we affirm. We thus set limits on our comunity, define outsiders from insiders, and judge the adequacy of the community's present living out of its vision.

Each Sunday's worship is a kind of cyclic rite, a time to gather and be reminded of who we are. Without these regular, sustaining gatherings, a community quickly loses its identity, breaks apart into subgroups and cliques, confuses its Story with other stories, and fails to integrate sufficiently its young or its initiates into its life together.

Inattention to the community's particular myth and ritual is one of the first signals of community disintegration. Part of that disintegration is due to a breakdown of the ethical structures and standards members have a right to expect from their group because without these no one knows what is expected or how to act.

Anthropologists note that, beyond their educative and preservative functions, both crisis rites and cyclic rites provide a supportive setting from which we may venture forth into new modes of behavior.

Erik Erikson has studied the common adaptive significance of children's play and adult rituals.[9] Like the child's playpen, adult religious ritual provides a place apart from the daily social progression and the predictable world-as-it-is. Here we can envision a new world. All good worship has a shockingly gratuitous character: We do it for the fun of it. In play or in ritual we literally make believe the world looks different than it appears in the ordinary humdrum pace of things. Children dress up and make believe they are adults as they are becoming adults. We

THE SERVICE OF GOD

make love as we are falling in love. Christians dress up and make believe they are truly brothers and sisters, courageous saints, obedient disciples as they are becoming Christians. In this way, ritual moves from its stabilizing function to its subverting function: Ritual not only helps protect the existing order but also helps us envision a new order.

As I have noted:

> Many of our religious rituals are cast between the tension of a world in process and the fixed, certain world that is. A ritual can only be helpful to us as it maintains a healthy balance between these two poles. It is thus a servant of human adaptability to an often threateningly ambiguous world. It helps us encounter a new world without fully owning that world, a new selfhood without fully relinquishing our old self. Out of such experimental, playful, ritualized encounters comes the opportunity for creative adaptation and growth.[10]

The analogy between play-acting and ritual has important ethical consequences. These playful rituals help us get the feel of a proposed course of action.

> Before they go out to hunt dangerous animals, many tribes have a ceremony of incantation, and it commonly includes some hunting actions. . . . What can be their purpose? They are said to give the hunters courage. But it would be truer to say that they give them the feel of the hunt: they make the Pygmy hunters at home with the pursuit, and take them into coming turns and surprises with the sense of action already in their muscles.[11]

Analogously, we "learn" what it means to be married by watching other people getting married and then going through marriage ourselves. We get the feel of it, we learn the moves and the words needed in order for "God to bless your marriage and sustain your home in peace."

John Dewey called ethics the "imaginative rehearsal of various courses of conduct" that occurs in our minds when we think ethically about some action. In such moments we playfully envision consequences and possibilities. Such deliberation, says Dewey, is dramatic, active, and playful—

not merely mathematical, calculating, or impersonal. It is something of the heart; intuitive, emotional rather than essentially rational.[12]

A good example of this "imaginative rehearsal," done by a group in worship, were those long prayer meetings which took place in Black Baptist churches in the South before major freedom marches in the sixties. Here the marchers sang, prayed, saw visions of freedom, gained courage to face the consequences of their actions, and, in general, acted out what it meant to be courageous disciples before leaving the church to be courageous disciples. The worship was a serious act of the imagination before doing the work.

When we become lost in the familiar words, patterns, gestures, and beat of a liturgy, ritual relaxes the tight grip of the status quo and frees us from the frantic treadmill of reason and reflection. We relax, let down our defenses, dream. Those who criticize worship for being a retreat from real life fail to see that there is nothing inherently wrong with Sunday worship as a sanctuary from the frenetic pace of modern life. In such relaxed, potentially contemplative environs, we are given space for creative, imaginative reviewing and revisioning of our lives. There are worse sins than sleeping in church.

By giving us a safe, boundaried, protective "world," ritual contributes to the spontaneity necessary for human growth and creative adaptation—or for a bold and creative ethical life. Many of us think of ritualized behavior as the very antithesis of spontaneous action. However anthropologists have noted that some of the most heavily ritualized societies (e.g., Japan) are often the most adaptive. Rituals provide us a secure homebase, a pivot point where enough things are tied down, so to speak, that we have the security to roam in new areas of thinking and acting because we always know where "home" is. Some of the most radical liturgical innovation has occurred in the most "ritualized" churches. Only the person who is secure in his or her identity can afford the risk and the threat that come from experimentation with new forms of being and acting.

We live in a time of great dis-ease and social dis-location.

In such a time, the locative function of ritual is especially important. In a society that idealizes openness and mobility, where "sin" is most often defined as a lack of freedom to move and change perpetually, the ritual life of the church will be caricatured as overly restrictive, conservative, and maladaptive. But the Archimedian claim, "Give me a place on which to stand, and I will move the world," is demonstrated in reverse by the apparent impotency of modern humanity to change anything in significant or courageous ways because we have nowhere to stand amid the swirling vortex of contemporary uprootedness.[13] In such a time, freedom, change, and perpetual openness will be celebrated as the supreme virtues: a celebration that masks the lack of meaning many feel because they have not experienced the sustained, orderly growth, the sense of place and identity true human freedom requires.

The timidity, the over-scrupulosity, and paralyzing anxiety that one observes among many may be testimony that we live in such insecure, unpredictable, homeless, deritualized circumstances that we dare not venture far in our actions lest our painfully inadequate sense of identity be obliterated by the chaos of uncertainty. This is not the stuff of which bold, courageous, ethically responsible action is made.

Liturgical Contributions
to Christian Character Formation

Let us now be more specific about ways Christian liturgy may influence Christian character.

1) *Liturgy helps form Christian identity.*

In the sixties and seventies, many theologians emphasized that the true *Sitz im Leben* ("life situation") of Christians was in the world.[14] As far as coming in for worship was concerned, it was said that "we are inside only for the sake of those outside."[15]

Talk of this kind made some interesting assumptions. It

assumed "the world sets the agenda" and, if God were active, it was everywhere but inside the church (a claim that could be easily disputed by empirically examining the average congregation). This appealed to the pragmatic, utilitarian, secularized American church in particular, a church that was never sure about the value of corporate worship. After all, what good does all that singing and praying do anyone?

Even Vatican II, mapping the way for renewal of Roman Catholicism, said on the one hand, that "the liturgy is the outstanding means by which the faithful can express in their lives, and manifest to others, the mystery of Christ and the real nature of the church";[16] but on the other hand, it gave such heavy emphasis to God's actions outside the church and in secular *diakonia,* that it implicitly cast doubt on the importance of *leitourgia*—prayer, preaching, sacraments.[17]

Admittedly, on many moral issues (the civil rights movement, the women's movement) it seemed as if the world had to reveal the gospel to the church rather than the other way around. Sometimes God's will is revealed, not through the church, but in spite of the church. I fear that after two decades of this thinking, the church finds it is losing its identity, its integrity and coherence in its marriage with the world. The world has become the transformer of the church rather than that which is being transformed. The church which let the world set the agenda has now forgotten why it came to the meeting.

Within my own denomination we celebrate a theology that affirms "pluralism" as a great theological virtue and social principles that speak much of "freedom of choice" and "personhood"—theology and social values without biblical foundation and without distinction from prevalent opinions within American society as a whole. While pluralism, freedom of choice, and self-affirmation may be important values for keeping things balanced and running smoothly in a multiracial, multiethnic, democratic society with nothing to hold it together but aggressive self-interest, it is doubtful whether such values are specifically Christian.

But how do we know? Cast adrift from our biblical roots,

our tradition, our Story, our rites and rituals; we are left with few criteria for judgment.

In the rites of the church our Story is told and retold. This is where the Christian vision is seen and shared. The liturgy of the church thus becomes a primary source for a Christian's identity.

Any claim for the importance of Christian liturgy in moral formation rests upon certain anthropological assumptions. How are human beings made? Is the human being inevitably a creature who needs communal rituals and symbolic actions to express and effect the basic consensus a society needs for survival? If so, ritual is powerful. The rituals that exercise power over us may be Christian or not, but they will have their way with us. They may be the rituals of chauvanistic nationalism, communism, egocentrism, atavism, or some other secular faith. We are formed in countless ways by these secular "liturgies." The only way the church will remain distinctive and lively in this world is through close attention to her identity-forming liturgies and rites. The term "anonymous Christian" is a theological nonsequitur. How can there be disciples who are unidentified with the Master or indistinguishable from those who are not disciples? How is there a Messiah without a messianic community?

No church can be entirely out of the world because the church is a sociological institution living under the same tendencies and drawing its members from the same world as any other human group. So the question is not *if* we will be in the world but *how*. The answer to that question, if it is a truly Christian answer, must be a biblical-theological-liturgical-ethical answer. I do not know how to act as a Christian unless I first know who a Christian is. True concern and action in the world can come only out of the nature of Christ himself—"we love because Christ first loved us."

That imperative love is, in great part, identified, acted out, experienced, and given specific content and meaning within the worship of the church. As Paul Ramsey has noted;

Church and synagogue are communities of adoration, remembrance, celebration, worship, and praise. The communities engage in faith-ing whenever by common liturgical action or profession they say forth their faith by doing; or when by song, recital, confession, reading or preaching they, by saying, do. These acts-speech and speech-acts are understood to be human performative. Each of these faith-acts and faith-statements of a congregation is at the same time a way of talking about ethical talk, a way of conveying and fostering what the community means by righteousness.[18]

2) *Liturgy creates a world for the Christian.*

The human brain constructs a picture of the world, various interlocking bits of information, which is more than a mere data bank of shelved facts. Our picture of the world is the sum of the implications and inferences which we have drawn from our experiences with reality as well as our personal ordering, incorporation, and interlocking of these experiences.[19]

Liturgy creates a world for the Christian, world in the sense that it is often used in the New Testament. When Paul refers to "the world" *(cosmos)* he is not referring to the physical world, the planet, but to the social reality; the world of values and institutions into which we have been socialized. We live in this world, and it lives in us. It is thus an inner and an outer experience. Our world is our unified structure of meaning, the result of our natural human capacity to unify our experiences of reality and to project this unified image. But this world is not a merely subjective phenomenon, a fanciful tableaux. It is the expression of the relationship between humanity and the things-that-are.[20]

Liturgy reveals the world of the Christian faith, which is not part of our natural, inborn perception. It is rather something to which our eyes are gradually opened. The liturgy is not merely an expression of this particular world, it is an exposure of it. Unless this "world" of faith is revealed, our ethics will merely adapt to the contours of the status quo, conventional wisdom, and the safe confines of contemporary values.

In the liturgy, we are enabled to see things as they "really are"—as Christians see reality. How often have Christians been told, in recent years, to get out of the sanctuary and back into the "real world." But this reverses the traditional order. In past times, when the Christian entered the sanctuary and its liturgy, it was not a matter of leaving the world, but rather of entering the world as it *really* looked in its full, transparent reality—as the place of God's love and activity. That divine love and activity takes place, of course, outside the "world" of the liturgy, for the whole world outside is God's world. But due to our defective vision, our inadequate perception, sometimes it is difficult for us to see that divine busyness. So, as Leo the Great once said of the Eucharist, the liturgy "makes conspicuous" the world as it is, a world to which we might otherwise be blinded.

The liturgical endeavor to help Christians see the world more accurately could be illustrated by referring to the words, the choreography, or the music; but I most often feel this cosmological function at work through liturgical architecture. For instance, the fifth-century tomb of Galla Placidia in Ravenna, a marvelous gem of Byzantine mosaic art, is an example of how the interior space of a church can be used to create a Christian world. One enters the building in almost total darkness. The only light comes from four small alabaster windows. As one's eyes become accustomed to the darkness, golden images appear from the upper levels of the building. The mosaics glisten and glimmer. First one sees St. Lawrence, the early Christian martyr. (Figure 1) Lawrence literally dances to his death by fire, carrying the sacred book for which he gave his life, as well as the cross which he bears like a battle standard. Here is the cost of discipleship. Above Lawrence, one's eyes are led up to the small dome to see, set in a mystical, deep blue sky studded with gold stars, a victorious cross. Over the cost of discipleship, over the cosmos, here in this "new heaven and new earth" stands the cross.

Turning around, as one leaves the building, after having

prayed or received the Eucharist; one is confronted by the beautifully compassionate "Christ the Good Shepherd." (Figure 2) The youthful Christ clutches the same battle cross Lawrence carried to his death. Now, in paradise, the cross is fully triumphant. One's eyes have moved from the cost of discipleship to the prize. One emerges from the building, having made the pilgrimage with the saints from life, to death, to life beyond death. One's eyes have been opened, and one has been given a mystical vision of the world as it is—not the world when this mosaic was made in which the emperor was losing control, barbarian hoards were at the door, and the classical world was disintegrating—but the *real* world where all stands under the sign of the cross and the sometimes hard path of faithfulness leads to peace and fulfillment in Christ.

This is not to say that the liturgical "world" is always an accurate depiction of the Christian vision. The world that liturgical words, ceremonial, music, and architecture create must be judged and refined by using the Bible or church tradition or whatever criteria the church uses to test its visions.

One may find the vision of Galla Placidia appealing. One may not be as favorably impressed by the vision of the architectural cosmos of the average church—the rigid rows of pews, the distant and lifted up clergy, the sentimentalism of the stained-glass depictions of the faith, the blandness of it all.

Washington Street United Methodist Church in Columbia, South Carolina, contains the type of windows popular in many American Protestant churches around the turn of this century. (Figure Three) The colors are muted pastels. The scenes are romantic views of the Holy Land as some nineteenth-century American artist thought it should look. There are no people in the scenes. As one sits in the church, looking at the windows, one realizes that the artist intended to make it appear that one is in the countryside of the Holy Land of the first century rather than South Carolina of the nineteenth century. From one window, the little town of Bethlehem is visible; the hill of Golgatha in another. Once

FIGURE 1

FIGURE 2

FIGURE 3

again, the worshiper has entered a world different from the world outside.

My point is not that the world of Galla Placidia or the world of Washington Street Church is an adequate representation of the normative Christian world. My point is that the liturgy, including the architectural setting, is the window, the vantage point through which a Christian is urged to see the world. That seeing shapes our moral life because it helps form our moral vision. The world vision one might subtly receive while praying at Galla Placidia might give one hope by envisioning a city "not made with human hands." It might inspire one to bold discipleship, in the footsteps of St. Lawrence. The world vision of Washington Street Church might foster inner peace to face one's troubles or sentimental romantic flights of fancy to escape one's troubles. Either world would have ethical consequences.[21]

Secular society provides a distinct cosmos to foster the identity of those who live there. The self is dependent upon this social cosmos for its identity and direction. This vision of the world makes this person, this person—not some other. It also influences the person's shaping of the continually emerging world—for the world is always in process of construction, and none of us receives our world in merely passive fashion.

Christian ethics is dominated and determined by Christian reality—or, more accurately, the Christian perspective on human reality. What to others in the "world" appears to be merely human action and interactions; life, death, and decay; appears to the Christian to be communion, acknowledgement, and rejection by God—part of the extravagant involvement of God with God's world.

3) *Liturgy is a primary source of the symbols and metaphors through which we talk about and make sense out of our world.*

Liturgy is a symbol-laden endeavor. The chalice, the loaf of eucharistic bread, the open Bible on the pulpit, the preacher in a black robe, the vivid language, the cross on the altar, all are powerful symbolic statements.

Social change is primarily symbolic chage. In order for us to change, our symbols must change. Our symbols must change because they determine our horizons, our limits, our viewpoints and visions. In his book on the decline of the Roman Empire, E. R. Dodds concludes that fundamental change in Rome came from change in her basic symbolic vision and outlook.[22] Rome's vision of herself was one of decay and decline rather than growth and ascendancy. This change was not always related to the "facts" of reality—but it might as well have been.

When women were at last given leadership positions in the liturgy of many churches, we soon realized how much symbolic change needed to be made in order to adjust the metaphors and symbols to the church's clearer vision of the role of women in the church. We realized how limited many of our old, male-dominated, heierarchial images were— God the Father; the Heavenly King; Lord over All; Rise Up, O Men of God. There could be no basic change without change in the symbols and metaphors through which we attempt to grasp reality and reality grasps us.[23]

The liturgy reminds us that we are more image-making and image-using creatures than we think. We apprehend reality only through symbols, sacraments, gestures, and metaphor. Even our language—which we use to describe ourselves as abstracting, rational creatures—is a symbolic system. Through these symbols we make sense out of the dismaying multiplicity we encounter. This renders our world apprehensible and manageable.[24] We cannot even speak of symbol or metaphor without cmploying metaphor and symbol. By the use of these, we predetermine, to a great extent, what we will be able to see and say about reality.

With the loss of vitality of some of the historic symbols of the faith (when such things as sheep, crosses, and kings pass from our daily existence) Christians have often been unable to grasp some aspects of reality or have substituted inadequate secular images for traditional Christian ones. In chapter 2 we noted how the exclusive use of the command-obedience metaphor as a way of describing the Christian life has impoverished Protestant ethics by focusing on only one aspect of the moral life. We also noted how the new metaphor of freedom, borrowed from modern existentialism, when applied to the ethical life resulted in a sub-Christian ethic.

So, today when Christians discuss an ethical issue like abortion, too often their speech is not much different from that of the secular society. Christians argue over the "freedom of choice" of the mother or the "right to life" of the unborn—metaphors one would be hard pressed to find in Scripture. This is the language of secular, pluralistic, capitalistic, Western democracy—not the language of faith. Only God has a "right" to our lives or our bodies—for only God is the giver and taker of life. "Freedom of choice" is not the supreme virtue for a servant of Christ. The debate is being waged by Christians without the use of specifically Christian language. When this happens, is there any likelihood that the resolution of the debate will be specifically Christian?[25]

Our character is relative to the kind of community from which we inherit our primary symbols and metaphors. The Christian expects to see and say things differently than the non-Christian for each will be employing different symbols of their world.

Because we say and see things differently, we have different characters. Without careful attention to the specific symbols and metaphors that the Christian community uses, we will be unable to form specifically Christian character.

4) *Liturgy aids in Christian imagination.*

One unique characteristic of humans is our ability to operate in the mind with images not present to the senses. This is our second language with which we carry on a continual discourse within ourselves, with which we debate, dream, argue, file away, and weigh what is happening to our lives. This is how humans rise above mere instinct—we imagine out of our remembered store of images, and we imagine beyond the present moment.

Many have the opinion that both liturgy and morality have exclusively conserving functions. They view the religious life as essentially an effort to conserve older values, to conform to a relatively static and closed set of precepts derived from the social or historical repository. But this overlooks the imaginative, transcending, ecstatic functions of religious experience.

Liturgy is mind-expanding work on a Christian's imagination. It helps us to transcend our immediate situation, to see "a new heaven and a new earth," to release the tight grip of the status quo.

To ask, what good participation in worship does for one's moral life, is rather like asking, what good being a friend of a certain person does for one's moral life. Any "good" that comes from these experiences will be as much a part of the imagination, the intuition, and emotion as of a discernible, cognitive, cause-effect relationship.

In his essay on epistimology, *The Identity of Man,* Bronowski makes a distinction between the ways of knowing in science and the ways of knowing in art that may help us to understand how liturgy may influence our ethical life.

Brownowski notes that poetry has no moralizing purpose. If art attempts to moralize and make some ethical point (whether it be Norman Rockwell kitsch or Chinese Marxist posters), it is perverted art. Art gives no rules or advice. Rather, it soberly sets out the human dilemma without moralism or programs for resolution.

> The universe of art is one in which there is a suspension of decisions. . . . There are no morals in any work of art. There are no specific lessons to be learned . . . no advice to be followed. There are many implications in a poem which enrich our experience of life: but it is a many-sided experience, and we are not asked to come down on one side or another. . . . Here the imagination explores the alternatives of human action without ever deciding for one rather than another. And in this tense and

happy indecision, and only in this, the work of art is different from the work of science.[26]

How similar is this work of art to the work of worship. We rarely finish a service of worship with a recipe for action. If we do, we have probably participated in a moralistic pep rally, which is less than true worship of God. We usually end worship having been stimulated by an experience in which we have willingly entered into a kind of experiment, a drama that has invited us into the divine-human action in a playful way. Like children at play or the reader of a novel, we experiment with how it feels to be another. Unlike a scientific experiment that has as its aim to choose between alternative hypotheses, leading the researcher to some single path of decision or action, the "experiment" of art or liturgy does not tell us how to act. It suggests *how to be*. It tells us how to be human by identifying who we are and who others are. It gives us that most fundamental requisite of all moral action—self-knowledge—not only knowledge of our foibles and sins but also of our possibilities.[27] As Piaget said, "Play is the serious business of childhood." So also the imaginative play of worship is the serious business of Christians, the criterion and starting point for faithful Christian imagination.

The imaginative work in art or liturgy can be a painful experience. Good art, unlike bad art, exists over against us. In our encounter with it, we are forced to surrender to its stark, objective, picture of reality. Good art shows me reality with such clarity that I am forced to admit, though it pains me, that I am not accustomed to looking at the real world at all. I do not read a story by Flannery O'Conner without realizing how warped and defective is my perspective on myself and the world. I am brought to my knees by the sheer truthfulness of its vision. As Iris Murdoch says,

> Good art shows us how difficult it is to be objective by showing us how differently the world looks to an objective vision. We are presented with a truthful image of the human condition in a form which can be steadily contemplated. . . . Art transcends

selfish and obsessive imitations of personality and can enlarge the sensibility of its consumer. It is a kind of goodness by proxy.[28]

This objective, self-forgetful, startlingly truthful vision is the gift of good liturgy. "Goodness by proxy" comes in those rare moments when liturgy becomes a poetic mirror to reality and, rather than through a glass darkly, we see truth face-to-face and say, "That's it, that's how it really is in my life."

Even funerals can have ethical import when seen as an artistic exercise of the imagination. I have been to many funerals in my part of the country where, during the funeral sermon, the pastor turned toward those present and sought to elicit some response, holding over them the threat of their own death. Here is a virtually verbatim account from one such sermon:

> It's too late for old Joe. He has gone to meet his Maker in judgment. *But it is not too late for you.* Joe has breathed his last. He might like to have done this or that, but now he is dead. You are still alive. You can still choose. You can, this very day, this very hour, come to Jesus and be saved. You can commit your life to Jesus Christ as your Lord and Master. Don't put this off. Someday it will be too late for you.

Many of us would react negatively to the blatantly manipulative, coercive, fear tactics of this sermon. We question whether this is the proper function of a funeral sermon. However, the preacher spoke what was true. We do not live forever. Someday it will indeed "be too late for you." Our days are numbered. Today is the day for decision.

While I would personally not preach such a sermon at a funeral, it does have a precedent. The Psalms, as honest a part of the Bible as one could hope for, contain these words that are traditional at funerals:

> Thou turnest man back to dust,
>   and sayest, "Turn back, O children
>   of men!"

For a thousand years in thy sight
    are but as yesterday when it is
past,
or as a watch in the night.
Thou dost sweep men away; they are
    like a dream,
    like grass which is renewed in the morning:
in the morning it flourishes and is renewed;
in the evening it fades and withers. . . .
So teach us to number our days
    that we may get a heart of wisdom.

                              (90:3-6, 12)

In a death-denying culture, does not the funeral perform a potentially prophetic, morally determinative function by helping us confront that which we seek to avoid? Funerals, even at their pagan, cosmetically adorned worst, at least point us in the direction of our morality, at least set us in the context where we can start to become honest about our finitude. What does it mean to "number our days," except to know that we will die? Because we will not live forever, today *is* the day for decision. While we must not turn funerals into an occasion for morbid, moralistic exhortation and tear-jerking appeals to the living, neither must we conceal that we are dealing with death. The simple honesty of the Psalms is our model. They have long had a central function in our historic burial liturgies because in their poetry and honesty, these passages urge us to confront boldly the truth of our mortality and its consequences.

It is not so much by some Herculean effort that we are able to be honest or to love or to see. Reality entices us from our self-centeredness. Without this self-forgetfulness, this denial of the self (as Jesus might say) ethical freedom is another illusion of our self-preoccupation. Hauerwas says, "The greatest prerequisite for true moral freedom is humility."[29] Bad liturgy, like bad art, merely confirms our warped vision, our truncated perspectives, our obsessive self-concern, soothing the "heart all curled in upon itself" rather than humbling us with love and truth.

So, through the imagination, liturgy, like art, may act upon a person to lead that person to goodness, not by direct command, but by a more subtle and complex interaction. Christian ethics, in spite of how it sometimes presents itself—a tidy, logical discipline of thought and problem solving—is a much more ambiguous, imaginative, interesting, mysterious, intuitive enterprise than we admit. There is no way to be free from the ambiguity of our ethics, to land in some pristine world of clear principles and directives for action. The task is ambiguous because we humans do not know everything, because we are limited and cannot see everything. To deny this fundamental ambiguity is the essence of sin itself.

The ambiguity not only reminds us of our dependency, our need for grace and forgiveness, but also keeps our ethics open. Our imagination, exercised in the liturgy and elsewhere, takes advantage of ethical ambiguity as an opportunity to envision, dream, to be patient and wait, to roam the uncharted territory of new possibilities. Sometimes the most valuable thing ethics can do for Christians is to help us preserve ambiguity in the face of our absolutist claims. Because of its liberating, imaginative function, art (and therefore religion) is among the first activities to be censored in a totalitarian state.

Ethics can help by reminding us of our mixed motives, the impurity of our decisions, the rationalization within our reasons. When ethics is put to the task of minimizing moral ambiguities rather than exploiting them, limiting alternatives rather than suggesting them, cutting through the proliferation of possibilities rather than envisioning them; it has failed in its imaginative task. The liturgy, in its richness and ambiguity, is a guard against any Puritanism in ethics that attempts to eradicate the luxuriousness of a Christian's ethical possibilities.[30]

5) *Liturgy is a primary source of the Christian vision.*

"The moral life is a struggle and training in how to see."[31] Human beings differ from one another, not only because their vision is selective, seeing some things in the world as morally significant and other things as insignificant, but also because they see a different world. Our morality is made, not only of principles and choices, but also of vision. Jonathan Edwards describes the converted person as one who has been given "new sight."

This is why ethics cannot abstain from commending the best way of seeing the world. Systematic ethical reflection, at least since Aristotle, usually begins by telling us what, in the end (the *telos*), we are supposed to "see." The *eudemonia* over which the Greeks puzzled, the *felicitas* for which the Romans searched, is said, by the Christian, to be found in a vision of God. "Christianity came into the world to offer men the vision of God and to call them to the pursuit of that vision," wrote Bishop Kirk.[32] Irenaeus' often quoted, *Gloria Dei vivens homo*, "The glory of God is man fully alive," ends in the less frequently cited, "and the life of man is the vision of God." Here Irenaeus' account of Christian ethics begins. Aquinas knew that all ethical action is *propter finem agere* ("action in view of an end") and that therefore the place to begin ethics is at the end, *De ultimo fine et de beatitudine*. The opening question and answer of the Westminster Shorter Catechism (1647–48) makes the same point.

> What is the chief end of man?
> Man's chief end is to glorify God, and to enjoy him for ever.

Our ethical motives are not some inner power that causes our behavior. They are descriptions of our response to our vision of the world. Identification of our motive simply states the reason, the goal, the world vision we had in mind when we did or did not commit a certain act. I did not steal the money because I believe that it is wrong to steal (my world view tells me that I have no right to other people's property).

Christian ethics is an attempt to cope with the problems of looking into the sun. Our ethics cannot be reduced to the study of rational argument precisely because of this visionary beginning and end of ethics. That vague, intuitive feeling within us, indicating that we ought or ought not to do something, usually arises from our blinding vision of what the world is. Those intuitions and feelings, those reckless and inexplicable deeds of love are as important as all our carefully reasoned arguments and principles—maybe even more important.[33]

The vision of this faith is not static, but is rather a constantly unfolding, transforming reality, which is itself the working out of God's purposes. The goal of liturgical revision, this painful and exciting venture of the past few decades, is literally re-vision: seeking appropriate language and forms to keep alive, in worship, the church's vision of God.

We must periodically withdraw from the world in order to worship because our vision needs the focus and concentration that occurs in worship. Such withdrawal is confrontation rather than escapism. Thus Bernard Häring sees the sacraments as *signs which sharpen our vision to the divine presence,* not exclusively in the sacraments themselves, but in the world. The sacraments thereby enable us to shape our deeds in configuration with Christ's deeds in the world so that we ourselves become sacraments to the world.[34]

When the moral life is little more than a procedure for detemining What ought I to do? ethics has failed in its essential task. The teleological, visionary, What kind of person do I want to be? is the first question ethics should teach.

The disconnected Western modern man or woman—a mosaic of conflicting rules, a wardrobe of quick-change social skills, healthy, independent, preeminently adaptable, generally secure from the ravages of disease and oppression, yet cut off, without a past and only the slightest hint of the future—is the product of a modern world view. From such a patchwork of conflicting claims and values, how can a person answer What ought I to do? A prior question might be "What kind of person do I want to be when I'm sixty-four?"

The puny horizons of modern humanity, its impaired vision leads to a truncated ethical life. We either see or we perish, the Bible says (cf. Prov. 19:16). When the environment in which we live becomes a scientifically objectified place to be used for our own ends, it is not long before people in that world start using one another in the same way. A truncated liturgical life—in which "worship" is used to assuage our guilt by rationalizing and justifying our values and actions, or to confirm our delusions of self-control by moralizing about our need to save the world (since we believe that we are the only ones to save it)—corresponds to our truncated ethical life. Both the ethics and the worship are results of the myopic vision.[35] In spite of his rather privatistic tendencies, I think that Whitehead beautifully expresses the visionary nature of worship, whether it be worship in public or private:

> Religion is the reaction of human nature to its search for God. . . . The non religious motive which has entered into modern religious thought is the desire for a comfortable organization of modern society. Religion has been presented as valuable for the ordering of life. Its claims have been rested upon its function as a santion (sic) to right conduct. Also the purpose of right conduct quickly degenerates into the formation of pleasing social relations. We have here a subtle degradation of religious ideas. . . . Conduct is a by-product of religion—an inevitable by-product, but not the main point. Every great religious teacher has revolted against the presentation of religion as a mere sanction of rules of conduct. Saint Paul denounced the Law, the Puritan divines spoke of the filthy rags of righteousness. The insistence upon rules of conduct marks the ebb of religious fervour. Above and beyond all things the religious life is not a research after comfort. . . .
> Religion is the vision of something which stands beyond, behind, and within, the passing flux of immediate things; something which is real, and yet waiting to be realized; something which is a remote possibility, and yet the greatest of present facts; something which gives meaning to all that passes, and yet eludes apprehension; something whose possession is the final good, and yet is beyond all reach; something which is the ultimate ideal, and the hopeless quest.
> The immediate reaction of human nature to the religious vision is worship. . .

The vision claims nothing but worship. . . . The power of God is the worship He inspires. That religion is strong which in its ritual and its moves of thought evokes an apprehension of the commanding vision. The worship of God is not a rule of safety—it is an adventure of the spirit, a flight after the unattainable. The death of religion comes with the repression of the high hope of adventure.[36]

Worship is a place of vision. "Worship is the place in which the vision comes to a sharp focus, a concentrated expression, and it is here that the vision has often been found to be most appealing."[37] The acts of worship we will examine are instruments whereby the vision is clarified and transmitted through time. Worship is not only a place to dream and envision a "new heaven and a new earth" where the deaf hear, the blind see, and outcasts come to a feast; worship is also a time set apart to focus our attention on and attach ourselves to something and someone outside ourselves.

Iris Murdoch uses the analogy of being in love with another human being to illustrate the moral results of being in love with God.[38] Being in love releases our energies, focuses our attention, redirects our goals, determines our perspective and posture. Kantian, existentialist talk about the will being so important in ethics fails to appreciate that being in love is not a matter of will—something one can decide to do, and, conversely, something that one can decide not to do: it is an attachment beyond the bounds of mere reason, command, and will.

We humans are inherently attaching creatures. We do not so much decide to be good or just or courageous, as we become attached to some object of love and attention that refocuses and releases our energies so these good things are done, not as an act of reason or will or response to a command, *but as response to the beloved.* We are obedient to whatever absorbs our attention. If this be true, then Christian morality should endeavor as much to focus our attention on the beloved (Christ) and on gaining a clearer vision of the beloved as to elucidate principles and decisions for correct action—until in seeing we become as we see, and in loving we become as him whom we love. As Augustine said, "We imitate whom we adore."

> Whatever is true, whatever is honorable, whatever is just, whatever is pure, whatever is lovely, whatever is gracious, if there is any excellence, if there is anything worthy of praise, think about these things. What you have learned and received and heard and seen in me, do.
>
> (Phil. 4:8-9a)

Christian worship or Christian ethics is thus a matter of training in how to pay attention.[39] It is practice in attentiveness of heart and mind. Until we become sufficiently attentive to God, our selves will be mired in the illusion, self-hate, self-defensiveness, and anxiety that occurs when we are forced to create and sustain our own significance.

Every time we worship, we should be reminded that the Christian life is not a response to a code of moral conduct or a response to the memory of a noble person who once lived. The Christian life is response to a reality, a personal reality, a presence which evokes—not mere obedience—but an effective relationship.[40]

In beholding God's glory, we come to reflect it in ourselves, (II Cor. 3:18). We now see "through a glass, darkly," but one day we shall see "face to face" (I Cor. 13:12). We shall then bear God's image which, heretofore, we have only dimly reflected.

Sometimes, in worship, we receive certain codes or guides for behavior—the recital of the Decalogue, the hearing of scriptural commands, the affirming of vows. Sometimes we hear and affirm certain guiding principles and ideals for the Christian life—self-sacrifice, justice, kindness, humility. But the main "good" we receive in worship is a relationship with God, the one who loves and is therefore loved.

Years ago, Kenneth Kirk, while speaking of worship in a more private and contemplative sense than I do here, saw the integral relationship between the vision of God in worship and the service of God in life.

> The doctrine "the end of life is the vision of God" has throughout been interpreted by Christian thought at its best as implying in practice that the highest prerogative of the Christian, in this life as well as hereafter, is the activity of *worship;* and that nowhere except in this activity will he find the key to his ethical problems. As a practical corrolary it follows that the principal duty of the Christian moralist is to stimulate the spirit of worship in those to whom he addresses himself, rather than to set before them codes of behaviour.[41]

6) *Liturgy is a major source of our Christian tradition which enables us to rise above the present and envision the future.*

One important way human beings differ from other animals is that animals cannot reach back any distance into their past. They have only habit to do the work of memory. Only the human is truly personal, a person, because only the human is able to carry in his mind what he was. Only the human tells stories. Only the human is able to conceive of a "future," because only the human recalls the past.

Ritual, religious or otherwise, is an inherently traditionalist activity. Part of ritual's power is its sameness, its repetition, its predictability. It provides the rudder for our lives in the midst of a sea of change. The worship of the church strikes us as the most traditionalist of all the church's activities: the archaic language, repetition, outdated vestments, resistance to innovation, the same old stories again and again.

In recent years the church has been engrossed in liturgical change. I have been an advocate and active participant in such change. We must be open to the Spirit's leadings, keeping liturgy related to life, modifying the liturgy to meet the changing needs of people. But it is also important, particularly after these past two decades of rapid, unsettling liturgical change, to recognize the positive values—particularly for Christian ethics—of the liturgy as a repository of Christian tradition.

Somewhere Jaroslav Pelikan distinguishes between "traditionalism," which he calls "the dead faith of living men"; and "tradition," which he calls "the living faith of dead men." Liturgy is often a place for archaism and antiquarianism, a place to hold on to the cultic vestiges of a dead faith. These traditions can and should be dispensed with as an affront and a subversion to living faith. But tradition is another matter. Tradition is the origin, not in time, but origin in substance of the community, the wellspring of faith itself.[42] It is good that liturgy has a kind of inertia. The worship life of the church seems to hold doggedly to certain time-honored truths, repeating them over and over again in the face of new truth claims, making new revelation fight for itself.

The liturgical year, with its round of seasons, keeps the essential features of the Story before us. As we live through this year, we not only hear the Story, we enact it until it becomes our own. Those churches which do not observe the liturgical year often find that they suffer from a truncated story. Their worship fails to hit the full range of notes within the Christian narrative. The result can only be a truncated ethical life. It is important to tell the Story, the whole Story, again and again until it is our own.

In its sameness, liturgy gives the requisite identity, security and stability from which exploration can proceed. The liturgy must be the church's supreme skeptic in the face of change, that one aspect of the church's life which continually honors the past and respects the wealth of the church's experience, the complexity of the church's Story in the face of modern manipulators of the liturgy who claim the past was too limited. These innovators endanger the church by imposing only purely contemporary standards.

In affirming the wealth of the church's tradition, the liturgy is not only holding on to what is important in our past, but is also prodding us forward to everwidening realms of importance. Memory is the major source of foresight. We push into the future mainly on the basis of inherited images from the past. Tradition is also the major critic of the church. Present detractors are never as tough on the church as our own story in its criticism of us. Tradition gives the church a fresh perspective which rises above the conventional folk wisdom of present culture and frees us from the tyranny of those who know only what they have personally experienced.

I heard a sermon recently in our university chapel which urged us to "put meaning in our lives" by "reaching out to touch other people, opening ourselves up to other people, and getting beside other people." On the way out, I asked a student what she thought of the sermon.

"Well, it was O.K. But it wasn't much different from the kind of thing you would have heard if you had stopped the average college Freshman and asked, 'What is the meaning of life?' I'm sure you would have heard all about 'reaching out' and 'touching' and 'being open.' If the preacher had stuck with the Bible passage for today and preached from the Bible rather than ignoring it, he might have had something interesting to say—even something shocking to say."[43]

A rich and multifarious tradition can be a great help to a church. Churches whose liturgies are less "rich," tend to have a paucity of images, themes, metaphors, and patterns to draw from when confronting present ethical dilemmas.

There is no utterly spontaneous behavior. We are never totally free, in our action, from our histories. The richer our personal and institutional histories, the more options we have for creative response to our world. Our decisions are both liberated and channeled by our past. Many of us think of our tradition, our history, as that which puts the mind in a mold, closing it to alternatives for action. But tradition can also stretch the mind. Memory gives what Chesterton called membership in "the democracy of the dead"—the courageous refusal to submit to the notions of "the small and arrogant oligarchy of those who simply happen to be walking about."[44]

———— · · · ————

The identity, world, symbols and metaphors, imagination, vision, and tradition which the church receives through its liturgical life enable the church to be the church and enable individual Christians to engage in *diakonia* without forgetting why they are in service and whose service they are in. The memory and hope they receive in their *leitourgia* thrusts them into, and sustains them within, their *diakonia*. Their *diakonia* provides the context and the need for their *leitourgia* until, in *leitourgia* or *diakonia*, worship or service, it becomes difficult for the Christian to distinguish between the two. This may, after all, be the point of it all.

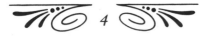

Praying, Believing, and Acting as Christians

The human response to God in Jesus Christ is not left "monotonous, colourless and formless" but "articulated, colourful and contoured," wrote Barth.[1] Using the perspective of the ethics of character, I earlier criticized Barth's ethics of obedience as lacking sufficient attentiveness to the substantial, long-term formation of the moral self. But this does not mean that Barth sees the Christian life as a structureless, nondescript, sporadic affair. While ethics is more than dry legalism, the Christian life must also be preserved from the boggy marshes of individualized subjectivity and foggy mysticism.

The Christian life is a "formed reference" says Barth; it will have a "peculiar character" to it, a definite "outline" that will be recognizable and congruent with the person and work of Jesus Christ. Or, as Paul Ramsey translates Barth's aesthetic terms into geometric ones, "the *convex* of God's action determines the *concave* shape" of human response.[2] What Barth said of Christian ethics, can be said of Christian worship. The Christian life is a formed reference, a peculiar response to, and acknowledgment of, the divine event. All Christian ethics has an essentially liturgical character in its responsiveness. Our ethics is doxological, oblational, our good deeds are done *ad majorem Dei gloriam*, as are our prayer and praise.

The *lex orandi, lex credendi, lex bene operandi* (law of prayer,

law of belief, law of good work) are all part of Christians'
response to God. We speak and listen, believe in and trust,
and imitate whom we adore. Our praying, believing, and
good deeds are three mutually enriching ways of responding to the God who has first loved us in Jesus Christ. Our
praying, believing, and acting must be described and judged
by how well these responses are formed in reference to the
divine event. That divine event is forever evoking, shaping,
and judging our response. For Christians, the most
interesting ecclesial, liturgical, or ethical questions are
always theological questions. The divine reaching out
determines our human response.

In the last chapter, I viewed liturgy as a primary source of
identity, world, symbols, imagination, vision, story, and
tradition of Christians. In this chapter, I examine more
closely the lively dynamics of our mutually enriching
responses of worship, work, and belief.

The Making of Christians

"Christians are made, not born," Tertullian observed. For
all his crubbiness, Tertullian knew that we do not grow into
this faith by natural inclination or birthright. One must be
trained, formed into this faith.

A Christian ethic is rather unique because it is formed by a
stance of faith. All activity is responsive, reflexive to God's
activity. "We are," says Luther somewhere, "more acted
upon than acting." As H. Richard Niebuhr reminded us, we
act "in answer to action upon us."[3] Our ethics is always
doxological, part of our overall gratitude, a fitting response
to actions done to and for us. Therefore there can be no
purely rationally received or legalistically closed systems in
Christian ethics. The fixed point of Christian ethics is Jesus
Christ. Beyond that, absolutes like "love," "justice," or
"right" are difficult. All moral criteria are relative to God's
will. God's will is the ultimate criterion for Christian moral
action—not rules, not our self-made goals, not what we
deem permissible and possible.

Christian ethics cannot avoid being Christocentric—

beginning with the Incarnation, with the astounding story that Christ rules, that God is with us. This mystery of God's human presence in the world, this sacrament of our encounter with God, is where it all begins—not in the safe confines of rules, the urbane discourse of human reason, the murky waters of mysticism, the high-sounding platitudes of noble and abstract ideals. The truth for us is a person, personal, relational.

As Christians we are to love God—and our neighbor. But many Christians wonder if we have not suffered a divorce of these two loves. We sometimes feel caught between the devotional love of God, on the one hand, and the activist love of neighbor, on the other hand. Jesus' "as you did it to one of the least of these my brethren, you did it to me" (Matt. 25:40), suggests to some contemporary expositors that love of God is realized _only_ in love of neighbor. But such an equation is not supported by the New Testament writers who consistently imply that love of our neighbor has its source in God's prior love toward us. Our love of neighbor is in response to God's love of us. That divine, originating love, that invigorating relationship is most often experienced in our times of worship—otherwise the divine love is reduced to the level of a past event with no direct influence upon us in the present.

Christ did not come to urge us to love each other. He came to establish the condition and the context where, even for poor souls like us, love is possible. Christ's command to love is not an abstract command which can be separated from the astounding story that, in him, God is loving us, showing us the way home from the far country, working for our redemption as children of God. "The Gospel is not about love," says Hauerwas, "but it is about this man, Jesus Christ. The ethic of the Gospel is not a love ethic, but it is an ethic of adherence to this man as he has bound our destiny to his, as he makes the story of our life his story."[4]

Whatever Christian ethics does with that Story, whatever we do in our lives in response to Christ's presence, we must never lose sight that we are dealing first with a relationship. Ethics must refrain from advocating a single ideal arising out of that relationship. We are talking about a path, a posture, a direction, an obedience, a multifaceted way of response. Ethics can help by clarifying the boundaries and shape of that relationship, giving direction, illuminating the way for responsible action. It can never replace the primacy of the relationship or the necessity for action with abstract principles, rules, reason, or other temptations to reap the fruits of the relationship without entering into the relationship (as those who seek the fruits of marriage without actually practicing love or fidelity). In other words, it would be meaningless to speak of "Christian" ethics without the prayer, praise, adoration, and worship, which are the sources of our relationship with Christ. It would also be meaningless to speak of "Christian" worship without the active, lifelong response that is the fruit, the testimony, the expected result of that relationship. *Lex orandi* and *lex bene operandi* go together. The *lex credendi* is also joined to our prayer and ethics. Without the theological predication of value we know not how to act or to what end.

We owe God trust, not works, said Luther. We owe the neighbor works. Trust in God gives us the freedom to love the neighbor selflessly. How do you get good works? The Lutheran response is that you get righteous work from righteous people. You do not seek apples from a thorn bush. The faith relationship is the necessary antecedent for ethics—at least in the classical Protestant view.

There can be no Christian ethicist who does not pray as a Christian. Nor could we call any liturgy "Christian" that avoids loving work and courageous action in God's world among God's cherished ones. This is said, not as a general principle, but as an operational observation of the way things function in Christian ethics—and these arise out of Christian faith. The ethical imperatives or obligations Christians follow arise out of our communal participation in the indicative faith statements of what God has done for us.

This raises an old argument in ethics. How can one logically derive an imperative ("Do this, and you shall live") from an indicative ("Christ, the light of the world")? How is belief joined to action? Many have wondered how a creedal statement like "I believe in God the Father Almighty, maker of heaven and earth" might lead to actions that treat all people as brothers and sisters, or the earth and its resources as God's creation. The troubling observation that many who affirm such creedal statements are not led to act in accordance with their creed adds to the suspicion that our indicatives do not logically lead to imperatives. How is it possible for Paul, in many of his writings (e.g., Romans) to move from his indicative faith statements to his detailed ethical instructions by a mere "because" or "therefore," linking indicative and imperative? One way to make sense out of this movement from indicative to imperative, from belief to action, is to remind ourselves about the nature of Christian discipleship.

When a believer is related to Jesus Christ, that person is not simply related to an objective body of information and beliefs. The relationship is more self-involved. It is one of trust and fidelity in God and in God's actions upon the believer. To say, "I believe in God the Father Almighty, maker of heaven and earth" is to claim a relationship that is personal, engaging, and innervating. I am in a relationship to truth, yes, but this truth is personal, present, active Truth—not a body of religious information. In this relation, I am not so much the one who understands as the one who stands under this Truth. I am the one who has been understood and grasped by this Truth rather than the one who has understood and grasped it.

If I were to say, "I believe in marriage," and you were to observe that I do and do not do certain things in regard to marriage, you might be correct in assuming that you have observed a case in which indicatives do lead to imperatives, beliefs are linked to actions. But you would be wrong if you assumed that my actions arose out of some purely rational, or even purely emotional, attachment to the general idea of marriage. To say, "I believe in marriage," is a belief statement which, for me, cannot be separated from a specific person, a specific relationship, a way of life in which I am now engaged. I do not risk much for the preservation of "marriage" in general, but I will struggle with that person who has committed herself in marriage to me and who therefore deserves my total commitment.

"Therefore"—"because," of a certain relationship, I do certain things, live in a certain way, I can be counted on to respond rather consistently in certain ways. To say that I have character is to say that I have been formed and ordered into a coherent, congruent, recognizable self by holding certain fundamental indicative notions. Christians, so far as they are recognizable and describable selves, are those who have heard the indicatives of the gospel in such a way that they now embody the gospel imperatives. The indicatives tell us who we are. Hear this early baptismal sermon:

> You are a chosen race, a royal priesthood, a holy nation, God's own people, that you may declare the wonderful deeds of him who called you out of darkness into his marvelous light. Once you were no people but now you are God's people; once you had not received mercy but now you have received mercy.

(I Peter 2:9 10)

Then come the imperatives:

> Beloved, I beseech you as aliens and exiles to abstain from the passions of the flesh. . . . Maintain good conduct among the Gentiles. . . . Be subject for the Lord's sake to every human institution. . . . Live as free men, yet without using your freedom as a pretext for evil; but live as servants of God.

(I Peter 2:11-13, 16)

The indicative states who one now is in Christ ("you are a chosen race, a royal priesthood, a holy nation, God's own people"), the imperative summons the believer to actualize who one now is in Christ. The imperative is the result of confrontation with this peculiar truth, which calls us not simply to assent but to become part of a holy nation, a way of life that is ecclesial, political, and social.

Christians may disagree over the imperatives of faith no less than we disagree over the indicatives of faith. Agreement over the indicatives will not lead all Christians to the same imperatives. Christ's indicative, "Blessed are the poor," leads some Christians to nonviolent actions in behalf of justice for the poor. It has led some Christians to potentially violent revolution. The movement from indicative to imperative is not a cause-and-effect relationship that denies the diversity of gifts and visions within the church.

However, that relationship is not a purely subjective, purely intuitive one. When I am yoked to Jesus Christ, I am not a disciple of just any good teacher but of this Jesus of Nazareth. Therefore, it is possible to speak of certain actions as being in accord with or in discord with Christian beliefs, or as consistent or inconsistent with the Christian faith. Most Christians, for example, perceive an inconsistency between faith in a Lord who blesses the poor, prays for daily bread, and feeds the hungry, and action showing disregard for the poor in our midst. We can speak of actions as characteristically Christian, that is, actions characterized by the Christian faith, actions expected of those whose characters are formed in reference to Jesus Christ.

In the perilous task of deciding what we ought to do, of discerning the imperative, we have often claimed to know too much. The easy identification of our program of action with God's program has led, and continues to lead, to horrors in human history. But the current pattern of moral life seems to claim to know too little rather than too much. "What can we know of God's will in regard to abortion or marital fidelity or nuclear power?"

Are our theological affirmations, the *lex credendi*, the indicatives of our faith, of so little assistance in answering What ought I to do? Does the *lex credendi* contain so little specific content that we are left to go it alone? Is the shape of the Christian response so amorphous and protean that talk of the Christian life as a "formed reference" is virtually without substance?

I agree with James Gustafson's observation that contemporary ethical agnosticism—which presents itself as great humility—may in reality be the very height of human conceit.[5] Since God is so obtuse and obscure in revealing his will to us, moral agnostics say, we must take matters in our own hands. Since the Christian community is so untrustworthy in its guidance, we must rely exclusively on self-guidance. We must decide what is reasonable, practical, and appropriate. But is it true that we know so little of God's ordering activity, of God's reconciling work in the world, that we are basically on our own? Is the Story so bare? The Spirit so limited? The community so void of support?

I doubt that our problem is only in the indicative mode. While we can delude ourselves in our claims to know too much, the claim that we know too little can be just as deluding. The ethical dilemma is not only What ought I to do? *Action*, more than knowing, is the final ethical dilemma. Our moral paralysis and our moral antinomianism both stem from our failure to be obedient and truthful, to discipline our lives in accord with the requirements of discipleship, to submit to reformation of our thoughts and actions. We are talking about character again, about sanctification.

The old Reformation claim that right actions flow from a justified man is true insofar as that justified person remains attuned, informed, and constantly re-formed by the person of Christ. This underscores the moral necessity of the persistent, lifelong, communal cultivation of virtues, habits, and attitudes that are the substance of Christian character. Our relationship to God in Jesus Christ is the source, not only of our knowledge of the *lex bene operandi*, but also of the will to *do* the *lex bene operandi*. From this affection for and relationship to the truth flow our response to the truth as Jesus Christ.

All this is to substantiate the necessary relationship between praying, believing, and acting as a Christian. The link between the indicative and the imperative is forged in the character of the Christian, in the natural process of behaving in accordance with who one *is* by virtue of one's relationship. Likewise, the motivation for acting upon the imperatives of the gospel lies in our desire to imitate whom we adore, to act in consistency with our relationships.

A Christian's worship is the necessary counterpart of ethics—ethics that acts in response to God's actions toward us, that does the will of God because one has been loved by God and by the people of God.

Self-Forgetfulness

Praying, believing, and acting as a Christian requires not so much that we know Christian truth, or even that we act upon the claims of that truth. The sacrifice of the martyrs, the reported cheerfulness and confident assurance with which countless Christians have braved the crowd, faced the mob, and been willing to part with life itself—all suggest something more compelling than the rational process of careful decision and determined action. Courageous, virtuous, visionary acts require more than clear discernment of what is fitting or even the willingness to be obedient. Radical Christian response requires a virtue I can only designate as self-forgetfulness.

The danger of the ethical enterprise, the peril of deciding what I ought to do and if I ought to do it, is one of self-centeredness. I become so enmeshed in my moral dilemmas, so concerned to keep my slate clean, to justify my actions or lack of actions, that I take myself more seriously than I ought. I set myself up as the supreme arbiter of truth, the final judge of what is right. In asking what *I* ought to do I make myself the source of value. Such self-centeredness, as Paul showed, ends either in pride or despair.[6]

Christians are not forced to conjure up moral vision or definitions of the true and the good from within themselves. Truth requires "disinterest" because the truth is not of our own making. The truth lures us to itself, enticing us out of our self-made, self-contained, self-sustained world of illusion. It is a risky business to get involved with this truth, this truth which offers to save our souls by allowing them to be lost in service to the truth.[7]

Aristotle set great store in that aristocrat of the moral life, the "magnanimous man," who attempts to be intellectually and morally superior to the common rabble—and is. But Christian ethics must commend a different path, one that advocates a humility due to our honest awareness of creatureliness—humility, not as a virtue, but derived from our belief in a Creator. "He is the image of the invisible God, the first-born of all creation; for in him all things were created, in heaven and on earth; visible and invisible, whether thrones or dominions or principalities or authorities—all things were created through him and for him" (Col. 1:15-17).

Christians tend to humility in their approach to moral knowing and doing, not as a virtuous achievement or cowardly agnosticism, but as their assessment of the way things really are in regard to creatures and Creator. Noninterest in self is a by-product of the otherness of reality, a result of confrontation with the holiness of God. Once again, we see the essentially theological basis of our ethics, the movement from *credo* to good works.

Religion is concerned with states of mind as well as qualities like a pure heart and a meekness of spirit. Such states of mind become purifiers of our vision, "Not I, but Christ," says the believer as he or she attests to the presence of One who helps us see and do and be. Anything—our creeds or our prayers—that helps "create in me a clean heart O God," renders vital service to the *bene operandi*. Anything urging us to look less at ourselves and more upon God is in service of the truth. Without a vision of that truth beyond ourselves, without this objectivity and realism, this humility; all talk of what is moral and good is premature.[8]

Humanity is inherently incapable of bearing the full weight of the truth. Modern concepts of humanity tend to be too grand, too promethean, too naïve in their faith that through education or act of the will we can be rational and free. Liberation theology, and its Marxist utopianism, assumes only the rich are capable of evil. After the revolution, they say, all will be justice and light. Theologies of human potential naïvely assume that, given the proper self-affirmation, I'm O.K.—you're O.K. To be human is to be a weaver of illusion.

As Gustafson says, "Man's dispositions, affections, and intentions are biased toward improper self-interest; man is curved in upon himself. This he never overcomes in a human perfection of his moral capacity; . . . the problem is a disorientation of their basic direction, and this also must be overcome."[9] In other words, "sin" is the opposite of worship. Sin is the heart curved in on itself, contracted, eyes turned inward. We become as gods to ourselves, impotent to rise above our own myopic vision.

Modern ethics of choice adopts an inadequate anthropology in asserting that we ourselves can change our moral selves through bold choices. Thus we increase or legitimize our excessive self-concern by stressing choice rather than vision, courage rather than character. But this overlooks how strenuous a task it is to see the world truthfully. The harsh light of reality is painful. The gospel says this. Unable as we are to discover truth, truth is revealed to us. Unable to make ourselves good, we are justified by God's action. Unable to bear the truth about ourselves, Christ's death and resurrection show God confronting the harsh truth about us and redeeming us for divine purposes.

Virtue requires selfless attention to God. The chief enemy of excellence in morals is our never-ending personal fantasy that we are the chief fabricators of truth and goodness, "the tissue of self-aggrandizing and consoling wishes and dreams which prevents one from seeing what there is outside one."[10] We do not see the truth simply by opening our eyes—we are anxiety-ridden animals who cling to fantasies and false images out of our anxiety. The chief evidence that we are, in the words of the old *Book of Common Prayer,* "miserable offenders," is that we loudly persist in the notion that we are *not* miserable offenders. As Luther said, the frightened human mind is a permanent factory of idols. Our minds are usually self-preoccupied. The selfless love that Christ shows and urges upon us is the tough ability to see someone or something other than ourselves, and, when looking at ourselves, to see ourselves accurately, as God sees us. Love, as an ultimate goal for Christians, is the freedom from self and self-aggrandizing fantasies—not simply the freedom to choose what one wants. "Freedom," says Iris Murdoch, "is the disciplined overcoming of self," in order to see what is real—painful though that vision may be.[11] Once such realism is attained, right conduct is the fruit of this soaring vision.

> Have this mind among yourselves, which you have in Christ Jesus, who, though he was in the form of God, did not count equality with God a thing to be grasped, but emptied himself, taking the form of a servant, being born in the likeness of men. And being found in human form he humbled himself and became obedient unto death, even death on a cross.
>
> (Phil. 2:5-8)

Morality is not something that is switched on and off on specific occasions when choice is demanded—as we argued in our ealier criticism of Barth's ethics of obedience or Fletcher's situation ethics. Morality is deeper than choice. Morality is a sustained, disciplined product of character, an activity that occurs between, and prior to, choices. Thus we must pay as much or more attention to the sort of persons we are as to the choices we make.

Human beings differ because we see the world differently from one another. Our conceptual and experiential filters are different. However, the church claims the presence of certain moral "facts" no less real because only a portion of humanity sees those facts. These are the facts of life to which one must eventually give one's assent in order to enjoy the "abundant life." Evangelism is one with morality in attempting to proclaim the gospel in such a way that one can say, "I see."

The "real" in our world is not existentially created. It is discovered, or, truer to the biblical witness, it is disclosed to us. The final authority of morality is not What is possible? or What works? but What is real?[12] Once again, ethics has a duty to examine how a person's vision of the world is formed and maintained. In regard to specific moral arguments, the church should expend less energy debating basic principles (e.g., "right to life" versus "freedom of choice" in the abortion debate) and give more effort to changing a person's world. We change our minds only when we see the world differently. Christian morality is the fine art of seeing and then encouraging others to see a new source of life that is real. The difficulty of the truth, as we see it, is that it not only beckons us ("Come to me all ye who are heavy laden") but repels us by its otherness ("My ways are not your ways").

At times Christianity allowed itself to be presented as a moral system with the religious, the transcendent, reduced to little more than an emotional tinting upon its humanistic ethical scheme. This is a mutation. The religious, the theological is the very ground of our ethics, the reality from which morality is possible. Thus, *worship is an ethical activity in itself*.

An example comes to mind from my own pastoral experience. After an Advent sermon on the story of the pregnancy of Mary, a woman in my congregation said this:

Parishioner: I'm rethinking what I once thought after Sunday.

Pastor: What are you rethinking?

Parishioner: Well you know how I've felt about this issue of abortion.

Pastor: No, I don't think I do.

Parishioner: I guess I pretty much followed the standard line.

Pastor: Which is?

Parishioner: Which is that it's O.K.—if the mother, if the parents, think it's the best thing to do.

Pastor: And you've changed? Why?

Parishioner: I don't know. It wasn't so much the sermon.

Pastor: Yes, I didn't even mention the topic in the sermon.

Parishioner: It was the scripture, I think. When you read about Mary getting pregnant: Her song, her joy, her vision about what God had in mind for her baby. I said to myself, "What do we think we're doing? This baby is what God wanted for the world. It wasn't our idea." It put me in touch with the birth of my children, the birth of children in the world—even poor children. Maybe I ought to say especially poor babies and their mothers.

Here someone sees things differently as a result of hearing something in worship. "What do we think we're doing?" is a characteristically humble question. The realization that God is God and that God may see things differently than we do is a freedom-producing vision, a mind-changing, behavior-changing situation. The process of ethical change is thus considerably more subtle than overt moral arguments. *Exposure of the self to God, the function and goal of our moments of prayer, praise, and worship is an integral part, a necessary qualification for the ethical life.* The *lex credendi* and the *lex bene operandi* are linked to the *lex orandi*.

Our times of worship, of major and minor *ecstacy* (literally "to stand outside oneself"), those times when the liturgy sweeps us up, "lost in wonder, love, and praise," are the supremely self-forgetful moments that are the very heart of morality. The liturgy at its best is the church's dangerous attempt to let God be God in the church, to preserve a healthy tension between creature and Creator. This glory, this majesty is as much over against us as it is for us—against our incipient Pelagianism that claims a basic goodness for us apart from God, against our urbane Arianism that sees the Christ as simply a good friend and blesser of our values. False worship, like false ethics, invariably ends up as another petty, but nonetheless disastrous, attempt to forget God rather than ourselves. "He has put all things under his feet and has made him head over all things for the church" (Eph. 1:22). The next two chapters, in which we examine the sacraments of Baptism and the Lord's Supper, are attempts to specify some of the self-forgetfulness that happens in our worship when we view and re-view the world *sub specie aeternitatis*.

My emphasis upon vision and self-forgetfulness may not be enough for the many that hear this view of morality as almost entirely intuitive and irrational, as liable to the same error and illusion of any human enthusiasm. Have we exchanged the rationality of man-the-chooser for the irrationality of man-the-lover?

I refer to my comments at the beginning of this chapter. The human response to God in Jesus Christ is not "monotonous, colourless and formless" but "articulated, colorful and contoured," says Barth.[13] Moral formation is a disciplined affair. It is not platonic love in the abstract, nor is it erotic love in the heat of passion. Moral formation is love in the manner of love in marriage—*a lifelong attention to the other in such a way that one is drawn out of oneself into the life of another.* Christian life, quoting Barth again, is a "formed reference." We are disciples of this Jewish carpenter's son from Nazareth, recipients of these canonized Scriptures, participants in this Story, inheritors of this church tradition, actors in this liturgy—not some other.

To affirm the moral value of self-forgetfulness, affection, and character is not to deny the continuing worth of specific features of Christian morality such as laws and principles. We simply want to keep laws and principles relative to the blinding revelation of God in Jesus Christ. While avoiding pure rationalism and legalism, we can also avoid pure intuitionism. "Thou shalt not kill." "You shall have no other gods before me." "Love your enemies." "Whoever receives a child receives me"—these are all aspects of the specifiable, rich contours of this faith, this story, this person who has lured us forth from our limited selves.

The liturgy, as a primary source of Christian belief, vision, history, laws, preaching, prayer—in short, the substance of our faith—is the primary safeguard against the Christian vision's subversion by other mutant or opposing visions. The primary place in which the majority of Christians come into contact with a creed, or the Decalogue, or the stories, or prayers, or scripture of the church is the church's liturgy. A continuing context for the Christian's emotional, affectional engagement with the truth of this faith, is in Sunday worship. Therefore we must be vigilant in our preservation of the substance of this worship. Orthodoxy—"right praise"—is a never ending concern for liturgiologists. The *lex orandi* will have its way with the *lex credendi,* and therefore with the *lex bene operandi,* so we had best be sure that we are truly praying, preaching, and singing as Christians rather than as pagans.

Those of us who are heirs to the free church, pietistic

tradition may be at a disadvantage when it comes to this matter of liturgical substance. Sunday services that are at the mercy of a preacher's whims, limitations, and pet crusades may leave the worshipers without sufficient substance, without a sufficiently challenging and continuing encounter with the given contours and narratives of the faith.

In its stress on instantaneous conversion and warm feelings, American evangelicalism reveals an inadequate appreciation for the depth of human sinfulness and therefore an inadequate stress on the long-term formation of the moral self. In its highly individualized songs and hymns, ("Amazing grace how sweet the sound that saved a wretch like *me./I* once was lost but now am found, was blind but now *I* see.") Much evangelical worship has fostered a "Me and Jesus" mentality and morality that actually added to our preoccupation with self. If, as we have argued, moral goodness is not automatic but rather a product of long-term discipline and attentiveness to the art of self-forgetfulness (rather than sporadic surges of emotion accompanied by heroic choices), then the churches of American evangelicalism are at a disadvantage when it comes to worship as a context for moral formation. In our worship renewal, in our attempt to recover substance, we may be at a disadvantage when compared to the so-called liturgical churches. It is more difficult to reintroduce what has been lost than to reshape what is still present.

And so Reinhold Niebuhr criticized the worship of Methodists a half-century ago.

> When the old evangelical piety is dissipated and there are not powerful theological and liturgical forces to preserve the Christian faith and feeling the tendency is to sink into vulgarity or into a pure moralism. In all sectarian churches there are today types of vulgarized Christianity in which both sermon and service seek to intrigue the interest of the religiously indifferent masses by vaudeville appeals of various sorts. This represents the worst form of disintegration. The best form is to be found in the championship of various moral and social causes. . . . The vulgarization of sectarian Christianity is partly due to its

difficulty in finding proper forms for the social expression of its faith.[14]

Later Niebuhr would write that,

the trouble with American Protestantism is that its protest against the various forms and disciplines [of worship] led to their destruction. It may be possible to have a brief period of religious spontaneity in which the absence of such disciplines does not matter. The evangelism of the American frontier may have been such a period. But this spontaneity does not last forever. When it is gone a church without adequate conduits of traditional liturgy and theological learning and tradition is without the waters of life.[15]

Perhaps Niebuhr would have modified his position had he been witness to the recent resurgence of lively sectarian enthusiasm and our growing recognition of the continuing vitality of some sectarian liturgical expressions. Could he have said, for instance, that the American black church, a mainly sectarian and nonliturgical body, is without the waters of life? However, his observations are an apt description of the current malaise of many "mainline" denominations. As one layperson put it to me, "You can't have a revival fifty-two Sundays a year. Something more has to happen."

The current liturgical reform movement is, in part, an effort to recover the substance of the liturgy, to tell the whole Story rather than one subplot of the narrative, to help bring the church back to the wellsprings of the faith. For those who tried to subsist on one scripture lesson a Sunday, haphazardly gleaned from the canon (usually one of the Gospels), the new three-year, ecumenical lectionary enables exposure of the faithful to a wider range of scripture in a more systematic way. For those who attempted to nourish the congregation on the preached word alone, new liturgies offer opportunities to experience the Reformation intention of word *and* table, eucharistic worship on a more regular basis, to move us from our stiffling subjectivism to more corporate worship. Those trapped in a year of Good Fridays need the full liturgical year. The recovery of Scripture, the Eucharist, and the church year are examples of how liturgical renewal hopes to preserve the substance of the Christian faith in our worship.

Malformation

Christian theology has traditionally contended that the root sin is idolatry rather than atheism. We will have our gods, be they false or true. And they will have their way with us. The sins of indulgence and greed (thing-idolatry), the sin of pride (self-idolatry) stem from this root sin.[16] The problem of human sinfulness is rooted in the liturgical problem of worshiping a false God. Idolatrous worship is malformation of the moral self as surely as true worship is moral formation. We imitate whom we adore.

Our idolatries of materialism, sex, reason, money, nature, health, and the state are certainly significant. However, the most significant type of unbelief I encounter is not one that denies God in an aggressive, articulate manner but is a mere shrug of the shoulders. Christianity appears to the modern Western world hardly worth denying because it seems innocuous in the first place.[17]

In the liberal, mainline Protestant apologetic attempt to speak to the modern world, we have fallen into its trap. In our effort to be relevant, we have become indistinguishable from the regnant culture. Religion is reduced to the civility of civil religion. In my own denomination, pluralism is a goal rather than a fact to be confronted by faith. Tolerance is substituted for conviction. "Live and let live," we say when confronted by truth claims alien to our own,[18] "Every religion is simply a different road to the same kingdom." But this denies the facts. Are all religions, at bottom, the same? Clearly not.

When acceptance is elevated as an ethical value, God becomes the great accepter *par excellence*, a cosmic Rogerian counselor who excludes no one and no behavior from his oozing grace. How could such a God have ended up on a cross? How could such a God invite us to his kingdom since, without boundaries on divine acceptance, there can be no kingdom?

The New Testament clearly acclaims Christ to be decisively different, singular. This divine deed is not on a continuum with other religious ideals or human aspirations. Yet this singular event is not a gnostic phenomenon, available only to those in the know. As Peter told the wondering crowd at Jerusalem, "this promise is to you and to your children and to all that are far off, everyone whom the Lord our God calls to him" (Acts 2:39). The gospel call is to go to those "in Jerusalem and in all Judea and Samaria, and to the end of the earth" (Acts 1:8).

Unfortunately, in its desire to show forth the good news into all the world, the church is always in danger of being subverted by the world.

In the history of the liturgy, unintentional syncretism has often been our response to cultural pluralism. For instance, in the fourth century the church adopted imperial court ceremonial into its worship, and with all the trappings of the empire, Christian worship became a very different affair. When bishops began dressing like Roman consuls, wearing stoles, rings, and other symbols of power, Christian ministry was well on the way to imperial lordship.

In church history, the central question is not How can the church be involved in the world? but How can the church resist being conformed to the world? The church forever deludes itself into thinking it can get some political or social or ideological handle on the way the world is run and then transform the world. The worldly, monarchial papacy of the Middle Ages is a historical example. The call for Christians to take up the gun and participate in violent revolution is a contemporary example. Alas, invariably the world transforms us. We fit the world's standards into a roughly Christian framework that results in merely residual Christian ethics.

Some current theologies of liberation appear to have switched one form of politicization (Western, capitalist, imperialist) for another (Third World, Marxist, Socialist).

In neo-Constantinian fashion, the church exchanges bedfellows, based on its assessment of who will be in charge once the revolution is over, substituting a little worldly wisdom for the foolishness of the gospel. When the revolution is over, whoever wins, will the world need the gospel any less than it does now? Will the eschatological claims of the gospel not relativize Marxist claims as surely as they do those of the capitalist? Is political success analagous to Christian faithfulness?

We must learn once again to trust the gospel to reveal the human situation. We need not ignore social, economic, political, or psychological analyses. But these secondary insights must be related to our primary theological claims. In a pluralistic society, the church can best serve that society by responsibly discerning and being obedient to our Story. Hans Conzelmann says:

> The Christian community declares publicly who is its Lord. The confession not only demands a decision but has the power to produce one. . . . Christ's rule is confessed before the world because his domain is not only the Church but the world. Thus the Church knows, whereas it is hidden from the unbelieving world. Therefore the Church must go on disclosing to the world the truth about itself.[19]

Worship, as a distinctively Christian activity, becomes a continual recalling back to the source of our faith, a continual retraveling of the path to which we have been called, a continual naming of *the* Name and telling of *the* Story so that we do not forget who we are, in whose image we were created, and to whom we are to conform.

The Church's Adversary

The interrelationship of the *lex orandi, lex credendi, lex bene operandi* is not always a harmonious one. At any time in the church's life one mode of Christian responsiveness may step to the fore and correct the other modes. In the Reformation, the *lex credendi* launched a reform of the church's liturgy based upon the doctrinal judgment that the Mass had become misguided. In the 1960s, social activism's *lex bene operandi* called the church off its comfortable pews, out of its solemn assemblies, and into the streets. Now, in a period of malformation and unconscious subversion of the church's belief and action, the *lex orandi* may be calling us to remember who we are.

Liturgy cannot, on its own, settle questions of right belief or right action. But it sets us in the context where distinctively Christian believing and doing must begin. In the liturgy, we encounter the indicatives of the faith over and over. Knowing that much of our moral formation arises from experience and discourse which, on the surface, have no moral import, we must pay attention to the subtle forces at work in the liturgy. What is the ethical import of a funeral where we confront human limits and mortality, or a Eucharist where we are in the presence of God, or a Baptism where we feel the burden of God's claim upon us? The subtlety of such influences makes them no less significant—perhaps they are more significant precisely because of their subtlety. In the following chapters, I hope to show specific instances of how liturgy is both content and critic of the church's ethics.

The liturgy, this embarrassingly primordial foe of all abstraction, rationalization, and self-interest, keeps inviting us to venture forth from the safe confines of life in post-Christian America and meet the truth—truth not as a principle but Truth himself. Christ came preaching, not love, but discipleship. He becomes truth and love embodied, sacramentalized, in the flesh. "Love" has no meaning apart from his life and work. He was nailed to a cross because he was a prophet who was not acceptable. The ability to love is the hard business of following this Lord. Liturgy—its icons, crosses, bread and wine, metaphors, images, and preaching—keeps beckoning us back to gaze upon this Lord, painful though it may be.

And so, while the liturgy is the church's source of life and identity, it is also one of our most persistent critics. Time and again it reminds us that although we are loved by God—we are not God. Although we are in the world—we are not of the world.

It is all too obvious that the church fails to form people who consistently pray, believe, and act as Christians. But our liturgy not only tells us that we are sinners. In helping us to confess sin, it offers us grace. In dealing with our failure to be Christians, the liturgy sets us within the sole context whereby it is possible, even for us, to become Christians.

Reading the catechetical lectures of Cyril by which he instructed the newly baptized in fourth-century Jerusalem, or the catechetical instruction of Augustine, I am amazed at the determination of these early fathers to evangelize the world without falling victim to their own astounding evangelical success. One marvels—in our time of cheap grace, warm fuzzies, Madison-Avenue strategies for church growth, and the promiscuous baptism of everything—at the continual attempt of the early church to define itself, particularly in its worship, as over against the world so that it might truly be for the world.

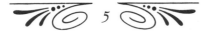

Baptism: Deadly Work

T he American church lives in an ethically debili-
tating climate. Where did we go wrong? The
urbane self-centeredness of Peal's *Power of
Positive Thinking* and its therapeutic successors?
The paternalistic, liberal, civic-club mentality of the heirs of
the social gospel? Or was it our cozy alliance with passing
intellectual fancies of American secular culture? Who can
say for sure? Now American churches waver between
evangelical TV triumphalism values or live-and-let-live
pluralism that urges open-mindedness as the supreme
virtue. In my own mainline Protestant setting we reflect the
latter. All we need is a little more love since we are all
basically nice people just the way we are. Triumphalism—
whether it be that of medieval catholicism, American
evangelicalism, or liberation theology—adopts the world's
standards of what is right and then sets out to defeat the
world on its terms. The battle ends before it begins.
Theological and ethical sentimentality reassure people that,
whatever the gospel means, it does not mean obedience; not
death. Love, divine or human, could never be so costly, we
tell ourselves. After all our culture is at least vestigially
Christian, and isn't that enough?

A few years ago, during the height of the Iranian hostage
crisis, I talked with a secretary who told me how she had

befriended an Iranian student on a nearby campus. His funds were cut off at the beginning of the revolution in Iran, and he offered to do some odd jobs around her house. When his financial condition got worse, she invited the boy into her home, gave him a room, and let him eat his meals with her family. Her neighbors did not like it, but she assured them that this was the way it was; the boy stayed.

"How does he feel about what's going on over there?" I asked. "Does he agree with his government?"

"Well, he's an Iranian," she said. "He thinks the revolution is just fine. We have had some arguments."

"How did you come to befriend someone like that?" I asked in amazement.

She pounded her fist upon the desk. "Because I'm a *Christian,* darn it. You think it's easy?"

In such moments, one has the impression that one is close to the truth of the gospel. This is the primal *via crucis* that gave birth to our church and made it vigorous.

Luther says I became a theologian not by comprehending, reading, or speculating, but by living, and indeed *dying and being damned.*

The Cleansing Bath

The Synoptic Gospels all begin with strikingly similar accounts of John the Baptist. This prophetic "voice crying in the wilderness" appears, "preaching a baptism of repentance for the forgiveness of sins" (Mark 1:4). John prepares Israel for the New Age by calling Israel to a water-bath of baptism.

The time is short. The day of judgment is near. False hope and security must give way to repentance and righteousness. To those who sought safety in the old order, John warned,

Do not presume to say to yourselves, "We have Abraham as our father"; for I tell you, God is able from these stones to raise up children to Abraham. Even now the axe is laid to the root of the trees; every tree therefore that does not bear good fruit is cut down and thrown into the fire.

(Matt. 3:9-10)

John's "baptism of repentance" was prophetic. Like the prophets before him, John proclaimed the triumph of a God who would bring the fire of judgment upon Israel's unrighteousness. Even the Chosen People must be washed. The only possible response was whole-hearted self-surrender and fruit worthy of repentance. Baptism became the action of that repentance.[1]

The Gospels show Jesus' baptism by John as the inauguration of his ministry (Mark 1:9-11 and parallels; John 1:32-34). But why, in light of Matthew 3:14-15, was the manner of inauguration an embarrassment for some early Christians?

It was an embarrassment precisely because it is a "baptism of repentance." This act of self-surrender is an unexpected way for a Messiah to begin his mission. Jesus' own self-surrender sets the beat for how his followers are to march to the New Age. Initiation into this messianic community is repentance. Later, when Peter's preaching of the good news led some to ask, "Brethren, what shall we do?" Peter responds *"Repent, and be baptized* every one of you in the name of Jesus Christ for the forgiveness of your sins; and you shall receive the gift of the Holy Spirit. For the promise is to you and to your children and to all that are far off, every one whom the Lord our God calls to him" (Acts 2:38-39).

Cleansing, death, birth, refreshment, illumination, the Spirit are all New Testament baptismal themes. But none of these negates the essential image of baptism as participation in the converting, life-changing, submission-evoking power of the gospel, the good news of a kingdom which begins with a cross.[2] Rich New Testament baptismal images underscore the life-changing nature of baptism: Birth (John 3:3-5), a funeral and burial (Rom. 6:1-11), a bride's nuptial bath (Eph. 5:26-27). The bath ends by arraying the body in new clothing (Gal. 3:27) for baptism sets Christians apart as specifically as circumcision set Jews apart (Col. 2:11). So radical, complete, and primal is this experience of baptismal *metanoia* that only the most limnal, primal human experiences can convey it: birth, marriage, death, bathing.

The preaching of Jesus will not leave us as we are. We pay dearly for this gift. The concrete reality of the life-changing gospel proclamation is baptism.

The New Testament gives few baptismal formulae, no detailed rubrics about method or mode. We have embarrassingly little guidance (considering later post-Reformation arguments over baptism) on the age or qualifications of those to be baptized. We are told only to baptize as a sign of repentance, entrance into the church, and participation in the mission of the church "in Jesus' name." We are to do for the world (Matt. 28:18-20) what John did for Israel in the Jordan—doing it now "in Jesus' name"—in the mode and manner of the Jesus story.

The starkness of this command provides a pattern for our interpretation of baptism. We may draw baptismal significations from the richness of water itself, but all these interpretations must be rooted in the primal repentance activity that began at the Jordan.

In the New Testament, when baptism is described to those who have not been baptized, verbs are in the future tense. When it is described to those who have been baptized, verbs are in the past tense, as we heard Peter say to the unbaptized: "You shall receive the gift of the Holy Spirit" (Acts 2:38). But when described to those who have been baptized, it is all past tense. "But you were washed, you were sanctified, you were justified in the name of the Lord Jesus Christ and in the Spirit of our God" (I Cor. 6:11).

How strikingly objective are these statements about baptism, especially when compared to the subjectivized faith of our age. To those who are not baptized, the message is one of promise: "Come, be washed, and you will come forth as a different person, you will be transferred to a different kingdom."

To those who have been baptized, the message is of an

alteration in the person's reality. "You are now washed, you are not who you once were, God has gotten hold of you, you have been moved to another location."

As in the baptism of John, when the abrasive prophet pointed to the inbreaking of a new reality, so Christian baptism testifies to, and invites one to participate in, a new reality. Baptism is a call to repentance, *metanoia*. This repentance is not a mere change of mind or heart. It is not an emotional feeling-sorry-for-my-sins. Repentance is the fitting response to the presence of the Kingdom, the only way left, the necessary choice between either self-abandonment or self-delusion. This baptismal work is something done to us rather than by us. Faith is a gift, says Paul. The passive baptismal verbs of the New Testament indicate that repentance is a gift too. The baptismal *metanoia* is not a heroic act, but rather the self's letting go of all attempts to be heroic. Baptismal repentance is a falling back into the waters, submitting to the power of God for better or worse, letting oneself be swept up like a dependent child into the movement of the Kingdom.

That Kingdom is both good news and bad. Repentance is a movement as painful as birth itself, as threatening as death; all the more painful *because* we are essentially passive participants in the process. The gospel call as signified in baptism is much more radical and painful than a mere, "Be clean!" It is: *You will be made dead!* The rite in the old *Book of Common Prayer* prayed for the newly baptized, "Grant that the Old Adam in these children may be so buried, that the new man may be raised in them."

Jesus' baptism not only inaugurated his messiahship but also revealed its shockingly unexpected nature. As John pushes him into the waters, Jesus says they are fulfilling all righteousness. His baptism becomes a foreshadowing, a microcosm for his whole ministry. And what will be its shape? On two different occasions, Jesus uses the word "baptism" to refer to his own impending *death*. He asks his half-hearted disciples, "Are you able to drink the cup that I drink, and to be baptized with the baptism with which I am baptized?" (Mark 10:38). As his ministry takes him toward the cross, he says, "I have a baptism to be baptized with; and how I am straitened until it is accomplished!" (Luke 12:50). His death is his ultimate submission, obedience even unto death, his "baptism." As he submits to John's baptism of repentance, Jesus shows the radical way in which he will confront sin, meeting it on its own turf, submitting even to death.

In Jesus' baptism, begun in the Jordan and completed on Golgotha, John's repentance motif is pushed to its ultimate limit, the *metanoia* of John is intensified, its ultimate implications are played through even unto death.

John presented baptism as the washing of sin, a turning from self to God and God's righteousness alone. Jesus seeks even more radical *metanoia*. The Old Testament prophetic call to righteousness cost something. John himself would pay with his head. John's washing was not cheap. The baptism with fire that John predicted, the winnowing, judging work of God in Christ is not cheap either. It has become present in Christ, who "is to be plunged, not into the water but into calamity unto death."[3]

Perhaps this is why we have no record (in the Synoptics) that Jesus or his disciples baptized during his earthly ministry. Jesus' call was no simple prophetic call to human repentance. Jesus' call was an invitation to be transferred by God from one kingdom to another, to be moved from death to life. Jesus' baptism, his submission to the righteousness of God, his going under the waters, was the first step in obedience. There would be other steps along the way—all leading to self-abandonment on the cross.

There, on the cross, his saving work—begun and intimated in his baptism—was finished. The depth of divine love, the seriousness of human sin, the subtlety of evil, and the power of God were revealed with an intensity that could have been but dimly seen before the cross. "It is accomplished," Jesus pronounces as he dies.

Now, the saving work done, the baptismal process completed, the disciples are to begin their saving work. Now the Kingdom is inaugurated, now the community of death and resurrection can be formed. "Go therefore and make disciples of all nations, baptizing them in the name of the Father and of the Son and of the Holy Spirit" (Matt. 28:19). The words thunder forth. "Repent, believe the gospel, take up the way of the cross, and be saved."

The Drowning Flood

When Paul described the Christian life, he seems not to know whether to call what happened to him "birth" or "death." It felt like both at the same time. Whether birth or death, Paul knew firsthand that conversion meant change. He frequently contrasts his old and new life, the old Adam with the new (Rom. 5:12ff; I Cor. 15:20ff), the Spirit with the flesh (Gal. 5:16ff). Baptism is clearly the demarcation between the old world and the new, between death and life.

All conceptions of the Christian life that see converts as basically nice people who gradually become nicer, or see Christian moral formation as orderly development or minor tinkering and fine tuning of fundamentally good people are inimicable to the way Paul sees it. Nothing less than death will do, nothing less than baptism.

The earliest and fullest exposition of the ethics of baptism is Romans 6:1-11.[4] Paul begins his Letter to the Romans with his most extravagant claims for the free, unmerited, undeserved grace of God in Jesus Christ. We are justified, not on the basis of our righteousness, but by faith (5:1). Salvation comes as a gift (5:15). But some ask, Since God's grace is free, should we not continue in our sin so that God may be even more gracious? (6:1). Why not continue in our old self-indulgence if our sin will be forgiven anyway?

One response might be, "You must not continue in sin because God will punish sinners." That is at least implied by Paul, but it is not the heart of the matter. Paul responds in Romans 6 by referring to baptism. It is too late for such questions. You are now those who cannot meaningfully say such things. The Romans were once like that—and their past life is the basis for their now meaningless babbling. But something has happened—baptism. That past event determines objectively who the Romans now are or are not. In baptism they have turned, or more to the point of the passive verbs in this passage, they *have been turned* toward new visions, new goals, new names. The past tense of Paul's argument is itself the answer to the Romans' "Are we to continue in sin that grace may abound?"

"Do you not know," Paul asks (implying that they do), "that all of us who have been baptized into Christ Jesus were baptized into his death?" (6:3). Baptism has detached us from our old lives and old allegiances. The verbs imply that we were co-buried (v. 4); we have "co-grown" (v. 5); we were co-crucified (v. 6); so that we might co-live (v. 8) with Christ. The Romans share in Christ's death and therefore in his separation from the old self. Self-centered concerns of reward, self-indulgence, and self-preservation are rendered irrelevant because, in baptism, we have been detached from the self, detached from the world.

One cannot be "in" Christ, in the words of the early baptism formulae, without being "in" his death. Those who sign on with this Messiah sign on for the cross. Christ himself defines the content of discipleship—submission even unto death.

This talk of dying and rising with Christ may sound excruciatingly mystical. Commentators like Albert Schweitzer thought they saw a Pauline debt to the Hellenistic mystery cults in which the initiate appropriated the life of the deity by ceremonial washings.[5]

Most commentators now agree that Paul's baptismal theology is not "mysticism." Nor is Paul's talk of death in baptism a purely eschatological reference with only future significance (as Martin Dibelius argued[6]).

Paul's extravagant claims for baptism call attention, not to his mysticism, but to his realism, not to his expectation of Christ's work in the future, but of Christ's work in the present church. His language is strikingly realistic. Neither Paul nor anyone else in his time would have understood what we post-enlightenment moderns mean by "merely symbolic."

What is the basis for Paul's astounding (to our ears) claim

that "all of us who have been baptized into Christ Jesus were baptized into his death" (Rom. 6:3)?

Earlier, in Romans 5:12-21, Paul contrasted Adam and Christ, not as individuals, but as representative, corporate persons. Without losing their individuality, these persons included others. In our profoundly individualistic society, it is difficult for us to comprehend this manner of thought because we have lost touch with the idea of a representative, corporate person. But analogies are possible. When Martin Luther King was invited to the White House, a prominent black leader stated, "At last we are in the White House where we can be heard." We experience some people as representative persons. This brings us close to Paul's talk of being "in Christ." And yet Paul says more. Christ and Adam were more than representatives of the whole. Christ determines the shape and character of those who follow him and his way.

For Paul, when we are baptized "into Christ" we become participants in Christ. But this participation is not some mystical experience or manner of heightened consciousness. Our experience and our consciousness have little to do with it. He is talking about *an objective transformation wrought in the believer by the work of God in baptism through the church.*

This objective act has subjective consequences. When one is baptized, one is transferred from one state of being to another. If, as we have implied earlier, our doing proceeds from our being, to change our being is to change our ethics.

This is what Paul claims. A person cannot simply decide not to participate in Adam, flesh, law, or sin. One cannot simply decide to live in France and still live in England. Apart from participation in the liberating event that incorporates the self into a new structure of living, such a decision is futile. The event of Jesus Christ and of his church is that alternative structure. Paul says that emancipation from the bondage of one structure is possible because initiation into another is available. We are moved from one country to another.

Paul sees humanity as torn between conflicting participations. Our problem is not that we do not act upon our beliefs.

Our problem is that we are enslaved. We can never do more than act in accordance with our situation.

Obligation is the correlate of sovereignty. We serve whom we worship. To have faith in Christ, to trust him, does not abrogate obligation. Our obligations flow from our Sovereign. Caesar is not in control here. Faith in God and life in Christ transfer the self to another domain where another king rules. Being emancipated from the domain of sin means becoming a "slave" to God and a new righteousness. Ethical obligation is defined by this new situation. The basis of Paul's ethics is his soteriology, his Christology, his ecclesiology.

The pattern for our obedience is Christ himself who lived by the demands of God's kingdom, obedient to those demands even unto death.

Baptism is the sacrament of participation in Christ's death and therefore constitutes an end to sin. God raised Jesus to a life in which death has no more dominion. In Christ, believers are called and enabled to walk in newness of life. Here they live, not in the anxious, self-seeking, self-preserving world of the old self, but in a new world. We are "dead to sin and alive to God in Christ Jesus" (Rom. 6:11).[7]

Of course, Paul knew that Christians still commit sins, even if they are "freed from sin" (6:7). He is not talking about a sinless, perfect existence of perpetually good behavior, as his exhortation shows, "Let not sin therefore reign" (v. 12). He is talking about living in the church where Christ rules. The problem is in recognizing the proper ruler and in living in the right family. He is talking about transfer from one domain to another.

The baptismal aorist tenses reflect God's "objective" action toward the baptized: we *were baptized,* we *were buried;* we *were crucified.* But these have their counterparts in the active aorists, which are equally baptismal.

And those who belong to Christ Jesus have crucified the flesh with its passions and desires.

(Gal. 5:24)

So you also must consider yourselves dead to sin and alive to God in Christ Jesus.

Let not sin therefore reign in your mortal bodies, to make you obey their passions . . . but yield yourselves to God as men who have been brought from death to life, and your members to God as instruments of righteousness. For sin will have no dominion over you, since you are not under law but under grace.

Thanks be to God, that you who were once slaves of sin have become obedient from the heart to the standard of teaching to which you were committed, and having been set free from sin, have become slaves of righteousness.

(Rom. 6:11-18)

The new life is for "walking in" (6:4). The passive verbs remind us that baptism can only be received. But the gift must be actively appropriated in the believer's life—therefore the ethical imperatives that Paul grounds in baptism. Faith is obedience, not necessarily to a command, but rather to reality. That reality has a past (our justification in baptism) and an anticipated future (our continued sanctification as God continues the baptismal work in us).[8] Our response is simply the appropriate activity, considering all that has changed since Christ. We internalize this reality, make it our own, through our lifelong, repeated response. We imitate our Master, obey him, and wrestle with his will. The tradition, scripture, and the church gauge whether our internalization is adequate (as Paul does with the Romans). Baptism is that radical reorientation of life that humanity needs, but only God can bring about, and which humanity then makes its own.

This human response, the basis for Pauline ethical imperatives, is not human-determined. That would reduce ethics to subjectively initiated activity, a notion Paul would not tolerate. When one is baptized, one is grafted to the church, the Body of Christ. Membership in this body is not a matter of voluntary association—look how Paul got in. We are thrust into it. Once in, this body quite unmystically determines our possibilities, horizons, and world view. Paul's extravagant claims for baptism are a function of his claims for the church.[9] "Private baptism," without the presence of the church, misunderstands baptism.

Galatians 3:25-28 is another example of movement from baptismal inclusion in the Body of Christ to radical ethical implications of that new ecclesial existence.

> But now that faith has come, we are no longer under a custodian; for in Christ Jesus you are all sons of God, through faith. For as many of you as were baptized into Christ have put on Christ. There is neither Jew nor Greek, there is neither slave nor free, there is neither male nor female; for you are all one in Christ Jesus.

The problem that gave rise to this discussion with the Galatians (or I Cor. 12:12-13) is the baffling disunity in the body. Paul takes them back to the objective fact of their baptism. Once the Body is created in baptism, all former differences are abrogated. So—whether they like it or not or feel like it or not or even behave like it or not, "now that faith has come," they *are one body*. The Corinthians and the Galatians might as well get used to it.

> For just as the body is one and has many members, and all the members of the body, though many, are one body, so it is with Christ. For by one Spirit we were all baptized into one body—Jews or Greeks, slaves or free—and all were made to drink of one Spirit.

> (I Cor. 12:12-13)

Permit me one more example of Pauline ethics arising out of his baptismal (and therefore ecclesiological) theology: I Corinthians 6:9-11.[10] Paul begins by cataloguing those who are among "the unrighteous." They are "unrighteous," not because of their bad behavior, but because they are not in the body—they do not yet know who they are and what the world is. Some of the Corinthians *were* among these folk (v. 11). But it is too late now. Now they can be among the adulterers only by self-contradiction. "You were washed, you were sanctified, you were justified" (v. 11). Paul uses these aorist verbs once again to accentuate the church as objectively created in baptism. Nobodies have been made somebodies. Christ has transferred the Corinthians from darkness to light, from rugged individualism to body life. Paul's whole justification theology is summed up in this baptismal passage.

One can see the same reasoning in passages like Titus 3:3-7. "We ourselves were once foolish, disobedient." Then comes the reference to the objective, saving action of God in baptism followed by a string of ethical injunctions.

How different is this line of ethical argumentation from that we usually make. Our social action preaching says, "You who have been justified by grace must try hard not to continue in your racism, sexism, and nationalism because that would be bad." But such preaching does not defeat human subjectivity and self-reliance—it encourages it by making faith a psychological state, salvation the result of successful believing, and ethics an achievement of individuals sincerely trying to be good. Paul will have none of this, knowing from personal experience that such exhortation leads either to a "let us sin so that grace may abound" situation or to moral despair at our inability to be and do good.

By taking the Corinthians back to their baptism, to that objective fact of life in the body, Paul reminds them of the end of their essentially self-directed, self-seeking lives. By water and the Spirit, Christ has transformed their reality. They must now either live by the facts of life or appear bafflingly out of step with the way things are.

Post-baptismal sin is baffling. The Pauline rhetorical, "Do you not know . . . ?" (Rom. 6:1ff., I Cor. 1:10-13) shows that he is stupefied by post-baptismal immorality. It seems so strange that those who have participated in the reality of Christ should persist in the fantasies and delusions of their old lives. First John claims, "No one born of God commits sin" (3:9). And yet the same epistle admits to sin among Christians (1:8-9, 2:1).

In Paul's thought on this issue, he comes close to Luther's *simul justus et peccator*. The redeemed are redeemed from sin but not from sinning. They still sin, yes. But sin's power is defeated. They live as naturalized citizens of a new country. Occasionally, their former accents will crop up in their speech and they react according to their old nation's standards. But they hold citizenship in a new land that determines who they are and how they live.

It is almost as if sin is the result of defective vision, the inability to see things as they really are. The tradition often speaks of baptism as *illuminatio* (Greek: *photismos*)—a lighting of human darkness.

> Awake, O sleeper, and arise from
>   the dead,
> and Christ shall give you light.

> (Eph. 5:14)

We have been born into the darkness of this world. The church is here to bring us to light. Baptism is enlightenment. While our darkness is primordial ("original sin"), the gracious enlightenment helps us see things as they are.

The *simul justus et peccator* metaphor can mean (as it does in some Lutheran theologies) resignation to the inevitability and inconquerability of sin, resigned antinomianism. But it need not—as Paul's detailed ethical injunctions show. The believer is engaged, with the prodding and power of the Holy Spirit, in a continual growth out of the old nature, in a continuing, lifelong process of radical transformation due to a radically different way of seeing things.[11] This is why the current interest in "moral development" is not an adequate concept for describing Christian growth. Baptism reminds us that Christians are not chosen for "development" but for conversion. We are not to become more autonomous and independent but more appropriately dependent on the One who is the source of our life. We are not expected to be mature or self-sufficient. We are only expected to be holy. Nothing less than conversion, lifelong, daily, body-yoking conversion can do that.

In baptism, our "old Adam" is drowned. But as Luther

says, old Adam is a mighty good swimmer! Nothing less than daily repentance, daily turning from ourselves and turning to God is required. Baptism is a once-and-for-all experience, requiring only a few minutes to initiate, but taking our whole lives to finish. Daily we turn, daily we take up the cross and follow (Luke 9:23). Our *metanoia* is always out ahead of us, never done in a moment. Baptismal repentance is not a sequential event; this rite is not mechanistic or magical. It requires a lifetime. As Tertullian said, we "begin our life in the water, and only while we abide in the water are we safe and sound." This takes seriously our historical existence, with all its pitfalls and temptations toward darkness rather than light. It also takes seriously the active divine love that has embraced us in baptism. The post-baptismal period is one long, tough process of learning how to keep our eyes focused on the light.

Post-baptismal sin is a constant encouragement, not to despair, but to repeatedly *reditus ad baptismum*. Sin is still present, but it no longer reigns. We remember our baptism and thereby remember who we are, whose we are, and where we are. Without this remembrance, this repeated return to baptism, the Christian life would be unbearable. Every Sunday's worship is such a return, an invitation to continue exposure to the promises of our baptism and the correction of the community.[12]

The Corinthians are those who have participated in the justification of God "in the name of the Lord Jesus Christ," incorporated into the obedience and death of Christ, sanctified "in the Spirit of our God" (I Cor. 6:11). They continue to grow and continue to be drawn into the life-death reality of the body. Baptism is the sacrament which justifies us and that gives the gifts and sets us within the communal context where sanctification is possible. We shall have more to say about sanctification in the next chapter.

In the midst of our anxious ethical striving, our vain, individualistic attempts to justify ourselves, to make ourselves pure and holy by ourselves; in the midst of our attempts to preserve the church's life through our standards of success (triumphalism) or through our heroic efforts to keep it all together by live-and-let-live open-mindedness (pluralism), we are called back to the reality that challenges our ethical subjectivity. All the questions must now be asked differently. None of the old answers can be counted on. Old securities of reason, right, acceptability, and convention must give way because the Christian life cannot be self-sustained. We must now live as dead people who have given up hope in ourselves and the old certainties, people who have let go. Our hearts cling to a different world. Like our Lord, we have passed through the waters to the other side. "For you have died, and your life is hid with Christ in God" (Col. 3:3).

Baptismal Ethics

To be baptized "into" Christ and "in the name of" Christ means to be incorporated into a way of life that character- ized his life.

What was the shape of Christ's life? The most important Pauline christological passage is the hymn in Philippians 2:6-11.[13] The context is Paul's desire that the Christians at Philippi live in response to the gospel. "Do nothing from selfishness or conceit, but in humility count others better than yourselves. Let each of you look not only to his own interests, but also to the interests of others" (Phil. 2:3-4). How is such self-forgetful behavior possible? "Have this mind among yourselves, which is yours in Christ Jesus" (v. 5).

> Though he was in the form of God, did not count equality with God a thing to be grasped, but emptied himself, taking the form of a servant, being born in the likeness of men. And being found in human form he humbled himself and became obedient unto death, even death on a cross. Therefore God has highly exalted him and bestowed on him the name which is above every name, that at the name of Jesus every knee should bow, in heaven and on earth and under the earth, and every tongue confess that Jesus Christ is Lord, to the glory of God the Father.

(2:6-11)

This hymn portrays the shape or the movement of the Son's mission. Rather than aspiring for, grasping, or reaching toward the divine, "he emptied himself, taking the form of a servant" (or slave).[14]

For Paul, the shape of the Incarnation is its downward mobility, the humiliation, weakness, and obedience of the Son (see II Cor. 8:9). Those who looked upon Christ did not recognize God in the flesh, otherwise they would not have hung him on a cross (I Cor. 2:8). Christ won his victories through obedience, through self-emptying and suffering, not through miraculous powers. This is the stumbing block for Jew and Gentile alike (I Cor. 1–2).[1] "Although he was a Son he learned obedience through what he suffered" (Heb. 5:8).

That day at the Jordan, standing knee-deep in the cold water, with John the Baptist drenching him, the Anointed One signified his obedient journey toward the cross. His baptism intimated where it would finally end. His whole life was caught up proleptically in this single sign. Our baptism does the same.

The chief biblical analogy for baptism is not the water that washes but rather the flood that drowns. Discipleship is more than turning over a new leaf. It is nothing less than daily death. The Crucified One determines the pattern for our baptism, the adequacy of our present making of disciples.

Older understandings of infant baptism assumed that secular society was a prop for the church. Evangelism was not taken too seriously because it was presumed that culture itself was Christian to the core. People became Christians by osmosis, by simply living in the right neighborhood, so there was no need for catechesis. Can the church assume these things today?

The religious marketplace is crowded. Whatever privileged status the church may have had has been lost. We must now compete—like any other claimant to truth—for commitment. Any church, lying apologetically on the periphery of the world, hat-in-hand, awaiting government subsidies, tax breaks, and public approval is doomed.

But many of our present baptismal practices act as if nothing has changed. They assume the appropriateness of the neophyte just the way he or she is. Baptism becomes a public recognition ceremony of the child's essential goodness and completeness, a rite of passage into the human race rather than the church. Confirmation becomes a junior-high graduation out of the church. The shock and inconvenience of the water bath is reduced to a trickle; the scandal of the cross and the difficulty of the church become the right hand of fellowship and a pledge card.

From the beginning it was not so. At least since the second century, baptismal rites mainly concerned themselves with radical departure from the old to the new (an emphasis still maintained in Orthodox rites). Apologists like Justin Martyr (c. A.D. 150) and Irenaeus of Lyons (c. A.D. 100) reveal that the church was under pressure to clarify basic issues like conversion and faith in distinction from the surrounding pagan world. The church responded to a pluralistic religious environment, not by reducing its vision to the lowest common denominator, but by becoming more rigorous in its clarification of its vision and delineation of its boundaries. Baptism was administered to converts after an extended period of moral instruction and scrutiny. The church began by assuming that inquirers had to be *converted*—changed, metamorphosed, done over, reborn, initiated. The criteria for determining whether or not converts were called to this not-for-everybody faith were decidedly ethical. After being in contact with the church, have they honored the widows? Are they fit for life in the Body? Have they cared for the sick? Can they share? Do they now do good?[16]

In this missionary environment, the initiatory process was adult in character; the place of children of adult converts (whom we know to have been included at a quite early date) was derivative and secondary. Adult initiation set the standards for whatever was done to initiate children (unlike our own time when the standards are reversed).

The rite itself intensified and made visible the process of conversion and separation that the catechetical training had begun. Baptism was carried out against a background of Good Friday and Easter morning, beginning with a dramatic renunciation of paganism and a confession of the Christian rule of faith. One thus exchanged citizenship in one kingdom for another. The candidates disrobed so that "nothing alien might go down into the water." Nothing from one's old existence was to be carried into the new. After being thrust into the water three times, they were given a white robe to be worn at worship during the week following Easter. The sign of the cross was traced on the forehead in oil after baptism, marking the baptized person for Jesus Christ as a slave was branded for his owner and a soldier tatooed for his emperor.

This dramatically showed the transferral from one kingdom to another. In the Byzantine rite reorientation is dramatized in the apotaxis and syntaxis just before baptism: the candidate turns west, the place of darkness, in order to renounce Satan, and then turns eastward, toward the light, professing adherence to a new Lord.

The ancient rites remind us that baptism is always *contretemps,* unsettlingly paschal. It intimidates, not only the new convert, but also the previously converted, forever reminding us of the dangers of discipleship. The cross is not optional equipment for Christians.[17]

Kavanaugh describes how baptism sets the beat for the Christian life at the beginning. The church

> baptizes a convert not upon the basis of the convert's having been intrigued by some Christian doctrines, attracted by the Christian stance on some moral issue, or pleased by the aesthetic of some ceremony. It baptizes in the conviction that the convert either has begun by the Holy Spirit to live in Christ already or shows a marked likelihood of coming to do so at some future point in the fullest and most explicit ecclesial way. Faith, in this view, is not theology as it is practiced in academe: it is a way of life in Christ among his holy ones. Nor are these holy ones a loose association of the tasteful, the genteel, or the well-informed who desire to follow some of the teachings of a dead and absent Master. They are nothing less than those who corporately are strengthened by grace to bear the weight of God's pleasure of

the world first manifested in Israel and finally brought to term in the personal individuality of the incarnate Son. The Church is not a palm potted in academe or a psychoanalyst's office. It is a Tree of Life whose vast branches hold ensnared a living if bloody Lamb; whose taproot sinks deep into the rich and murky waters of creation itself. Who would live in Christ must learn to climb with muddy feet, for there is nothing conventional, neat, or altogether logical about a crucifixion or the Church.[18]

What happens at the font is the birth of the church, done in the death and resurrection of its Lord who, in baptism, brings us along with him on the perilous way. No cross, no crown (Phil. 2:3-11). The chief criteria by which a Christian is made and nurtured throughout life are always being refurbished at the font. This is the acid test, this bath, the taproot of it all, and any faith community is doomed if it departs notably from the terms that gave it birth. "Christ loved the church and gave himself up for her, that he might sanctify her, having cleansed her by the washing of water with the word., . . . that she might be holy and without blemish" (Eph. 5:25-27).

Practical Points

So-called believer's baptism arose as a critique of Christendom's practice of infant baptism. Radical inclusiveness produced radical exclusiveness. The church does not grow by natural generation sanctified by infant baptism; the church exists as an act of God, called into existence in each generation; God has no grandchildren, said the anabaptists. The church is the gathered body of the consciously converted.

Infant baptism, according to proponents of believer's baptism, depersonalizes baptism, turning the rite into magic and grace into an impersonal influence. For the anabaptists, a vigorous church is made of deeply converted people. Deep conversion is not an experience accessible to an infant, therefore infants cannot be baptized.

At its best, believer's baptism is a useful protest against

baptism as a social convention. Yet even this practice develops its own conformity. One church can produce youthful conversions as predictably as another brings its infants to the font. Baptist congregations have their problems with uncommitted members. Today's situation is not, on the whole, simply analagous to the situation of the church in the first two centuries. Believer's baptism has its appeal to an individualistic, self-help society.

In the future, those of us who baptize infants must take seriously the conditions which this practice requires. We will baptize those children whose sponsors and churches are ready to nurture them into the faith. But we must postpone the baptism of those whose sponsors need more guidance, support, or life-style changes until they and the church feel they can be effective agents of God's *metanoia*. Whatever we do in the matter of making Christians, business as usual will not do.

A new seriousness about the church demands a new seriousness about baptism. Whether baptism of infants or adults, we must cease promiscuous baptism. It is dishonest, if not downright cruel, to entice people with rosebuds, lace, sentiment, self-help, and end up tacking them on a cross. Pre- and postbaptismal cathechesis must strive to make clear what we are asking of converts and their sponsors.

Missionary, *metanoia* baptism is the historical and theological norm. The adequacy of our rites for the infants of Christian parents must be judged by how well these practices conform to the norm. Have the parents shown that they know the cost and are willing to pay? Will they be bold in leading their child down this narrow way? How will they insure that this new Christian continues to be caught up in the life-death dynamic of the gospel to be exposed to the workings of grace, to be grafted to the Body?

Appropriate prebaptismal questions for parents and sponsors: What do you need to give up or let go of now that God has entrusted the faith of this person to you? When this new disciple looks at you, how will he or she be able to see the weight of the cross on your shoulders? What skills can the church give you to enable you to help us make disciples?

The needs of the world are too great, the suffering and pain too extensive, the lures of the world too seductive for us to begin to change the world unless we are changed, unless conversion of life and morals becomes our pattern, unless we are disciplined to let go over and over again. The status quo is alluring. It is the air we breathe, the food we eat. Even if we manage to strike a blow for justice here and there, it's in the ball park of the world. The only other ball park is God's. Baptism takes us there.[19]

The question is not, What is the best age for baptism? but How do we best make Christians?

For some, baptism must be postponed until such time as the parents, sponsors, and the church can be faithful to the promises or until the child can answer. That time may be six or sixty years. We pray it will be soon, but we can wait. While we wait we can teach and witness before the young catechumen. For most of us, images of conversion must replace images of nurture in our Christian education. We are not talking anymore about fertilizing and watering a young seedling in warm, rich soil. We are talking about grafting a raw cutting onto the Tree of Life. The graft will work only if the cut is deep and the binding secure.

Above all, we can celebrate the rite of Baptism more robustly. A trickle of water will not kill or even clean anybody. On the bank of a dark river, as we thrust new Christians under the water backward, onlookers will remark, "They could kill somebody like that." To which the church will respond, "Good, you're finally catching on."

Baptism probaby never told anyone how to spend money, what to do for a living, with whom to eat, what to die for. But it tells everyone where these questions come from and how they must be asked if they are to be answered in a way that conforms to this cruciform faith. Baptism thrusts us down and then pulls us forth, naked, clean, fresh and sticky as a newborn; shocked, with eyes open, dripping wet, and then puts all the questions to us again—this time as those who have been buried and raised with Christ.

For example, the world has a race problem. But concepts like race, sex, and nationality do not work for us anymore.

We are not concerned with the race problem. We are concerned that the very idea of race be cast aside in the church, "In Jesus Christ there is neither Jew nor Greek, neither slave nor free, neither male nor female" (Gal. 3:28). All those old, sinful, distinctions do not impress us anymore. They get washed away in the baptismal waters. We have stopped trying to achieve maturity or decency. Now nothing will do except to let God put us to death, and give us birth—again and again. My self is a gift, not an achievement.

We see differently on our way back from the font, from the womb and the tomb, after our dress rehearsal for death and resurrection.

So an inquirer said to Tertullian one day, "I would be Christian, but after all, I do have to live don't I?"

"Do you?" the old man asked.

> We thank you, Almighty God, for the gift of water. Over it the Holy Spirit moved in the beginning of creation. Through it you led the children of Israel out of their bondage in Egypt into the land of promise. In it your Son Jesus received the baptism of John and was anointed by the Holy Spirit as the Messiah, the Christ, to lead us, through his death and resurrection, from the bondage of sin into everlasting life.

> We thank you, Father, for the water of Baptism. In it we are buried with Christ in his death. By it we share in his resurrection. Through it we are reborn by the Holy Spirit. Therefore in joyful obedience to your Son, we bring into his fellowship those who come to him in faith, baptizing them in the Name of the Father, and of the Son, and of the Holy Spirit.[20]

The Lord's Supper: Discerning the Body

Only a couple of decades ago, in the civil rights movement, people fought over who would be allowed to sit at a dime store lunch counter. One must give segregationists credit. They saw clearly that to share food with another person is to risk conversion. Something happens to people at a table. So Jesus came inviting people to dinner and preaching, "Blessed are you that hunger now, for you shall be satisfied. . . . Woe to you that are full now, for you shall hunger" (Luke 6:20, 25).

In this chapter, I discuss some of the ethical implications of the Eucharist by using Paul's writings on the Lord's Supper. Two main aspects impress the Apostle: (1) *Its formative, sanctifying power upon the church and individual Christians;* (2) *its efficacy as a paradigmatic experience for Christians.*

The Body

Throughout his letters Paul is concerned with what it means to be the church. When he addresses the *ekklesia,* he is usually referring to the local congregation (I Thess. 1:1), although he also uses the term in a more universal sense (I Cor. 15:9). When he turns his attention toward the moral life of Christians or their worship life, it is invariably for the ecclesial purpose of edification of the congregation (e.g., I Cor. 14:2-4; I Thess. 5:11).

The metaphor "Body of Christ" was Paul's unique contribution to the self-understanding of the church. "You are the body of Christ" (I Cor. 12:27), you were "baptized into one body" (v. 13). Baptism and the Lord's Supper are constitutive of this body.

In struggling to distinguish the Christian community from the surrounding pagan culture or Judaism, Paul turns to the church's worship as the defining or characterizing activity. Paul's thought on the Lord's Supper must be inferred from the tradition he reports (I Cor. 11:23-25) and from those sections where he uses the Lord's Supper to make a point about Christian behavior (10:16-17).

Paul calls the cup and the bread "communion" *(koinonia)* in the body of Christ. By this drinking and eating, the congregation shares Christ. Paul could argue that the Corinthians can no longer participate in the sacred meals at their local pagan shrines because the Lord's Supper makes them continuing participants in the reality of Christ (vv. 20-21), even as baptism initiated them into that reality.

It was this sacramental or realistic understanding of the Lord's Supper that got the Corinthians into trouble. The precise nature of their problems remains unclear; nonetheless, it is reasonably certain that they understood the Lord's Supper in a rather magical way. As the Christians at Rome had said, in effect, "Baptism has saved us, therefore let us continue in our old ways so that grace may abound" (Rom. 6), the Corinthians said, in effect, "The Lord's Supper saves us, therefore let us continue to eat as we always have so that grace may abound."[1] In responding, Paul exposes the radically ethical nature of Christian worship and thereby delineates the difference between pagan and Christian liturgies.

Here is the Corinthian context: We are in a house-church situation. The church probably met in the home of a wealthy Christian on Sunday, the first day of the week. (I Cor. 16:1-2). Wealthier members of the congregation brought food and shared it. People came as soon as they got off work.

Evidently those who arrived first began eating so that by the time everyone had arrived, some had had too much (11:21), while the poor were humiliated because they had nothing (v. 22). The Corinthians did not share with each other because they saw the Lord's Supper as personal, salvific, participation in the Lord, especially in the Lord's glory and power—The supper is an affair between me and the Lord; why should I worry about you? I shall ingest as much of this saving substance as possible; too bad about you.

This aggressive self-centeredness infected all aspects of church life at Corinth. They are fragmented (I Cor. 1:1-12). Some claim to have special wisdom and grace (1:18–4:21). Even the gifts of the Spirit have become a source of boasting, pride, and division (ch. 12). Their disunity is nowhere more apparent, and nowhere more appalling, than at the sacred meal.

To counter their abuses, Paul recalls the eating and drinking of the patriarchs (I Cor. 10:2-4). In the Exodus they "were baptized into Moses in the cloud and in the sea, and all ate the same supernatural food and all drank the same supernatural drink" (vv. 2-3). Manna and water from the rock in the wilderness are used as antetypes for the Eucharist and Baptism. "Nevertheless with most of them God was not pleased; for they were overthrown in the wilderness" (v. 5). The eating of the sacred manna and the drinking of the sacred water did not preserve them from God's judgment. Remembrance of their punishment should warn us in our eating and drinking (vv. 6-13).

What is the Lord's Supper?

> The cup of blessing which we bless, is it not a participation in the blood of Christ? The bread which we break, is it not a participation in the body of Christ? Because there is one bread, we who are many are one body, for we all partake of the one bread.

> (I Cor. 10:16-17)

We participate in Christ, says Paul. But what does that mean? *We who are many are one body.* Participation in Christ, in this meal, leads to communion, *koinonia,* in his body.

This is why the Corinthians' divisiveness is so shocking. Against the very essence of communion, "When you come together it is not for the better but for the worse" (I Cor. 11:17). "There are divisions among you" (v. 18). To the Corinthians' surprise, Paul asserts that because of this factionalism, "When you meet together, it is not the Lord's Supper that you eat" (v. 20). Why? They have not honored authoritative tradition? They have not followed official rubrics? They have not been led by certified clergy? No. Paul does not criticize them on the basis of any exclusively "liturgical" criteria. His criticism is that,

> in eating, each one goes ahead with his own meal, and one is hungry and another is drunk. What! Do you not have houses to eat and drink in? Or do you despise the church of God and humiliate those who have nothing? What shall I say to you? Shall I commend you in this? No, I will not.
>
> (vv. 21-22)

Through baptism, the Spirit-filled Corinthians thought themselves to be in possession of salvation, salvation which was constantly tasted afresh by receiving the holy substance of the sacred meal. Each person eats for himself (*idion diepnon*), gobbling down as much of the sacred food as possible. Perhaps the Corinthians confused the Christian sacraments with the washings and meals of their former pagan religions. In the Lord's Supper they tried to ingest the sacred, saving substance without regard for those who had nothing.

"It is *not* the *Lord's* Supper which you eat," is Paul's laconic verdict upon their meals. How can he say this?

First, Paul tells the Corinthian charismatics that, "as often as you eat this bread and drink the cup, you proclaim the Lord's death until he comes" (I Cor. 11:26). The Lord ate this meal on the way to a cross. As in baptism (Rom. 6) the Corinthians are being enticed into their Lord's *death*, not simply his power and glory. Paul reminds them of the servanthood and suffering of the historical Jesus lest they forget that aspect of their Lord in their exclusive focus upon the Risen Christ. "On the night when he was betrayed . . ." (v. 23). They need to remember the whole story.

As in his discussion of baptism, Paul also stresses the eschatological prospect, "until he comes." Lest the Corinthians overlook the not-yet quality of the time in which they live, lest they assume they are participating in a heavenly meal at the end of time rather than an earthly meal between the times, Paul reminds them that they are *in via* rather than *in patria*. We eat under the shadow of the cross, not simply in the glory of the resurrection. Christ is both savior and judge. Christ's suffering, serving love is the supreme qualification for the Corinthians' eating and drinking—as it is the great test for their spiritual gifts *(charismata)* (I Cor. 12–14). Thus Paul ends his discussion of the Corinthians' problems with his great hymn on love (ch. 13).

Second, Paul reminds the Corinthians that their forebears in the faith ate similar saving food in the wilderness, but "they were overthrown." Their behavior, in the midst of eating sacred food and drink, brought them to grief. The same can happen to the Corinthians. Sickness and even death have befallen those who have participated in the Lord's Supper unworthily (I Cor. 11:27). It is therefore important to discern the Lord's body while eating (v. 29). To despise one's brothers and sisters at the table is to despise Christ.

Insensitivity to the poor is a dramatically blasphemous act—particularly in the context of worship—because it is contrary to the very essence of *Christian* worship. The Letter of James castigates those who defer to "the man with gold rings and in fine clothing" while dishonoring "the poor man in shabby clothing" (2:1ff).The Letter of Jude speaks of people who "are blemishes on your love feasts, as they boldly carouse together, looking after themselves" (v. 12). The Corinthians were not alone in their failure to "discern the body."

The Body of Christ is not merely the bread, but also the church. The Body of Christ is gathered at the table. All are "baptized into one body" and all eat of one loaf. No longer can we act, eat, or be saved alone. We are in the body.

Christian worship is distinguished from pagan rites, not by its ceremonial, rubrics, language, or form. Christian worship, like Jewish worship before, is a uniquely ethical act.

As often as the body eats this bread and drinks this cup, the believers are nourished and strengthened in this new body-relationship that Christ has established. Christ is really present in this meal, in this body, in this bread and wine. But let us shift our focus from Medieval and Reformation questions of how and when Christ is present in the eucharistic elements to how the believers, in breaking the bread and pouring the wine, experience their presence in Christ as members of his body. Here ritual effects that which it celebrates. Here the Body of Christ takes visible form; here the church begins to taste, touch, and feed upon the miraculous assertion, "Now you are the body of Christ and individually members of it" (I Cor. 12:27).

The Normal Food of Christians

In my own free church tradition, Zwingli's practice of quarterly celebration of Communion has taken hold. That radical reformer from Zurich felt that quarterly celebrations of the Lord's Supper were sufficient lest the meal become too commonplace, too ritualized. This is an odd point of view. Odd because five hundred years of experience in those churches that adopted the Zwinglian practice shows that churches which commune less frequently value Communion less. Odd because of the biblical and historical testimony of weekly celebrations of the Eucharist. Odd because reformers such as Calvin and Luther hoped to establish weekly Communion.

John Wesley, founder of the Methodists, in "The Duty of Constant Communion," expressed the traditional Anglican view—Holy Communion as frequently celebrated, sanctifying sacrament. "As our bodies are strengthened by bread and wine, so are our souls by these tokens of the body and blood of Christ. This is the food of our souls: This gives strength to perform our duty, and leads us on to perfection."[2] Wesley is here speaking of *Communion as a sanctifying activity*. It is our sustenance along the way.

Sanctification is that life-long process by which Christians grow to be who they are called to be—saints. One of Paul's favorite terms for the church is "saints" (Rom. 8:27; 12:13; 15:25, 26; I Cor. 6:1; 16:1; Phil. 1:2). For Paul saints are not holy persons who stand out from the common herd of Christians because of their extraordinary spirituality or good works. Every Christian is a saint, a person made holy, a person sanctified by the working of God's Spirit. The Revised Standard Version's translation of Romans 1:7 and I Corinthians 1:2 is therefore inaccurate ("called to be saints")—as if sainthood were some future goal toward which struggling Christians aspire. The better translation is "called saints." "Called" here does not mean that these are labeled "saints." Rather, it means that they are called by God's act of including them among the elect. In the Old Testament, "saints" was a term for the elect of Israel. Now, in Christ, even Gentiles are called to be part of this sacred body (Gal. 6:16).

Obviously, when Paul calls folk like the Corinthians and the Romans saints, he does not mean that they are without sin. Rather, in addressing them so he reminds them that they are the ones who have been baptized, whose status has been radically altered, who are now citizens of a new kingdom. Therefore, they ought to be faithful to who they are—saints.

The process of becoming who we are is sanctification. Sanctification is a progressive work, according to Wesley, "carried on in the soul by slow degrees, from the time of our first turning to God."[3] A primary means of that strengthening toward holiness is our participation in the Lord's Supper.

As noted earlier, contemporary ethics has often presented the moral life as a rather sporadic, detached phenomenon. Ethics that stresses blind obedience to a principle, a feeling, or a situation gives little attention to the need for long-term formation of the self. Ethics concerned only with making autonomous decisions and choices often neglects the need for character and community which give vision, coherence, and order to our choices. Contemporary Christian ethics' neglect of sanctification is understandable. As tough as obedience to principles is, it is even tougher to submit to sustained, long-term obedience, to "be perfect even as your Father in heaven is perfect." It is much easier to simply do the right thing whenever the occasion arises than to become a saint. It is much easier to be sincere than to be perfect.

The Lord's Supper is a "sanctifying ordinance," a sign of the continuity, necessity, and availability of God's enabling, communal, confirming, nurturing grace. Our characters are formed, sanctified, by such instruments of continual divine activity in our lives.

Sanctification is a willingness to see our lives as significant only as we are formed into God's image for us. According to Paul, that image is always ecclesial, social, communal. In our attentiveness and response to this call to be saints, we find our thoughts, affections, sight, and deeds qualified by this beckoning grace. We become characterized as those who attend to the world in a different way from those who are not so qualified. Gradually, Sunday by Sunday, day by day, we are weaned from our natural self-centered, autonomous ways of looking at the world until we become as we profess. We are different.

As Christians obey their Lord in performing acts of justice and love, as they reshape the world with their Lord, as they accept their Lord's gifts, they are reshaped. They become what they eat. Christians do not simply live by certain external norms of justice and right, but by a general orientation that is the result of their peculiar way of looking at the world. Rules, norms, principles, and slogans do not change the world. Only people can do that. How people change the world depends on who they are, on what type of character they embody. The changes they effect in the world will be the results of how they themselves have been changed, on how tight the tension is in their own lives between the way things are and the way God wants things to be, on their ability to hope even in the midst of the world's

hopelessness, on their cultivation of daily, normal attentiveness to truth, the "single eye" as Wesley called it.

Among historic Protestant theologians, Calvin and
Wesley gave most attention to the need for careful
formation of the moral self—sanctification. Unfortunately,
Calvin does not often speak of *how* the self is determined,
except in rather abstract remarks about the self in relation to
law. Wesley, however, commends various disciplines for
spiritual formation. Chief among them is frequent participation in the Lord's Supper.

Without this inward orientation, this cultivation of the
whole personality attuned to God, our good works are
suspect. Wesley warns against exclusively outward religion
of good works. At the same time, Wesley opposed those
quietists and others who stressed inward piety to the neglect
of outward cultivation and expression. He thus maintained
a characteristically Anglican middle course between legalism and antinomianism. He saw clearly that our characters
determine our deeds and that our good works shape our
inward selves. Attention to both dimensions of the
Christian's life leads to Wesley's "Christian Perfection,"
Christian wholeness.[4]

Wesley could urge constant Communion because of his
Anglican stress on the benefits of Communion, as expressed
in the closing prayer of Cranmer's service:

O Lorde and heauenly father, . . . graunt that by the merites &
death of thy sonne Jesus Christ, and through faith in his bloud,
we and al thy whole church, may obtaine remission of our
synnes, & al other benefites of his Passion. And here we offre
and present unto thee, O lord, holy, & liuely Sacrifice unto thee:
humbly beseching thee, that all we which be partakers of this
holy Communion, may be fulfilled with thy grace & heauenly
benediccion.[5]

Cranmer's invitation to Communion sets the sanctifying,
ethically emphatic tone from the very beginning of the
service:

You that doe truely and earnestly repent you of youre synnes, and bee in loue and charitie with your neighbours, and entende to leade a newe lyfe, folowyng the commaundements of God, and walking fro henceforth in his holy wayes; Drawe nere, and take this holy Sacramente to youre confort.[6]

We approach the table with the intention of living in "love and charity with our neighbors"; we leave the table formed into a "lively sacrifice" for our God and our neighbors. At the table, the ethical implications of the presence of Christ in our midst become explicit; we grow to be who we are.

Sanctification asserts that the Christian life ought not be formed in a haphazard way. It takes constant, life-long attentiveness, habits, and care to embody this character.[7] The normality, the constancy of the Eucharist is part of its power. This meal need not be special, nor exhilaratingly meaningful (though sometimes it is both). This is the normal food of Christians, the sustaining, nourishing stuff of our life. We return again and again to the Lord's table, to the source of our life together, to the standard by which our life together is judged, as habitually and normally as we gather at the breakfast table. Contrary to fragmented, *ad hoc*, radically individualized or subjectivized views of the ethical life, the Eucharist is a sign of the necessity for continuous, habitual, ritualized, constant communal encounter with the presence of God so that we might be continually formed into God's people, the body we are meant to be.

In the Eucharist we proclaim the justice of God. We teach Christians how to remember, how to eat, and therefore how to live. We teach by the way we learn most important things—not in a lecture hall or classroom—but rather on stage, in a dress rehearsal where actions are learned through repetition, doing them again and again until they are assimilated into the personality. The Eucharist is a drama of repetition—first acted in the meals of Jesus with sinners and outcasts, now continuing to unfold in our day—until we find our places on stage, and know our cues, and it all becomes second nature to us so that our work is worship and our liturgy is life.

It is all so ordinary, so commonplace, so mundane, so *same*. It is the same bread you had for breakfast, the same wine you had at the wedding party; dare we bless it in Christ's name and call it holy? It is the same grocer whom you think cheated on last week's prices, the same smiling, neat secretary whom you know to be a closet drunk; dare we offer them the Body and the Blood and call them holy? The sameness of it all brings it so close to home, makes it so mundane, so concrete and near. Precisely.

Our relationship to the Jesus story is not one of logical deduction. It is a relationship to the person of Christ, an experiential, narrative matter rather than a logical one. Many are Christian, not through a tortured process of belief-doubt, examination-belief; but by simply following a way of life, eating at the family's table until their language, manners, memories, and tastes are such that they are one of the family. This can occur because the process of growing into this faith (sanctification) is not simply believing but also behaving, not simply conversion but also nurture. The Eucharist sets before us a feast, bids us eat and be filled, and thereby become what we eat.

Thank goodness, Jesus did not proclaim his kingdom by preaching abstract words like "reconciliation," "liberation," "atonement." For the sake of us poor animals, he ate and drank with sinners. He invited all to the table. He was among them as a deacon (waiter, butler, servant) rather than a master. He proclaimed the Kingdom by forming his kingdom around a table.

So, when the Corinthians wondered what the church was and who was a Christian, Paul followed his Lord's lead and pointed to the broken bread, the blood-red wine, and the sinners seated at the feast. At the table, this topsy-turvy, unexpected Kingdom begins to take visible form. The poor are filled with good things, the promised banquet of the New Age begins, and the hungriest of all get to sit at the head table.

Christian ethics arise out of Christian vision. But this

kingdom vision is so mundane, and yet so strange, that only constant attention, frequent repetition, and continual practice will enable us to discern the body, to see. Therefore we eat this meal and remember. This is a meal of "remembrance," not in the historical sense of the word, but in the sense of *anamneisis,* waking up, opening the eyes; in the sense of "remember who you are." We remember so that the body of Christ might be continually re-membered.

Blessed Are the Hungry

As it was for Paul and the Corinthians, it must be for us. When we think about the church, we must think eucharistically, in terms of the body gathered at the table. Here is the paradigm for how we are to be in the world, for how the church is to become the sacrament whereby the world encounters the Kingdom vision. Here we see the criteria whereby our present expressions of the church are called to task, even as the Corinthians were judged when they ate together.

The world still has its counterparts to the old mystery religions. Secretaries of Agriculture speak of American food as a weapon, health food faddists purify their way to immortality, a hungry world looks at a country where more perish from overeating than from starvation, a land of junk food and drive-through restaurants, of wide-spread obesity side by side with the sick, self-induced starvation of *anorexia nervosa*—my food is mine and to hell with you. Do we need more demonstrations of the potentially demonic, self-destructive, disruptive power of food? It is in such a world that the Lord's Supper becomes a revolutionary, counter-cultural act of protest, a subverting act of evangelism and social witness. Jürgen Moltmann compares our situation with that of the Corinthians before us.

> Anyone who celebrates the Lord's Supper in a world of hunger and oppression does so in complete solidarity with the sufferings and hopes of all men, because he believes that the Messiah invites all men to his table and because he hopes that they will all sit at

table with him. In the mysteries, the feast separates the initiated from the rest of the world. But Christ's messianic feast makes its participants one with the physically and spiritually hungry all over the world.[8]

From the first, the Eucharist was a protest against the way the world dealt with hunger, food, and community. The liturgy of this meal made manifest the essentially communal nature of this faith, the necessity of life in the body. Sharing in this one loaf keeps us tied to one body (I Cor. 10:16). Christian worship is joining with one heart and voice (Rom. 15:5-6), always *synaxis*, coming together (I Cor. 14:23).

In early celebrations of the Lord's Supper a number of ritualized activities made this communal, body-focus evident. The "holy kiss" (Rom. 16:16, I Cor. 16:20, II Cor. 13:12, I Peter 5:14), a common gesture of meeting and greeting, came to symbolize the *shalom*, the peace, which the Lord required among the faithful before offering their gifts (bread and wine) at the altar (cf. Matt. 5:23-24). The peace originally preceded the offertory, as Irenaeus and Cyril make clear. Later, in the Roman rite, the gesture was postponed and linked to the Lord's Prayer ("as we forgive those who trespass against us") and the Communion itself. In either position, the peace was a sign of the requisite community that must be present if this meal is to be the Lord's.[9] The peace made the ethical implications of the Eucharist obvious. Inability to make peace signalled inability to proceed to the table with faithfulness.

Even today, in spite of our deficiencies in eucharistic practice, the Eucharist retains words and gestures which are formative of the Christian ethical life.[10] The peace is being recovered. Many rites begin with a communal confession of sins against others. Prayers of intercession are prayed and the cup is shared, thus enacting basic symbols of the interconnectedness of human life. When someone in the congregation bakes the bread or makes the wine, when lay servers are used in the distribution, the everyday ethical implications of the offering and the giving are made manifest.

The doxological prayer after Communion in a new eucharistic service says:

> You have given yourself to us, Lord.
> *Now we give ourselves for others.*
> Your love has made us a new people:
> *As a people of love we will serve you with joy.*
> Your glory has filled our hearts;
> *help us to glorify you in all things.*
> *Amen.*[11]

Contrary to the views of the enthusiastic Corinthians and contemporary mystics, the liturgy is not a doorway out of the world, or a path deeper into the self, but a way into the world through an alternative vision. The instruments of sacramental worship are the worldly things of everyday life: bread, wine, water, touch, gesture, movement.

You cannot forget about your earthliness or creatureliness while chewing bread. You cannot presume to be some ethereal, glorified being who has risen above it all while your stomach growls and saliva flows. Nor can you convince yourself that God is unconcerned with the hungers of creatures and their material needs when this bread is lifted up and called holy.

As in the Jewish thanksgiving prayers which preceded them, Christian eucharistic prayers move through the basic stuff of life to an ever widening circle of praise until all of life is encompassed. The bread, when lifted up and blessed in the Eucharist, thrusts our vision both forward toward all God's gifts and backward toward the bread we had for breakfast, to the gifted and social nature of our existence, to the interconnectedness of worship and life.

The church has had a constant struggle with this interconnectedness. The temptation to return to our old ways of eating and drinking is ever-present. From the beginning, as Paul's Corinthian correspondence shows, privitization of the Eucharist was a major threat. The forces of perversion which would turn the *kurakon diepnon* (Lord's Supper) into the *idion diepnon* (your own supper) were ever present. These were fought by Paul, but became institutionalized in the Eucharist after the first four centuries. After the Constantinian peace, the church made adjustments in its relationship to the world. The old tension with the existing order relaxed. The initial, radical break with the old—Christian initiation—was reduced to social convention, Christening. The continual severance with the status quo, the Eucharist, became a celebration of the new harmony with culture. The church becomes the great civilizing, rather than the great evangelizing, agent. Having made an easy peace with the powers-that-be, the church obscured its unique vision.[12]

By the Middle Ages the Eucharist had become the Mass—a private thing, the confection of the clergy, doled out to individuals, an individual wafer set upon an individual tongue. The liturgical assembly had become fragmented. The Eucharist was no longer the mark of the church's unity. The cup separated the clergy from the people. There were private masses "said" by individuals for individuals—sometimes said even for dead individuals. Religion again made its retreat from the cauldron of human suffering and hunger to a more ethereal realm.

Many changes of the Reformation, while intended to restore Communion as a communal, participatory experience for the whole church, accentuated some of the most private, individualized aspects of the old Mass. Reformation eucharistic prayers offered private grace to private individuals for private sins in order that they might obtain private salvation. This introspective, didactic, pietistic, penitential emphasis aggravated the problem rather than corrected it.[13]

Looking over the history of the Eucharist and the constant struggle by the church to retain this meal as a communal, body-forming activity, one detects an unconscious attempt by the church to protect itself from the radical, communal, transforming power of this rite. Our individual prayers and prayer books, individual wafers and communion glasses suggest that someone is hoping to have a meal without having a meal: Me and Jesus without any messy leftovers or other people to worry about. Private devotion to Jesus is used to escape the church's inability to form a community of faith in Jesus. Far from confirming the irrelevance of the Eucharist to our human needs for community and communion, our history of aggressive attempts to defuse it is testimony to its threatening power. We only avoid that which would change us. We know we cannot sit down at this table, partake of this food with this host, and depart as we have come.

According to the Gospels, table fellowship with Jesus was always a radically communal affair. The charge against Jesus was not that his theology was bad but that "this man receives sinners and eats with them" (Mark 2:15-17, Matt. 11:19, Luke 15:1-2). He welcomed all to his table. His Great Exhortation manifested the radically inclusive nature of his kingdom, a kingdom that cuts across the barriers we erect between insiders and outsiders, the saved and the damned, the elect and the outcast—barriers often most rigidly enforced at the table.

Jesus offers his "blood of the (new) covenant, which is poured out for many" (Mark 14:24, Matt. 26:28). "Many" here is inclusive—not "many, but not all," but "all, who are many."[14] "The bread which I shall give for the life *of the world* is my flesh," (John 6:51) is the Johannine equivalent. The foretold messianic meal shows God's universal love. Isaiah says, "On this mountain the Lord of hosts will make for all peoples a feast" (25:6-9). "I tell you," says Jesus, "many will come from east and west and sit at table with Abraham, Isaac, and Jacob in the kingdom of heaven" (Matt. 8:11, cf. Luke 13:29). So Paul's appeal to the Corinthians to discern the body is not some imported meaning—it is at the heart of the table fellowship with Jesus. All meals with Jesus were parables of how the Kingdom takes form, the story that begins with the thundering declaration, "Blessed are you that hunger . . . you shall be satisfied" (Luke 6:21).

The eucharistic table is the one place where at least this much of God's kingdom is perceived, this much of Christ's real presence is felt: where suffering has meaning, where all are welcomed, where those who are elsewhere excluded, despised, oppressed, and left to starve are invited up to the head table. This is the way God intends the world to look, not just in church, but always.

> Now he told a parable to those who were invited, when he marked how they chose the places of honor, saying to them, "When you are invited by any one to a marriage feast, do not sit down in a place of honor, lest a more eminent man than you be invited by him; and he who invited you both will come and say to you, 'give place to this man,' and then you will begin with shame to take the lowest place. But when you are invited, go and sit in the lowest place. . . ."
> He said also to the man who had invited him, "When you give a dinner or a banquet, do not invite your friends or your brothers or your kinsmen or rich neighbors, lest they also invite you in return, and you be repaid. But when you give a feast, invite the poor, the maimed, the lame, the blind, and you will be blessed, because they cannot repay you. You will be repaid at the resurrection of the just."
> When one of those who sat at table with him heard this he said to him, "Blessed is he who shall eat bread in the kingdom of God!" But he said to him, "A man once gave a great banquet, and invited many . . ."
>
> Luke 14:7-10, 12-16

When our table is less than the fullness Christ's invitation intends it to be, we have failed to discern or actualize the body of Christ. The eucharistic table is the church's visible standard of measuring how well our concrete formations of the church embody Christ's will for the church. When there is an embarrassing gap between the actual life of the church and the values of the church as proclaimed in the sacraments, the sacraments are little more than make-believe. The sacraments become our judgment and we, like the Corinthians, are eating and drinking our own destruction.

The Eucharist is also the sign of the unity and communion meant for all people but which is now seen only prophetically in the church. Our church is a fundamentally political institution whether we like it or not. It is political in the sense that here is an institutional, sociological embodiment of what God wants for the world. Whenever the church is gathered at her Lord's table, our communion is judgment upon the world's inadequate attempts at community and a promise to the world of how community can be possible, but only possible, in Christ.[15]

Therefore, the first political act of the church is to be itself, not as a strategy or tactic, but as its primary mission. Only by being the body, the redeemed community, can the church establish the necessary boundaries between itself and the world so that the church can see clearly who it is and the world can see what it is. The world, in its myopic vision, does not know what it is. By being its distinctive self, the church serves the world by forcing the world to look at its limits. The world is powerless to form community on anything more substantial than mushy pluralistic relativism that claims our differences do not matter, totalitarian regimes, self-centered balances of competing rights, or a sub-group that rallys around common self-interest and calls its clique a community.

Our first political duty as Christians is to embody Christ's death and life in the church. The actual existence of such a body is crucial for any credible evangelism or radical social witness. We are to allow Christ to form the church as the one place in this world where love can be seen, where amazingly diverse people allow themselves to be formed by one Lord into one body around a table. In the church we are to pioneer those institutions and practices that the wider American society is still struggling to realize in the uneasy alliance of coercive social legislation and competitive self-interest. As Stanley Hauerwas says, the church "must act as a paradigmatic community in the hope of providing some indication of what the world can be but is not. . . . The church does not have a social ethic, but rather is a social ethic. That is, she is a social ethic inasmuch as she functions as a criteriological institution.[16]

The church must pay attention to those it welcomes to its table, where they are seated, and how it treats them once the meal begins. The meals of Jesus are our models. Eucharistic ethics would do well to examine meals and parables of meals in the gospels. Where are the little ones at our table? Do we include children? Where are the poor, the sick, the hungry, the weak, the retarded? Does our language include everyone?

A church that sides with the rich against the poor, with the strong against the weak, with the young against the old, with the intelligent against the retarded has nothing to say to the world. The world has taken sides with the successful and the powerful already. When Paul told the Corinthians to let the poor eat first, he was reminding them of the upside-down table etiquette for meals in this kingdom.

When Christians are divided at the table, when the church exists to fill the full even more, and to send the hungry away hungrier, the church is judged.[17] At the Lord's table, no one must be seated according to how much bread he or she has brought. On the other hand (contrary to some "liberation" theologians), no one should be seated according to who holds the gun. The seating arrangements are in accordance with the demands of and the invitation to the Kingdom alone. The church criticizes secular society by beginning with criticism of itself. Only then can the church be an imaginative alternative for policy in the larger society.

As the documents of Vatican II said so often, the eucharistic assembly is the *pracipira manifestatio Ecclesiae,* "the chief manifestation of the church."[18] At that table, the church is revealed for what it is and what it is not, even as Jesus was revealed at his meals.[19] Here the Body of Christ either takes visible form or is embarrassingly malformed. Here the church is reminded of the scandal of service to a Lord who received sinners and ate with them, a Lord who said at table, "I am among you as one who serves." Here the congregation sees that it is unable to commune with Christ unless it is in love and charity with one's neighbors and intending to lead a new life, "following the commandments of God, and walking from henceforth in his holy ways." One must discern the body. Here is an intensely communal faith that forms itself at a table rather than in a closet or before an altar, seeking all the hungry, whatever their hungers, inviting them to a table, breaking bread, pouring wine, and proclaiming to all who will listen, "The bread which we break, is it not a participation in the body of Christ? Because there is one bread, we who are many are one body, for we all partake of the one bread" (I Cor. 10:16-17).

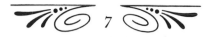

Preaching:
Responding to the Word

S o far we have been arguing for an integral relationship between liturgy and ethics, while admitting that in our worship this relationship is more implicit and general than explicit and particular. But ethics is no good if it offers only generalizations, platitudes, and clichés about love, justice, and right. The sermon offers the primary occasion in worship to be as specific and explicit as necessary in order to move toward truly ethical behavior.

If, as we have argued, baptism points us in the direction of discipleship, the sermon is a place where we can learn which step to take next. If the Eucharist gives us an overall vision and enactment of the story of discipleship, the sermon gives specific shape, content, concreteness, and timeliness to that story and vision.

There is no denying the efficacy of the nonverbal and the symbolic in the church's liturgy. But who would deny the necessity of the verbal? As Augustine said, without the word, water is simply water. Add the word to water and you have a sacrament. The word names, claims, and gives specificity to our liturgical symbols. Baptism symbolizes that we die to sin that we may rise to God; the baptismal sermon gives specific instances of the drowning in our safe suburban lives. The Eucharist shows that all are nourished at the Lord's table, the eucharistic sermon tells the many ways we are fed at St. John's, Brooklyn. The wedding liturgy proclaims that marriage is "an honorable estate, which Christ adorned and beautified with his presence in Cana of Galilee," the wedding sermon notes how the human union of John and Mary remind us of something divine.

But how specific dare we get? Perhaps we should limit our sermons to the enunciation of general principles and universal precepts. I can then preach about the need for justice in the marketplace but not mention the boycott of a nearby textile manufacturer. I can construct sermons about historic Christian views on war and peace, but not discuss registration for Selective Service.

Generalized preaching violates both the gospel and Christian ethics derived from the gospel. We are not dealing with a set of general principles and noble ideals. The gospel is the good news of Jesus Christ, the story of the life, death, resurrection, and ascension of this man, this Jew from Nazareth and the people he formed. To reduce this story to a set of principles or ideals is to say something less than the gospel. We cannot preach general principles and preach biblically, for the preaching of Jesus himself is concrete. The *kerygma* of the New Testament provides us no models for abstract, generalized, reductionistic preaching.

Abstract preaching reinforces our natural human tendency to generalize and so protect ourselves from the demand of more specific ethics.[1] How much easier it is to care about the poor across the world rather than to care for the poor across town. Everyone is in favor of justice until a specific oppressed group demands that I be just in a specific way. To say nothing is to say something.

Of course, there are dangers in being too specific. Is the pulpit the place to discuss complicated, sensitive, ethical issues? Is there a danger in the pulpit's becoming a platform for the preacher's moral agenda? Does too much specificity destroy some of the freedom and creativity required for courageous ethical response?

In this chapter we will examine the sermon as an ethically formative activity, its strengths and weaknesses, some of the pitfalls preachers encounter along the way to proclaiming what God wants us to do and be, and end with some suggestions for ethical preaching.

The Peril of Moralizing

The majority of sermons I heard while growing up went something like this, "If you are a Christian, you will do these things." Sometimes we were urged *to do* certain things: tithe, be kind, attend church regularly, read our Bibles daily. Or we were urged *not to do* certain acts: smoke, drink alcohol, be unpleasant to others. When the Bible was used in such sermons, it was a repository of noble precepts and principles or a catalogue of ideal personalities. The outline of these sermons was invariably: "here is a human problem; here is a religious course of action; now you go follow it."

By my late teen years, no one had to tell me how petty and inconsequential such preaching was. It was like the lectures often received from one's parents. When allegedly biblical principles were urged upon us, it was the "Always be a good boy and people will like you" lecture. When biblical personalities were enlisted, it was the "Why can't you be as nice as your sister?" lecture.

To be fair, this preaching was easily understood by the congregation—we are a nation under the influence of Dale Carnegie and Norman Vincent Peal, do-it-yourself religion. The platitudes and six easy steps of these sermons needed no artful homiletician to make them plausible in such a society. It gave people something specific to take home after the sermon, and isn't the function of the sermon to get specific and concrete?

A person hears a sermon. The preacher makes a point. The congregation responds, "So what?" This preaching took the "So what?" seriously.

But there were weaknesses. Those parts of the Bible that could not be reduced or allegorized into six easy steps were either force-fitted or omitted. Over the years, the principles being urged got scaled down, the behavior being advocated became more individualized, more private, more petty.

Such preaching failed to do justice to the hard facts of human existence or the hard choices involved in the ethical life. It underestimated the complexity of evil in human nature and overestimated the power of human beings to do good. It reduced the gospel story to simple imperatives. Rather than preaching truth, it was content to preach practicality. Its failure was the chief danger in explicitly ethical preaching—*moralism.*

Moralizing usually occurs when the preacher attempts to draw simple moral inferences from a biblical text. The gospel is presented in the form of suggestions for better living, principles for correct behavior, or obligations to be met. Originally, a moralistic sermon meant quaint domestication of the gospel into a set of rules for personal behavior. This privatized, pietistic morality was usually coupled with a laissez-faire attitude toward public, social morality: Stick to saving individual souls by urging individual morality and stay out of larger political and economic matters. Today, the role seems to be reversed: private antinomianism and public moralizing. In our governmental regulations and denominational pronouncements, we are confident of what people ought to do in regard to national public policy, and we tell them what to do. But we are reluctant to prescribe standards for behavior in a bedroom. We are private antinomians, tolerant of and open to all sorts of private behavior, but coercive and legalistic in our control of other people through the safe anonymity of public policy and church polity. Whether it is advocated publically or privately, such legalism is inimicable to the gospel.

A glance over my old sermons proves that moralizing occurs in all forms. I may not moralize over the small, private sins, but I still moralize. The story of Jesus telling the disciples to cast their nets on the other side of the boat becomes, "If at first you don't succeed, try, try again." The story of the miraculous feeding of the five thousand becomes "ways that we can cure the world's hunger problem through sharing." Jesus' "Blessed are the meek" becomes "How to practice meekness in everyday life."

Is it wrong for a preacher to offer moral directives? Does not the Bible give moral directives? Because moralizing represents the attempt to preach in an ethically formative way, we need to know why moralism, contrary to our expectations, usually fails to be either ethically formative or true to the character of Christian preaching.

1) *Moralizing tends to distort the Bible.*

Homileticians agree that preaching ought to be biblical—that is, it ought to be done in a manner that is true to the message, manner, and content of a biblical text. It is possible to preach a Christian sermon without reference to a biblical text, but this is the exception rather than the rule.

Moralizing sermons transform biblical narrative into a repository of moral precepts and instances. Every parable, story, historical event, and personality is said to bear a message for the modern reader. The narrative nature of scripture is seen as a hindrance to the message rather than the message. The purpose of the preacher is to explicate the text in a way that reveals its ethical content. Allegorization is the usual result; fancifully reading a message into the text, regardless of its plain sense. The pearl of great price becomes anything the preacher considers to be worth great sacrifice. The parable of the laborers in the vineyard is an example of how employers must not be restricted by government regulations concerning treatment of employees!

Moralistic preaching also distorts the historical context of the Bible. It idealizes and romanticizes the past—in a way that is utterly alien to biblical treatment. Moralistic sermons overlook Jacob's deviousness in their praise of his shrewdness. They forget Peter's betrayal in their commendation of his faith. "Oh, if we could only be like those people of the Bible." But, God help us, we already *are* like them and that's our problem! The answer is not more scolding, advice, or calls to be better. The answer lies only in the gospel.

2) *Moralizing sermons tend to confuse the traditional understanding of moral obligation.*

Traditionally, moralizing was criticized because it obscured the relation between law and gospel. Paul claims that the law is not God's definitive means of dealing with humanity (Gal. 3). He calls the law the "dispensation of death" (II Cor. 3:7). The law deludes us into thinking that we can obey the rules, fulfill all righteousness, keep ourselves pure and thus make ourselves righteous without God. Self-salvation is the hope of legalism, and we are all born legalists. But as Paul says, "If a law had been given which could make alive, then righteousness would indeed be the law" (Gal. 3:21*b*).

Moralism attempts to accomplish, with the law, what only the gospel can do. But both the accusing and the encouraging imperatives of God are derived from faith, from our communal relationship to the story of the grace of God. Our sanctification is the result of walking by "the law of the Spirit of Christ" (Rom. 8:2), rather than by meeting the obligation of the law. To be in Christ is not simply a matter of "exchanging an external law for an internal one (i.e., swapping a demanding statute for a nagging conscience), but of exchanging the extrinsic demand for the indwelling Christ," as Richard Lischer says.[2] Moral motivation under the law tends to be based either upon fear or pride. Moral motivation arising out of life in Christ comes from *eucharistia* (thanksgiving) and *doxa* (praise) for what God is doing in us and in our world. As Luther noted, the law can help by illustrating our sinfulness and great distance from God. In the larger society, law can help keep order. Pedagogically, the law can help by offering basic guidance on how the externals of the Christian life appear. But none of these functions can, in themselves, produce the initial motivation or the carefree, risky freedom Christian ethics demands. Only life in Christ and Christ's church and continual confrontation with the amazing grace of God can do that. Not law but, "The love of Christ controls us" (II Cor. 5:14).

Homiletical exhortations to do things can easily be heard

as a call to return to the false security of life under the law, putting law before gospel, and thus turning the Christian life upside down.

Moralism is an affront to the gospel both in its implicit faith in humanity to do good on its own and its implicit lack of faith in the power of God to work in us to do good. It urges sanctification without justification, making sanctification a human achievement rather than an act of divine grace. Its aim is not life in Christ but individualistic protection from life in Christ and his terrible, ecclesial claim upon us and our actions.

3) *Moralistic preaching misunderstands how human beings behave.*

As it reverses the order of law and gospel, so it reverses indicative and imperative. Our obedience rarely arises out of submission to abstract, external demand. We act out of our relationships, our communities, our basic commitments, our way of viewing the world. We are called to be before we are called to be good. As a young preacher, Reinhold Niebuhr quickly discovered the limits of moralism.

> You may be able to compel people to maintain certain minimum standards by stressing duty, but the highest moral and spiritual achievements depend not upon a push but a pull. People must be charmed into righteousness. The language of aspiration rather than that of criticism and command is the proper pulpit language.[3]

People do not become good simply by being told they ought to be. If they could, they would. People are trapped in a tangled web of self-delusion, warped vision, fear of death, and a host of other masters that make autonomous, self-initiated, self-judged, self-sustained goodness an impossibility. Graves must be full of worn-out preachers who went to their deaths wondering why their parishioners would not become better when told in sermons to be better.

If we could become better by ourselves, we would need neither the church nor Jesus' dying and rising to save us.

Moralistic preaching provides a safe defense against God. It subtly assures our superegos that all we need is a little better instruction, a little greater effort, and we will be like God, as good as God, without God. Albert Outler says,

> One wonders how many sermons there are which are aimed at the superegos of the congregation, either to condemn or reassure without deep analysis of the ordeal of man's responsibility before God? How often is worship designed to rush up reinforcement to flagging moral endeavor, or to substitute propitiatory forms for the actual divine-human encounter?[4]

Ideally, worship is the enemy of moralism. Wherever moralism would domesticate the faith and tame the Christian life into socially approved conduct, worship proclaims that God is greater. Our participation in the liturgy suggests that the ethical problem is not so much law versus gospel or indicative leading to imperative but is a matter of *attention*. We are called to pay more attention to the story of God's dealing with us than to ourselves. Gospel differs from law, not because it urges us to be free and independent of all moral constraints, the gospel urges us to be appropriately dependent upon God and God's people.

While the law/gospel metaphor is helpful in analyzing the nature of Christian moral obligation, it is not wholly adequate. In its fear of works-righteousness, the law/gospel concept fails to recognize the need for the self to grow, to conform our lives to what God is doing. Luther's law/gospel metaphor conceived of the Christian life in a rather isolated, individualized manner, stressing justification without sanctification. Membership in the Christian community makes a Christian's adherence to norms and laws intelligible. The question is, not whether I ought to live by law or by gospel, but what story am I a part of and how does my life conform to that story?[5] Am I the story of the self-made man made better by earnest effort or the story of the man made better by the work of God in my life?

Wherever moralism focuses all attention upon us and our individual superegos, worship would wrench our gaze off ourselves and charm us toward God. God alone is good. God alone is great, the liturgy of the church would say. But, alas, moralism even creeps into the liturgy. I have noted, in contemporary liturgical speech, the exchanging of moralistic imperatives for original theological indicatives: "We ought to be new creations in Christ." "We ought to be a chosen race, a royal priesthood." "We ought to be one body with many members." We can urge behavior upon people as easily in a corporate prayer of confession as in a sermon. Of course, that is speaking to people rather than to God—a sermon rather than a prayer!

Safeguards Against Moralizing

The primary safeguard against sermonic moralizing is careful attentiveness to scripture as the basis for Christian preaching. Faulty exegesis followed by faulty hermeneutics is necessary for consistently moralistic preaching. When the preacher's biblical interpretation jumps too quickly to the So what? the preacher is apt to draw simplistic moral inferences not justified by the text. Vast portions of scripture have no *immediate* moral message. Much scripture is the narrative of what God has done, is doing, and will do in human history. Prescriptions for human behavior can be only secondarily inferred from these texts—if they can be inferred at all. Careful exegesis helps us ask such questions as: Does this text urge *us* to do or be anything? Or does it proclaim who *God* is and what *God* is doing? Exegesis helps us recover some of the original context and purpose of the biblical text lest we abuse it by twisting it to suit our contemporary questions and purposes.

Contemporary exegetical practices arising out of the historical-critical method sometimes give the impression that the Bible can be revelation apart from a community formed and sustained by scripture. Outside a community of faith, scripture has no authority; scripture is not scripture. All claims for the authority of scripture are unintelligible except when seen as political and social claims. To claim that certain writings are scripture is to say that a faith community relies upon them in a morally decisive manner.[6]

Perhaps this is why for some modern ethicists, the moral claims of scripture make no sense. "Thou shalt not kill" or "Thou shalt not commit adultery" only make sense as the narrative of a God who suffers and is faithful and a community that allows itself to be formed by that narrative. The Bible is the church's book rather than a repository of universally applicable concepts. It is not enough to speak of the "biblical view of . . ." or to make unsupportable claims about the ethical unity of scripture. This is an attempt to legitimate the loss of a faith community that is the source of and the product of the Biblical narrative. The Bible is unconcerned with the establishment of a universally applicable ethic. It does not care if the American democratic experiment works, or if the world applauds its point of view. We have scripture to enable the church to be a community, one formed, across the generations, by continually retelling and reliving the story of how God is with us.

Our present Service of the Word, in which we read and preach from scripture on Sunday morning, has its roots in the synagogue services of Israel. Many scholars believe the origin of the synagogue lies in the Babylonian Exile. Whether or not the Exile was the origin, the service of the word has proved to be an ideal setting for exiles and sojourners in strange lands. The systematic reading and exposition of scripture through preaching, reminds us that the moral use of scripture lies in its power to help the church remember the stories of God. The church, like Israel before it, lives and grows by remembrance and remains the continual foe of the liberal notion that we grow by freeing ourselves from our past and our family's stories.

Moralism takes an essentially anthropocentric approach to biblical interpretation. It begins with our questions: So what? What's in here for us? It seeks answers to our questions, guides for our behavior, and a one-to-one correspondence between the time of the text and our time. We start with ourselves rather than God, beginning with our moral anxieties, our need to keep our slates clean, our yearning for the security of the law, our attempts to save ourselves by ourselves, our need to prop up our institutions or revolutions. Careful exegesis reminds us that the scriptures, again and again, are focused primarily upon God and only secondarily or derivatively upon us. This is what I call the *theocentric approach* to interpretation.[7] I agree with James Sanders.

> One must read the Bible theologically before reading it morally. The primary meaning of redemption is that God has caught up human sinfulness into his plans and made it part of those plans. This theologem pervades the Bible, OT and NT, and so all texts must be understood theologically (in the light of that theologem) before any indication for obedience can be drawn from it.[8]

Jesus' own teaching and preaching display this God-centered approach to scripture. His Beatitudes are not guides for human behavior; they are proclamations of the inbreaking kingdom of God. His parables are not little object lessons for human conduct, they are revelation of the way things are now that God has entered human history. His teaching is primarily theocentric and only secondarily directed at specific human response.

> Jesus' preaching and his interpretation of the Scriptures center upon the revelation of God's identity and activity in the present. Because of this revelation, new and challenging responses are called for from adherents to the Kindgom. But these responses are *subsequent* to the revelatory, God-centered word that Jesus speaks and finds in the Scriptures . . . for Jesus the Scriptures always and everywhere speak of God and reveal his identity-for-us. . . . Our response to God can never be prior to the revelation of God's identity-for-us. Covenant stipulations (whether Old or New) are necessary because they constitute the subsequent statement of *our* identity; but matters of human response whould not make up the principal ground or starting point for our participation in the dialogue of revelation. . . . The

Scriptures function *primarily* as revelatory of God and *secondarily* as regulatory of our response.[9]

One can see this same theocentric approach in Paul's letters. The ethical parts of the epistles, the *paraenesis,* are not a string of imperatives laid upon his congregations, nor are they ethical ideals applicable to all humanity. They are illustrations from traditional catechetical formulae, which are the life-style changes appropriate for those who believe the gospel story and have begun to live in the gospel community through baptism. Preachers do Paul a great disservice when they isolate his household codes, his rules for the behavior of Christians, his thoughts on the relationship of husbands and wives, his sexual ethics, and put these forth as independent imperatives. We must pinpoint the ecclesial context and the kerygma, the theocentric proclamation, behind these ethical exhortations.

The Bible begins theocentrically, ecclesially and therefore liturgically. It thus reveals Christian preaching and ethics as essentially "liturgical," that is, God-centered, activities. If we begin anthropocentrically and individually, we immediately limit the scope of our inquiry to our own questions, our assessment of what is personally possible and permissible.

Admittedly, the liturgical or theocentric approach is less immediately satisfying than using the Bible as a repository of moral precepts, but it does seem more faithful to the Bible's own theocentric and ecclesial concerns. It helps to maintain the distance and the tension between where we are and where the Bible is. It reminds us that the ethical problem is in us, not in the Bible. It aids in the essential task of taking God a little more seriously and ourselves a little less so. We ask what God is doing in the world before we rush out to do God's work. We look for the form and content of God's kingdom lest we busy ourselves building that kingdom on our terms.

Patience is still an essential virtue for God's people. The patience required by the theocentric approach, the tolerance of the ambiguities within the text and our incomplete interpretations, the lack of an instant payoff, could lead to skepticism and hermeneutical agnosticism. But our homiletical work and scriptural interpretation are done within the supportive context of the worshiping community of faith. We do not anxiously search the scriptures, hoping to cull a set of divine moral directives whereby we can keep our slates clean. We are preserved from that anxiety through our weekly encounter with the grace of God in worship, through the weekly nourishment of the sacrament, through our enduring baptismal confidence that God does not let us go even when we are wrong, through our continual rehearsal of our story as God's people who have been saved from such anxious searching and posturing.

Now we begin to see how scripture is ethically significant in a dynamic sense. As we said earlier, the moral life is not only a matter of making decisions. And the preacher's duty is not simply to help us make better decisions. The moral life is a slow, complex process of character formation and sanctification. The moral content of the Bible has to do chiefly with the type of people who are being formed by listening to the Story, and the preacher should put us in conversation with the Story.

A pastor told me of a couple in his church whose baby was born with Down's Syndrome. The baby had a minor respiratory problem that required assistance from a respirator for the first few days. The attending physician immediately urged the couple to allow him to remove the respirator so that the child could die.

"Don't you know that statistics show that couples who keep these babies have a greater chance of marital break-up than couples with normal children? You also have your other two children to think about. Is it fair to ask them to sacrifice for this child? There is no way you can know the suffering this child might cause your family if you keep it," said the doctor.

The couple decided to keep their baby. "Our Lord Jesus suffered for us. And he loved people who suffered, especially people who suffer for other people. If he suffered, we can suffer too," they reasoned.

This couple simply looked at things differently than the doctor. They were participants in a different story, a different adventure which had formed them into certain kinds of persons who made certain kinds of decisions on the basis of the stories they knew by heart.

The function of the sermon as a liturgical act is not primarily exhortation, dissemination of information, or instruction on correct doctrine—though these functions may be performed from time to time in sermons. The primary function is proclamation—again and again naming the Name, telling the Story, keeping time, rehearsing the truth, stating the way things are now that God has come among us, announcing the facts of our adoption as children and heirs. Any ethical payoff from the sermon must derive from this essentially theocentric function. Ethos must not be allowed to precede logos. Indicative precedes imperative. Initiation into the community provides the initiative to go live the community's story. Communion at the community's table gives us the sustenance to continue in the story. We do not need a sermonic set of rules for action, we need a story that helps us make sense out of the conflict that circumscribes our moral experience, a story as complex and tragic as life itself. Without this sustaining narrative, action is impossible.

Worship as the Context for Preaching

While liturgy is not immune from the dangers of moralizing, recognition of the liturgical context of the sermon is an effective safeguard.

The liturgy's nonutilitarian purpose, the glorification of God, can lead to the ethically formative sanctification of humanity. The fundamentally theocentric focus of our liturgical life complements the theocentric focus of scripture. Like our sermons, our ethics often begin anthropocentrically, looking at ourselves. This is the ethical heritage of a misguided pietism that begins with the subjective and the individualized.

Corporate worship offers the opportunity to look in a

different direction. Any worship that is attentive to anything other than God is readily recognized as idolatry—the antithesis of divine service. Admittedly, our worship is sometimes misguided. We Protestants, particularly those of us in the pietist tradition, confess that we sometimes conceive of Sunday morning as a time to soothe, titillate, anger, convict, motivate, or do some other noble thing to the worshipers. Some sermons end with an invitation to come to the altar and join the church or recommit to the church or with a "hymn of dedication," urging the congregation to do or feel something. The implication being that the whole function of all the preceding acts of worship—including the act of preaching—was to get the congregation to do something. "We are only here this morning to get motivated to go out in service to the world," was how one pastor began her service. She thus began by assuming that service of God was somewhere other than in the service of worship. The function of worship, under this interpretation, is to move the congregation from point A to point B.

This utilitarian, anthropocentric view of worship is a perversion. It is primarily education or manipulation or harrassment or a pep rally for the lastest denominational program, but it is not the service of God. Adoration, glorification, reflection, and praise of God are the primary activities of our liturgical assemblies. We are gathered to be with our God. The purpose is primarily theological. Because this God is the God who has created, saved, liberated, chosen, and commissioned us, our secondary purpose is anthropological. But one does not arrive at the proper anthropology until one does the theology.

In its liturgical context, the sermon is an essentially theological endeavor. The sermon is one additional liturgical activity in which we are attentive to the God who is attentive to us. Moralistic preaching, at first glance, appears intensely "moral" by its great stress upon responsible human participation in God's kingdom. But it is morally defeating because it implies that we humans are the only active participants in the quest for righteousness. God is wholly passive. It is up to us to do right, or right will not be done. This is the Deistic "Christ has no hands but our hands" sermon.

Worship reminds us that the mighty acts of God are always prior to our acts. God is busy before we arrive on the scene and will be busy whether we arrive or not. Worship rehearses these mighty acts, tells the Story, recapitulates God's work, recognizes that God is loose in the world. As the Germans say, worship is *Gottesdienst,* "God's Service," implying not only that we are serving God, but that God is busy serving us in worship. It is not all left up to us in worship or in the world.

In the face of our radically subjectivized worship and ethics, the sacraments; the scripture, the sermon, the creed, all remind us that we need not subjectively sustain our faith or our ethics. There are certain facts of the faith. J. G. Davies sees these "facts" as the great gift of preaching to our ethics.

> To proclaim the Gospel is, in New Testament terminology, to act as a herald; but a herald is not expected to declare his own views; he has to announce objectively certain facts. He affirms what God has done and is doing in the world; he declares the coming of a new era, but his message is in the indicative and not in the imperative; he does not primarily urge, exhort or persuade but makes known what has happened.[10]

When moralistic preaching forgets that the sermon is an act of worship, and degenerates into an exercise in telling people what to do, it forfeits the capacity to celebrate God's grace and thereby undercuts the *sine qua non* for bold Christian action. In forfeiting the gospel story, it detaches people from their legitimate birthright as participants in that ongoing story. Failing to make contact with the wellspring of faith, the sermon urges substitutes for faith—trivial and reasonable codes of conduct or shrill advocacy of absolutes for individuals and society.

Moralistic sermons rarely affect our self-centered image of the world. It is from our image of reality (our faith) that our actions flow. Moralistic sermons expend too much energy interpreting the human situation, often using contemporary psychological or sociological constructs, in order to tell us what to do about it. Worship reminds us that our time is better spent inquiring into the story of what God has done and is doing about it. We ask, What is going on? before asking, What ought I to do?

In the account of Peter's Pentecost sermon, the ethical "Brethren, what shall we do?" (Acts 2:37) came *after* his kerygmatic telling of the gospel story. The story gives the shape and the criteria, the impetus for the doing.

The objectivity of the liturgy also helps us preachers maintain our solidarity with our congregations. The sermon is not a performance by a moral and spiritual super-Christian whose virtuosity mutates into moral condescension. The sermon is a humble, prayerful effort by the preacher to articulate the truth and then to allow the naked truth to stand equally against congregation and preacher.

The preacher articulates the church's faith, not simply his or her own faith. The sermon is confessional, revealing the preacher listening to the Word even as the preacher bids the congregation to listen. It must reveal the preacher struggling under the burden of truth as much as it attempts to lay that burden upon the shoulders of the faithful.

What right have we preachers to proclaim the end of their secular hopes, their delusions, their laws, their idols—if we have nothing more to offer than rules and principles which, if they be ultimately worthwhile, are ultimately unattainable? We cannot lure them from the safety of their law unless we can offer something stronger than the law. We dare not call them into the battle for justice, if justice is solely of their own creation. We dare not ask them to risk some great work, if there is no possibility of forgiveness for great failure. In other words, if we cannot commend them to God and God's people, then we best leave them be with their pious and petty regulations.[12]

As an act of worship, preaching becomes profoundly ethical. Prophetic preaching unites us with the transcendent. It frees us from parochial concern and anxious self-interest and leads us to self-forgetfulness by attending to God. It is evocative or declaratory before it is didactic or hortatory. It aims at a meeting between the faithful and their God. Its purpose is not so much to urge us to do something as it is to look at something, and thereby set the conditions in which our doing will be a response to God in our midst. When this meeting occurs, the essential prerequisite for Christian response is made possible. As Niebuhr said, "People must be charmed into righteousness." Only when we are lured out of ourselves, attached to something greater, are we moved to righteousness. Our congregations are those who have been claimed, who are here seeking to deepen their response to that claim.[13]

Guidelines for Ethical Preaching

Preaching forms Christian conscience by proclaiming the Christian story. The ethical payoff is mainly derivative. But this need not mean that preaching must avoid confrontation with specific ethical issues.

I agree with Walter Burghardt that "the pulpit is not the proper context to pontificate on complicated and highly controversial political and socio-economic issues."[14] But, as he is quick to add, the key word is "pontificate." In a sermon the time is short, there is no room for counterargument, and I must not be tempted to overly simplify and to become dogmatic about complicated questions.

However, I can allow the complex questions of the day to help me proclaim the gospel. The tougher and more specific the questions, the more perplexing the dilemmas, the greater the need for the grace, forgiveness, and judgment offered in the gospel. As preacher, I stand in solidarity with my people as we confront the tough questions of modern life. I can testify to the issues that I see brought before us because of our having been called forth as God's own. I can even tell people where I stand on these issues and why. But I tell them as my testimony of my convictions arising out of the particularities of the gospel, not as the gospel itself. In all issues, the first matter for the sermon is what the Bible, tradition, the teaching of the church, the liturgy, and then our own witness of the faith say about an issue. All possible responses or suggested courses of action must come later, as derivative of, as evoked by the proclamation.

Weekly use of a lectionary, in which texts are assigned for each Sunday, can help the preacher avoid putting forth his or her pet moral exhortations and social programs as divinely sanctioned. In using the lectionary, the text determines the subject of the sermon. Some texts may suggest specific ethical content, some may not. The preacher does not decide to talk on politics or pressing social issues, the preacher lets the text determine the sermon. Many times we cannot faithfully preach on a particular text without preaching about politics and social issues. In such cases, the preacher is not using the pulpit as a platform to push his or her personal concerns, the preacher is simply submitting to the Word of God as revealed in the text. Congregations are more likely to hear our prophetic preaching if they are convinced that it arises out of the church's weekly confrontation with scripture rather than out of the preachers's private need to be relevant, abrasive, and controversial. Of course, if our foregoing argument about the nature of scripture is correct, *every* text is political and ethical since all scripture is forming God's people.

The preacher summons the congregation to respond in concrete, specific terms and thus fulfill its identity as God's holy people, responding first at the Lord's table in Communion and then responding in the world as we join in the Lord's work. But first we "open the scriptures" (cf. Luke 24:32), we move aside and point the people to the God who has summoned us, telling them what we see and hear, then we help the church form its specific faithful response. That response may begin to be formed, in a preliminary way, in the sermon. It will mostly be formed in the latter, more mundane, ecclesial ways of teaching, discussion, debate, and day-to-day life of the congregation who takes its place in the ongoing gospel story. The first job of the preacher is to give them a vision so true, so concrete, so clear, so demanding, so gracious, so alluring that it evokes their most courageous response.[15]

Now to him who is able to strengthen you according to my gospel and the preaching of Jesus Christ, according to the revelation of the mystery which was kept secret for long ages but is now disclosed and through the prophetic writings is made known to all nations, according to the command of the eternal God, to bring about the obedience of faith.

(Rom. 16:25-26)

Promises to Keep

iturgically speaking, the rite of Holy Matrimony is mostly a promise. In the fifteenth century, the Council of Florence agreed that "the efficient cause of marriage is regularly the mutual consent uttered aloud on the spot."[1] Peel away the accumulated liturgical bric-a-brac from a modern marriage service and what you have is simply a set of promises uttered before witnesses. Promising of this kind can take place inside or outside of a church—in fact, many ministers have probably wished that they could move more marriages outside of the church! But when marriage promises are made and witnessed in the context of the church they take on special significance.

In this chapter I hope to show the moral consequences of this liturgical fact: *Marriage is no more nor less than a promise.*[2]

A quick perusal of the marriage services of any number of Christian traditions reveals that the language of the services is the language of promising. In all these services, amazingly little interest is shown in the qualifications of the bride and groom for the pact they are about to make. One cannot be licensed to drive an automobile without a driver's test, but the church seems to assume that just about any novice can

Portions of this chapter appeared in the December–January 1981 issue of *Quarterly Review*.

marry. While some premarital counseling with the pastor has become *de rigueur* for most couples married in a church, no consideration is given within the service itself to the results of much counseling. After all, the church seems to be saying in its older marriage liturgies, how much training is required to simply make a vow? Preparation may not be the problem.

At an obviously emotional moment in life, the traditional service of Holy Matrimony is unashamedly oblivious to the feelings of the bride and groom. While much time and effort has been expended during the couple's courtship on "this crazy thing called love," the marriage service barely gives a nod to love or loving feeling as prerequisite for wedlock. Where love is mentioned, it takes an inconspicuous place on the bench beside other virtues such as "honor," "cherish," and "keep." Whenever any virtue is mentioned in the marriage service, it is only there as a future activity, an expectation and not a prerequisite. Never does the minister ask, "John, do you love Susan?" The question is, "John, *will* you love Susan?" Love is here being defined as a promise, an act of the will, something one decides to do, the fruit of marriage, not its cause. That definition of love is counter to what we have been taught to believe about love. Hollywood will not buy it, romantics will chafe under so mundane a definition of what they have limited to the realm of gushy feelings, physical arousal, mindless oblivion, passionate abandon, and nothing more. But the church (when it has been at its best) has rarely cared what the culture was selling or buying at any given moment in history. Where "love" is being bought and sold, the church, in the marriage service, protests that what we moderns are buying is merely pagan love; feelings and nothing more, hardly anything substantial enough to build a life upon, nothing so hearty or risky as the love of which we speak. Nothing so creative. Only an unqualified promise can sustain *that* love, and so a promise is the only liturgical requirement for a Christian marriage, the only thing asked of a couple in a Christian marriage service. Marriage is no more nor less than a promise.

A friend of mine who is a pastoral counselor asked, "Is this saying enough? After all, a promise is just a set of words, nothing more. While the wedding service does contain some beautiful symbolic gestures, the service itself is only words, nothing more; archaic, old-fashioned sounding words at that." Perhaps, he argued, we should make careful distinction between a "mere wedding"—which is just a set of words with a lot of lace, candles, flowers, cake, and hoopla—and a "real" marriage which is a way of life, an experience of mutual growth, a lived relationship between two people. Or, say some of my liturgical friends, we should at least speak of marriage as a "sacrament," a "means of grace," or some other sacred designation that makes the wedding sound more sanctified, more dramatic, more effective than mere human promise-making.

Doing Things with Words

The suggestion that the service of marriage and its promises are "mere words" raises some fundamental questions about the nature of words and the relationship of our words (such as those used in a promise) to reality. If the liturgical act of a marriage basically involves the use of certain words to make promises, then we might step farther back and ask, "What does it mean to use words to make a promise?" Are the words of our promises mere words and nothing more?

In thinking about our words, whether they be words used to make promises or to order a loaf of bread at the corner grocery; we are heirs to two problems within the Western philosophical tradition that tend to confuse us about what words do. First, there is a belief that the meaning of a symbol (like a word) depends on its ability to faithfully represent some "real" object or idea. The meaning of a descriptive statement like, "The chair is red" is proved only by a careful examination of the chair itself. The proof of the statement, "I take you as my husband" is only in the actual intention and in long-term results of the taking.

Second, most Western philosophy has described the sole function of our words as the communication of truth.

Words describe, represent, express, point to, indicate the existence of some reality that the words merely communicate to our minds. Words are merely tools to help us get handles on certain truths. A major task of Western philosophy has been to "get behind" these verbal symbols to find the reality, the truth, the things in themselves that the words represent. Those who speak of our words, the words of promising or any other words as "mere words" are simply reflecting what Western thought has taught us to believe about the function of language.

In the late Middle Ages a debate raged over the relationship of words to reality. We need not restate here except to remind ourselves that the winner, so far as most modern secular and scientific thought is concerned, was William of Ockham. This fourteenth-century philosopher took a position which came to be known as nominalism. The pure nominalist believes that words do not refer to any objective reality as such. Words are merely names which we attach to certain objects and ideas but which do not represent the essence of those objects and ideas. They merely represent my own impressions of the objects and ideas. There is no necessary connection between the words and the objects they represent. For the nominalist, reality consists of individual objects or events. The mind abstracts from certain experiences and labels or "names" these abstract ideas (hence "nominalism"). Most people who have grown up amid scientific empiricism are nominalists. They are distrustful of any claim that our words are more than mere words, more than a set of culturally defined labels that we attach to given sets of experiences. Our words, to the nominalist, are merely conventional modes of expression, dependent only upon the speaker's and the hearer's particular understanding of a given experience. The truth of a set of words depends upon the understanding of the speaker and how the speaker chooses to express that understanding. "I believe in God" is a statement of no independent validity. It is only a description that depends upon my understanding of "belief" and my understanding of this set of experiences I choose to name as "God." In general, modern secular and scientific thought has totally and uncritically accepted the representational, nominalistic quality of language. A promise, to the nominalist, is *merely* a set of words that represents some inner disposition. The key to understanding a promise would not be to dissect the promise, since the promise itself has no meaning apart from my intentions in making the promise. For the nominalist, the way to understand a promise is to inquire into my disposition, understanding, or intention in uttering these words of promise.

The couple who seeks to end the vow of marriage by pleading that, "we did not really know what we were doing at the time we married," or "we no longer love each other," or some similar plea based upon a change or a fault within their disposition toward the words of the vow, are pleading from the standpoint of good nominalist philosophy. After all, who would urge people to stick with a marriage on the basis of a set of words when the disposition and affections that gave those words meaning have now dissipated? Are not the words of the vow mere representations of a piece of reality? When the reality is gone, the mere words are meaningless. In this view, the couple is not so much breaking a promise as re-representing its feelings about a given promise.

Situational Ethics (see chapter 2) is basically a nominalist approach to ethics. Fletcher denies that any values have abiding, inherent, intrinsic worth within themselves. There are only characteristics that happen to be meant and valued by persons.[9] Extrinsicism agrees with nominalism in maintaining that all meaning comes from outside the thing itself; only as meaning is given to things by the intentions of a particular person.

The nominalistic and extrinsic view of language and ethics has been challenged in our century. Twentieth-century studies in the semantics of language have led philosophers to deal with language in terms of diversity of *function* rather than simply in terms of abstract definitions of its essence. The way words are used and the consequences of their use are more important and diversified than a simple representation of reality. Representation of the world through the use of words, description of reality through the use of verbal symbols, is only one of the things language does.

The philosopher of language, J. L. Austin in his *How to Do Things with Words*, builds on Wittgenstein's work in arguing that there are some declarative statements that do not "describe," "report," or "represent" anything at all. They are not "true" or "false" in the sense of statements of fact. There are declarative statements which are, in *themselves*, activities. They are the making of facts rather than the mere description of facts. Our speech *makes* promises rather than reports on promises. Some speech can only be understood as doing something. For example, to say "I will give you a loaf of bread" or "I take this man to be my wedded husband," is not to describe what I am doing. It is to *do* it. It is not to report on a gift or to describe a marriage, it is to make a gift or to make a marriage. Austin calls this "performative language" or, in legal jargon, "operative speech." It is language that does something.[4]

Admittedly, it is hardly a gift to say, "I will give you a loaf of bread" and then never hand it over. It is hardly a marriage to say, "I will be faithful," and then lapse into infidelity. There are certain things that must be done and said if the statements are to do fully what they claim to do. We therefore demand that performative utterances be spoken "seriously." Joking or poetic license is not permitted. We also demand that performative utterances be spoken freely, without coercion. But if a performative utterance is spoken in seriousness and in freedom, the deed is done. To say, "I bless you" is not to describe a blessing but to bless. To say, "A curse upon you" is not to report on a cursing but to curse. To say, "I take you as my lawfully wedded wife," is not to symbolize or represent a marriage but to marry.

It is little help to speak of the words of a performative act like marriage as being an "outward and visible sign of an inward and spiritual grace," as many of our marriage rituals do. To speak in this fashion implies that we regard the words as only an outward description of some invisible, more important, inward performance.

Stressing the need for an inward and spiritual disposition for our outward assertions is not as ethically sound as it might appear. The words in this case are not "mere" or "superficial." The words are very "outward" and very public, and therein lies their chief significance.[5] To stress some inner, subjective disposition as the proof of our promises, the validation of our words, can be a way of weaseling out of the plain truth that our word is our bond. Accuracy and morality alike confirm that to say, "I promise" means simply that. I *do* promise. To say it is not to state it but to *do* it. A new fact of life is thereby created, a new reality is added to the world—my promise. This reality may be ignored, but it cannot be erased. A promise can be broken, but it cannot be undone once it is done (spoken). It may be repented, but it can never be retrieved. To break a promise is not so much to void a promise as it is to simply let the promise painfully hang there, done but not fulfilled, made but not completed.

The language of the service of Holy Matrimony is mostly performative language, the language of promising. The service is not merely some ceremony that may or may not relate to some other hidden or inward reality for which it stands. The service is the making of something new, creation, the doing of a deed, pure promise-making and little else. This is why little interest is shown, within the ceremony itself, in the inner dispositions or cognitive understanding of the promise-makers. The promise itself, spoken aloud and in public, is the act of greatest significance.

Common sense alone tells us that things do have value apart from whatever extrinsic worth we bring to them. A promise has an independent, intrinsic value and life of its own, apart from our intentions in making promises. Well-intentioned people can make promises. Poorly intentioned people can make promises. Our actions (including our action in making promises) have an intrinsic, objective importance that situationalists like Fletcher, in their overstress of intentions, motives, and the ends of actions, fail to appreciate.

Admittedly, sometimes the church has acted as if all meaning and value were intrinsic in things and acts themselves—*ex opere operato.* Medieval philosophy of objective realism went too far in this direction, implying that our intentions, disposition, and motives mean nothing. But now, in our nominalism, in our stress upon individual feelings and subjective values, we must not go too far in the other direction. There is a mutual interplay between the individual and the reality the individual is making or confronting.

Marriage as Promise

Once a wedding is "done" by the public exchanging of vows, the man and woman will never be the same. They are moved to a new life status by virtue of their promising. They can be widowed, divorced, separated, but they can never be unmarried. They may become estranged, but they will never again be strangers. An ontological transformation has occurred through their promising. They have a new identity that can never again be abstracted from this promising. The formerly "two" have become "one flesh." The promise of marriage becomes a central fact of their lives. That fact may be denied, resisted, ignored, or avoided, but it can never be erased. As Aquinas said, even God Almighty shares one limitation with us creatures, "Even God cannot make what is past not to have been."[6]

It is pointless to quibble, at some future date, about whether the promise made a "real" marriage or not. It is not fair to claim that one lacked an adequate understanding of the full implications of the promise, or entered into the vow with inadequate or questionable intentions. Such circumstances might make a promise more difficult to accomplish or put the promiser in a position more susceptible to surprises, but these circumstances cannot negate the promise. As the semanticists say, a descriptive statement may be "true" or "false," but a performative statement is simply a deed that is done. There are no such things as "real" or "unreal" promises, only kept or unkept promises. If a promise is made but not kept, it is not a matter that something was not a fact, not real, not true. It is a matter that someone's word was not kept. It is a moral matter, a breakdown in morality not a breakdown in reality.

I fear that our psychologically infatuated society has put, of late, far too much stress on the virtues of premarital counseling. Premarital counseling, like premarital sex, may yield certain untested indications for the success of a marriage, but such pre-promising activities tell us nothing essential about marriage. One can never know marriage except from inside the promise of marriage because, before the promise, there is no reality to understand. Like any promise, marriage is inherently full of risk—the risk of unknowing.

One of the difficult characteristics of all promises, those of marriage or otherwise, is that there is an inherently future quality about them. A promise is not kept until it is fulfilled. All promising places the promiser at the risk of the future. If I say, "I will meet you for coffee at ten o'clock," I am promising to meet you *in spite of* what the future between now and ten o'clock may hold for me. My promise places me at the mercy of the future, indicating that I will so order my life between now and then as to keep my promise, come what may. For me to quibble over the way the future shapes up and then to advance this as a reason for breaking my promise is unfair. Promises contingent upon shifts in the future are hardly promises at all. To say, "I will meet you for coffee at ten o'clock—unless something else comes up" is not to make a promise (performative speech) but rather to describe my present intentions (descriptive speech). That little word "if" makes all the difference. For the church to demand an unconditional, unreserved promise of fidelity on the part of a bride and groom—with no "if's" at all—is not only to make a theological statement about the unconditional, unreserved quality of love as the church defines love, but also to make a practical observation about the nature of promises. One cannot control a promise. One must put oneself at the mercy of it.

Of course, the future of some promises is rather short. I

promise to meet you for coffee at ten o'clock and, when I do, the promise is kept. It is fulfilled in one simple act. But some promises are not so simple and require a host of acts, a lifetime of response and faithfulness to the promise. The church has sometimes referred to such lifetime promises as "covenants." Marriage is that kind of promise, a promise kept only by faithfulness until death.

A broken promise is just that—a broken promise. It stands out as a kind of unnatural, severed part of life. Like a limb severed from a body, its stump remains there as a reminder that something wrong and unnatural has occurred. When a promise is broken, there is a major break in the parties involved since the promise constituted the reality of who they were. There will be a feeling of betrayal, unfaithfulness, deceit, because something has been torn from the other person, something basic to life—trust.

To promise, particularly to make a promise like the promise of faithfulness in marriage, is to move oneself to a new status—that of a trusted one, one who is reliable, faithful, dependable in the midst of life's vicissitudes. It is to give and to receive a gift. Both the making and the receiving of promises are significant moral acts. My promising is my exercise and enjoyment of my full and free humanity, an expression of my competence and creativity as a responding and responsible fabricator of life. The joy of marriage is the joy of giving and receiving a gift. Every promise, and the giving and receiving it entails, changes who I am. I find my self transformed, redone, converted in my promising. Perhaps this is why many couples report that, the longer and more faithfully one keeps the promises of marriage, the more unaware one is that one is keeping a promise. The promise becomes a natural part of who we are, so much so that fidelity becomes, not an accomplishment, but a characteristic of our lives together, part of our character. Perhaps that is why the church called marriage a "sacrament," an indisputable "means of grace."

My character is the result of my human capacity to determine myself beyond merely momentary acts, part of my unique human ability to project myself into the future as well as to build on what I have been in my past. This is the stuff of which true humanity is made.

> One who promises identifies himself as he is now with what he will be later. . . . The breaking of a promise would be a renunciation of himself, its fulfillment a holding fast to himself. . . . On this . . . depends a man's moral continuity in contrast to all nature and empirical instability; on it, therefore, depends at the same time the ethical substance of the person.[7]

The order, stability, and character of my life depend upon the promises I have made, and those made to me, and those I am still busy keeping. As Locke noted, the order, stability, and character of our society in general are based upon our "contracts," our promises. The world is held together by the tenuous threads of our promises. This is why any union of man and woman can never be a purely private affair. It must be a social, corporate, political, public event because nothing less than society itself is at stake in such promising. Future generations will be dependent on our ability to keep our word, on the reliability of our speech. Is the church overstating the case when it claims, in the service of marriage, that such covenanting has a cosmic, eternal significance? Are we demanding too much in asking men and women to love one another as Christ loves the church (Eph. 5:21-23)? Is the church going too far when it claims, in Holy Matrimony, that in the quality of our faithfulness to these promises, our very humanity is at stake? Is it an exaggeration for the church to say that it sees in the act of love, done in this man and woman, a human mirror of the love with which God has loved us in Christ?

Many today are saying that marriage has had its day, that the promises of Christian marriage are no longer relevant or tenable. What they may be saying is, not that the promises of marriage are out of date, but rather that they are difficult.

The courage to risk a public promise, the fidelity to keep a promise, are more gifts than natural human attributes. The promises of marriage are far too difficult and risky for any one man or woman to make and keep. Therefore they are made "in the presence of God and these witnesses," as the liturgy puts it, publicly asking the church for corporate support and God for love and grace for our marital union, confident that God's grace is sufficient.

Marriage:
The Question of Children

O lord archbishop,
    Thou has made me now a man! never, before
    This happy child, did I get any thing. . . ,
    when I am in heaven I shall desire
To see what this child does, and praise my Maker.

(King Henry VIII, Act V, Scene 5)

Some time ago, a student came by to tell me that she would be taking a leave of absence because she was going to have a baby. Having rejoiced with her upon the occasion of her marriage, and having high regard for her personal attributes, I now rejoiced with her at the gift of a child.

"I'm glad to hear you say that," she said, "since I was beginning to wonder if this were a gift or not."

When I asked what she meant, she replied that a number of others had reacted to the news of her pregnancy with something less than joy. Some women seminarians had expressed disappointment that "a person with your talents is having to discontinue your career" as if she had betrayed them; a faculty member had urged her to arrange for child care as soon as possible so that she could quickly return to

Portions of this chapter appeared in the Spring 1980 issue of *Religion in Life* and the Winter 1980 issue of The Duke Divinity School, *Review*.

her studies "with a minimum of inconvenience"; and her apartment manager had notified her that she and her husband would be evicted when the baby arrived: No pets or kids.

I was shocked that this future mother, at the announcement of the advent of a new person into the world, should encounter this response, especially from those who are engaged in the task of clear theological thinking.

Perhaps the experience of others has been different, but I have personally noted, as I have done premarital counseling in the past few years, a growing number of couples who consider parenthood a thoroughly optional aspect of marriage—an option many do not exercise. When I ask about their plans for children, I have received ambivalent responses such as, "We really haven't gotten into that question yet" or "Definitely not anytime soon—we'll have to wait and see how our jobs turn out." There was also the twenty-five-year old man who told me, after two years of marriage, that he was getting a vasectomy because, "Kids just don't fit into our career plans," to say nothing of the young couples who become parents but who within a matter of months, quickly dispose of their preschool children in day care centers or other child-care arrangements so they can continue to pursue their careers with a single-mindedness unhindered by children. This is not to mention the New Jersey couple who recently attempted to trade their fourteen-month-old son for a three-year-old black and silver Corvette.

A 1974 issue of *Esquire* asked, "Why do Americans suddenly hate kids?" Noting that the fertility rate was the lowest in our nation's history, that well over one million Americans are seeking voluntary sterilization each year, that the number of children for each married woman between the ages of 25-29 had declined from 2.3 children in 1967 to 1.8 children in 1973, an *Esquire* article by Gary Wills asked, "Are Young Americans *Afraid* to Have Kids?" Wills observed:

> Our culture is, especially in its younger married sector, afraid of and for children. The matter goes beyond mere statistics on

declining births. Even those who have children do it tentatively now, as with a lab experiment that may blow up. They would be fools not to. . . . It would be wrong to dismiss the dips and rises of the birthrate as cyclic adjustments, rather than as part of a growing spiritual drama and dilemma.[1]

In 1971 Ellen Peck wrote *The Baby Trap*[2] and founded the National Organization for Non-Parents, an organization that continues to point out all the economic, marital, and career risks of parenting. American abortions are running at about 1.5 million a year.

These tendencies toward non-parenting are continuing through the 1980s. Between 1960 and 1976, the percentage of Americans under five years decreased from 11.3 percent of the total population to 7.1 percent. There were over one million less births in 1976 than in 1960. More Americans are envisioning marital futures without children.

What disturbs me most in these apparent trends is the implicit assumption that procreation and parenting are thoroughly optional, even quite unnecessary appendages to marriage. From the beginning it was not so.

The Service of Marriage

At the very beginning of a marriage the church has traditionally proclaimed that procreation is one of the purposes of matrimony. In this chapter I will use the traditional service of Holy Matrimony as a source for thinking about the ethical implications of children in marriage. I use this method because if one wants to know what the church believes about an aspect of marriage, it seems reasonable to inquire into what the church says to itself and to couples getting married in its rites of marriage.

In the Service of Holy Matrimony of the old 1559 *Book of Common Prayer,* when Cranmer listed the three functions for which marriage was "instituted of God in paradise in the time of man's innocency," the first reason was "the procreation of children to be brought up in the fear and nurture of the Lord, and praise of God," followed by "to avoid fornication" and then "mutual joy, help, and comfort." As a liturgiologist, I find it interesting that the new *Book of Common Prayer* now reorders the reasons for marriage:

> The union of husband and wife in heart, body and mind is intended by God for their mutual joy; and for the help and comfort given one another in prosperity and adversity; and, when it is God's will, for the procreation of children and their nurture in the knowledge and love of the Lord.[3]

"The procreation of children" has, in this new service, taken a back seat to "mutual joy" and "help and comfort."

The United Methodists, in the commentary on their new Service of Christian Marriage, reject the possibility of procreation as a prime purpose of marriage within their supplemental rite.

> The view that marriage's prime purpose is procreation is theologically and practically arguable. This purpose needs to be understood, not as a universal claim of so-called natural law, but as a decision of conscience made in marital trust and based on grace. Such a decision may or may not result in a commitment to bear children. A Christian family may complete its love with no children, through adopting or fostering children, or by planning for natural issue.[4]

Along with Cranmer's service of Holy Matrimony, as well as the Western church's theological tradition, I would argue, in the face of a devaluation of parenthood and a reordering of the priorities for marriage, that *procreation is a major purpose of marriage.* For marriage in general, this should be obvious. For *Christian* marriage, this is fundamental.

We are speaking here of the *norm* for marriage when we say that the "normal" Christian marriage includes openness to the possibility of the gift of children. This does not deny that there would be legitimate alterations in the norm. Like any norm, it tells us what is basic, the standard by which everything is judged, the type of world we want to encourage. The liturgy's normal linking of the possibility of parenthood with marriage can be defended from a purely biological standpoint, arguing the necessity of marriage, or something very much like marriage, as an ideal setting for the conception, birth, and long-term nurture that the propagation of the race requires. While we human beings have a destiny that is something more than mere biological necessity, it is interesting how few ethicists today seem willing to take questions of biological function with any seriousness at all.

Or the point could be argued from a sociological point of view. The preservation and adaptation of a society is dependent upon men and women who give their highest priorities to the parenting of new members of the society. In *Marriage and Morals*, that grand old socialist, Bertrand Russell, even went so far as to say:

> In a rational ethic, marriage would not count as such in the absence of children. A sterile marriage should be easily dissoluble, for it is through it alone that sexual relations become of importance to society, and worthy to be taken cognizance of by a legal institution.[5]

Russell had the good sense to see that marriage and parenting are social acts of the highest order. It is indeed curious to find many who consider themselves to be social activists indifferent to the fundamental social questions raised by our current devaluation of the vocation of parent. It is not too much for a society to expect that normally, a seriousness about marriage will also involve a seriousness about parenthood.

Aside from the more mundane biological and sociological questions, for Christians, the most troubling questions surrounding this issue are theological. To assert that the norm for marriage is an openness to the possibility of children is to find oneself in the midst of questions thrust upon us since the advent of conception control. While previous generations had the option to limit their fertility, we are the first to possess so many easy ways not to bear children.

Roman Catholic moral theologians take a natural law stance on the question of conception control, noting various dangers of "unnatural" contraceptives, condemning most programs for planned parenthood and planned non-parenthood. Within this Roman Catholic tradition, norms are asserted (e.g., marriage is for the procreation of children), and then casuists apply the norms to specific situations. Thus, among Roman Catholics and Anglicans, couples are allowed to project non-parenthood for what the moral theologians call "serious reasons." The questions then revolve around such factors as: How serious are the reasons being given? Is this deviation from the norm warranted?

Generally, we Protestants have chosen to reject the official Roman Catholic naturalistic position in favor of what might be termed a more personalistic stance, rejecting the Roman position as too mechanistic in its application and too insensitive to the needs and responsibilities of individual couples to make careful, intentional decisions in regard to the bearing of children into the world. But the questions for us now are: Have we Protestants taken biological function, social responsibility, and theological stance seriously enough? Have we, in our reaction against what we perceive to be the rigidity of the Roman Catholic position on birth control, jettisoned some fundamental values?

A doctrinaire pro-parenthood or non-parenthood stance would be equally misguided. While the Old Testament does contain the Genesis command to "be fruitful and multiply," this can only be taken as a general, eternal principle by denying its probable historical context. In the New Testament there is no necessity, no general command to procreate. Human beings have a dignity and worth whether they marry or not. Celibacy and remaining single are fully legitimate vocations for a Christian. If the church has done a poor job supporting the married, it has done worse in strengthening the vocation of the unmarried.

Marriage has a dignity and necessity irrespective of whether marriage includes parenthood or not. To affirm

THE SERVICE OF GOD

that the theological norm for marriage is the openness to the possibility of children is not to deny that there may be legitimate exceptions to the norm, though these exceptions tend to prove rather than disprove the norm. Some marriages are involuntarily childless, due to some physical or emotional problem which prevents childbearing. We must in no way imply that these childless marriages are less than marriage. We may even admit the possibility of marriages that voluntarily do not have children, making a conscious decision not to have children because of some reason judged to be of sufficient consequence as to make the bearing of children into the world an undesirable or irresponsible, or even unfaithful act. We might make a further distinction between the temporary unwillingness to have children and the permanent unwillingness to have children. Young couples, for instance, may decide not to have a child until they are more mature or more secure financially, deciding, on the basis of their perception of a child's needs, to postpone the bearing of a child until they are better able to meet those needs.

A couple's decision permanently to refuse to bear children is undoubtedly a more serious situation. But any decision to refuse the office of parenthood, whether it be temporary or permanent, is a decision which may have far-reaching consequences for that marriage and for society as a whole. It may also be an example of some rather unhealthy trends within our society. Could the decision, among a growing number of couples, to postpone or permanently to refuse the gift of a child be an addition to the growing evidence which convicts our society of a hedonistic, narcissistic, self-centeredness—a self-centeredness which looks upon children simply as a worrisome bother which is best avoided rather than one of the chief services marriage renders to the community?

Sex, Selfishness, Sacrifice

For the traditional liturgy to assert that Christian marriage normally involves the willingness to accept the

176

office of parenthood is to link the marital relationship, as well as sex, which is part of that relationship, to responsibility for the new life that is brought forth in that relationship. One reason that the church has traditionally maintained that sex is best when enjoyed within the context of a lifelong, permanent, exclusive, commitment to another person is that future parental responsibilities are best fulfilled within such a context. Conversely, one reason that the church has traditionally maintained that parenthood should be an intention of every marriage is that marriage is blessed by the responsibility, demands, sacrifice, joy, wisdom, and growth children bring to a marriage.

But it is unpopular to use words like "office," "sacrifice," and "responsibility" to describe marriage today. Most talk I hear is preoccupied with "relationships," "freedom," "self-fulfillment," and "joy." The long-standing Christian virtues of sacrifice, of vocation as a duty and gift, of self-giving love rather than self-seeking love are bound to have rough going in a society which seeks (if Christopher Lasch was right) narcissistic self-gratification, which wants to be pleased rather than called, which zealously guards its personal "freedom" by carefully avoiding messy entanglements with other human beings. Children, who are notoriously demanding, weak, threatening, expensive (*Esquire*'s 1974, preinflation, conception-through-college estimates were, $188,981 for boys, $200,691 for girls), time-consuming, and attached to their parents, are best avoided by those suspicious of words like "sacrifice" and "responsibility."

Of course, marriage itself may well be avoided for precisely the same reasons. So a responsible pastor might respond to a couple who, on the eve of their marriage, say, "We want marriage, but we don't want the responsibility of children": "I appreciate your honesty about your irresponsibility." The central problem for the couple would thereby focus not so much on their misgivings about parenthood as on their misunderstandings of marriage.

The old Catholic moral theologians had it right. While they were willing to accept a temporary unwillingness to have children, they were suspicious of a permanent unwillingness to have children as a thinly veiled selfishness, which spelled trouble for the marriage and for the individuals. While they were willing to recognize certain "serious reasons" as legitimate for such permanent refusal of parenthood, the moral theologians rejected all "frivolous reasons." A couple's desire for comfort, fear of responsibility, desire for a higher standard of living, or even goals of career advancement were deemed to be fundamentally frivolous.

Speaking of career advancement, I find it disheartening that many American women seem to be uncritically buying into the same profession-career infatuation that has always infected us American men. Willingness to forego family and parenthood, to offer up these vocations on the altar of the almighty career, may be the unavoidable peril of living in a capitalist-consumeristic-materialistic society. But surely the gospel says there is a higher definition of our worth than our careers. Perhaps the time has now come when women *and* men need to remind one another of the relative importance and unimportance of our various vocations, again claiming parenthood as the vocation that deserves the best we have to give.

Even so noble a reason as overpopulation may be more frivolous than it first appears. In some parts of the world, overpopulation is a pressing reason to limit family size. This is not the case in our country. Our pressing problem may well be over-consumption, or a never-ending rise in individual expectations for all the material comforts of "the good life." Besides, if we have learned one thing in the past few years of efforts to reduce the world's birthrate, it is that birth conrol and contraception are only one part of the solution. Problems with economics, health care, care of the aging, and the status of women are much nearer to the heart of the problem.

An American couple who appealed to the population problem as a serious reason for the permanent refusal to bear children would need to demonstrate that their entire life-style was a response to the problem. Is the population argument an escapist politics for middle-class America that seeks to ignore hard problems of war, race, and poverty by stressing mere survival of the fittest as the supreme virtue?[6] Moreover, we are talking here, not in the context of under what circumstances it is right to decide to bear ten children, but under what circumstances it is right for a couple to decide to bear *no* children.

I would be grateful to hear even so questionable an appeal as overpopulation in justification for the permanent refusal to have children. More often what I hear is an appeal to individualistic concerns over career or economic status or personal freedom. Such frivolity based upon self-centered expediency is hardly morality. It is rather a self-centered "conjugal hedonism" within the context of a marriage that seeks pleasure without responsibility, remaining intentionally closed in upon itself and permanently nonproductive.

Contraceptive technology has enabled us to pursue conjugal hedonism with an efficiency unknown to previous generations. This is the inevitable result of the Baconian revolution by which greater knowledge is acquired in order to attain ever greater *control.* One of the most threatening (and valuable) aspects of childbearing is that it is a helpful reminder that our generation's goals are limited, that there are more surprises yet to be revealed to the human race, that even our most noble ideas and very best reasons will be judged by ones who are yet to come, that we are never fully in control of the future. As Karl Barth said, children are "an offer of divine goodness made by the One who even in these last times does not will that it should all be up to us."[7]

Many today say they refuse this offer of divine goodness because of their uncertainties about the future or doubts about their own abilities or insecurities arising out of the present state of their marriage. Let us be honest about the wretchedness of the present age. We do live in an age of anxiety, to recall the title of E. R. Dodds' book on the first Christian centuries.[8] The rampant self-centeredness and selfishness of our times may be in part a distorted asceticism and self-denial brought on by the anxiety and self-doubts of our age. We Christians have known this feeling before, as

Dodds reminds us. Whenever society came apart at its seams, ascetic theologies, false messiahs, and strange religions flourished. As the old empire dissolved and anarchy threatened, Tertullian complained, even in his time, of the overpopulation, overcrowding, and the overproductivity of humanity.

> The earth shows us that it is becoming daily better cultivated and more fully peopled than in olden times. There are few places now that are not accessible; few unknown; few, unopened to commerce. Beautiful farms now cover what once were trackless wastes, the forests have given way before the plough, cattle have driven off the beasts of the jungle, the sands of the desert bear fruit and crops, the rocks have been ploughed under, the marshes have been drained of their water, and, where once there was but a settler's cabin, great cities are now to be seen. . . .
>
> The strongest witness is the vast population of the earth to which we are a burden and she scarcely can provide for our needs; as our demands grow greater, our complaints against nature's inadequacy are heard by all.[9]

In a time such as Tertullian's, many Christians said this was no time to bring children into the world. Manichaeans called babies the "offspring of human darkness," gnostics fought sex, questioned marriage, and forbade children. Tertullian wondered what was the gain in merely packing hell with more souls and the venerable Chyrsostom urged the sincere Christian to "beget a new self in himself" rather than beget children. Monks debated self-castration, and Origen did more than debate it.

In times, Tertullian's or ours, when everyone senses that everything has gone wrong, desire must be cut back and human expectations must be cut back because our future itself seems cut back. Dare we bear new life into such a bleak prospectus? Thus we waver between crude, eat-drink-and-be-merry indulgence and ascetic, restrained, confined self-denial. Both are unhappy stances for parenting. Auden spoke for many when he wrote, on the occasion of his godson's baptism:

Who am I to vouch for any Christian
baby, far less offer ghastly platitudes
to a young man? In yester times it
was different: the old could still be helpful
When they could nicely envisage the future
As a named and settled landscape for their children
would make the same sense as they did
laughing and weeping at the same stories.
. . . Imageable
no longer, a featureless anonymous
threat from behind, to-morrow has us
gallowed shitless.[10]

Who would be so irresponsible as to bring children into such a world, or at least under this perception of our tomorrow? Perhaps voluntary childlessness is admirable self-denial rather than selfishness. Perhaps the responsible ones are those who voluntarily deny themselves the gift of children, basing their denial on the uncertainties, doubts, and insecurities of the present age.

But how do we know that we may not actually be allowing a calculating need for personal security to take precedence over confidence and faith in God? We are being naïve to think that previous generations were immune from insecurities and uncertainties about the future. As Tertullian shows, previous generations did not blissfully populate the future under the delusion that the future was assured. Parenthood is a risk, an incalculable venture—and always has been. That is the inherent nature of any long-term commitment: parenthood, marriage, or any other human covenant worth making. To plead reluctance on the basis of uncertainty over the future, one's own or the world's, may betray a lack of faith that is not only a commentary on the mores of the present age but also a judgment on the inadequacy of the church's proclamation of the gospel. Here is a call to the church to witness, to those who are paralyzed by doubt and uncertainty, that commitments, even commitments to persons so unpredictable and demanding as children, can be made and, by God's grace, kept. We have a problem of evangelism here rather than a problem of ethics. A problem of *faith*.

Many couples' current reluctance to bear children may attempt to present itself as an act of responsibility (e.g., to the world's population problem) when in actuality it is only an untrusting anxiety that causes an overwhelming need for personal security. Of course, it is difficult to know what are the true motives behind our decisions. But, as Helmut Thielicke noted, the decision not to bear children, whether it be a temporary or a permanent decision, confronts us directly with questions of responsibility, self-interest, and self-control. The dangers, uncertainties, and the heavy economic and emotional demands of parenthood furnish us with an inexhaustible stock of reasons that can be used in defense of the decision not to bear new life.[11] Our increased ability to limit new life by technical means with little personal risk increases our readiness to use this stock of reasons and call it responsible parenthood. Responsible to *whom* or to what values? Are our reasons arising out of responsibility to God and our fellow human beings, or are they arising out of our desire to evade responsibility for anyone besides ourselves?

The Burden That Is a Blessing

Our increased ability to control conception and birth gives couples the possibility of a new insight into children as a blessing. Parenthood now, for most of us, demands a clear yes, just as every gift of God demands a response if its gifted nature is to be fully realized. As Barth says, contraception may bring us to the "conscious and resolute refusal in faith of the possibility of refusing, i.e., the joyful willingness to have children and therefore to become parents."[12]

The yes to children will spring from faith, not necessarily faith in the future or faith in one's own abilities, but rather from faith in a God who holds the future and strengthens our abilities to be faithful stewards of God's gifts, including the gift of children. Our yes arises, not out of trust in the essential goodness of children, but rather out of trust in

God. We accept the burden of children, not in hope of being blessed by our children in the future, but rather because God gives children. God's gifts, whether they be experienced as blessing or burdens, are to be received with thanksgiving.

Children are not, so far as Christians are concerned, to be chosen or planned; they are to be received. Stanley Hauerwas thinks that our current talk about children as something to be carefully planned for and chosen is not as ethical as it might sound, at least from a Christian point of view.[13] Children are gifts, not achievements. They are not to be chosen, bargained for—and then manipulated, controlled, and planned. Whenever we "choose" children we not only choose to have a child, but we choose to have a perfect child, a child who will not be a burden, a child who will be, in short, like us. Children are gifts, surprises. We cannot control them for our selfish adult ends. We cannot tell God what to give us. God's gifts come as grace.

How many people today give up on their children because they chose to have them and received, not the perfect, obedient, fulfillers of all their unfulfilled adult dreams; but instead received independent or disobedient or ungrateful or retarded or handicapped or brilliant children instead of what they had in mind? Children are a gift.

In a world plagued by self-doubt and uncertainty coupled with the selfishness and irresponsibility which may arise from these, the bearing of children as a bold, conscious faithful response to God's offer of new life may become an evangelistic, even missional activity, a bold vulnerability springing from faith. The question is recurrently being phrased, "Can I, with the world in the shape it is in, responsibly bring children into this kind of world?" The question ought to be (for those who see children as a gift and the world as their responsibility), "Can I, with the world in the shape it is in, responsibly *refuse* to bring children into this kind of world?"

Here is where the church can help. One function of the church is to help us bear our vocations. Those who are called to the vocation of parent may require special support.

Children are too tough a gift to bear alone. The church can become the essential community where parents are given the encouragement, guidance, and forgiveness that Christian parenthood requires, and children are given the nurture, limits, story, and space that growth into faith requires.[14]

It is of crucial importance for the church to be a witness to the world in regard to children. As Hauerwas says, "The church does not have a social ethic, but rather is a social ethic. That is, she is a social ethic inasmuch as she functions as a criteriological institution."[15] The church is called to embody the truth she sees in Jesus Christ. We can best witness to the truth, not by mouthing platitudes to the world about the care of the poor or children or the hungry or the rights of women. We can witness best by embodying that vision.

Where are children when the church gathers for worship? Are they stuck away in a nursery so they will not distract adult worshipers? This is odd since Christ clearly taught that children are a way of seeing the Kingdom. Do we baptize children in some sentimental, romantic little rite and then forbid them to come to the Lord's table until they more closely resemble adults? How we treat children in worship is of crucial importance, not simply as a liturgical concern, but as an ethical concern. We are not forced to resort to either utilitarianism or sentimentalism to find a place for children. We receive them as gifts.

So, most of the new services of Christian Baptism specify that sponsors other than the child's parents present the child for baptism. In so doing the church is saying, "Parenthood is too difficult to do alone. We'll help you."

For so long now we have stressed the positive values of birth control as contributing to the joy of sex and marriage. Sex without fear of unwanted pregnancy can indeed be a positive benefit of our new contraceptive technology. But now is the time to let the liturgy remind us that *children can also be contributors to the mutual joy of sex and marriage*. Sex tends to lose its essential nature when practiced outside a willingness to be responsible, a willingness to expand upon the meaning and the experience of sex by being open to the creativity of our sexual unions, a willingness to expand the male-female encounter beyond the confines of the one-to-one relationship.

In spite of our inherent narcissism and attempts to evade responsibility, sex is most joyful when linked to the joy of responsibility to another, the joy of duty. When Philip Roth's *Professor of Desire* impregnates his lover, and the lover decides to have an abortion, this leads him to reflect on the human joy of doing one's duty in regard to children.

> On her own she decided to have that abortion. So I would not be burdened by a duty? So I could choose her just for herself? But is the notion of duty so utterly horrendous? Why didn't she tell me she was pregnant? Is there not a point on life's way when one yields to duty, *welcomes* duty as once one yielded to pleasure, to passion, to adventure—a time when duty is the pleasure, rather than pleasure the duty?[16]

Even those who temporarily refuse to bear children should be reminded that thereby they are denying themselves the experience of the full, normative, most basic function of sex; a denial which may limit their joy and the meaning of marriage since it decides to close off the major possibilities for extension, creativity, duty, and sharing of the love of that marriage. Such decisions can be made, but surely they should be made with fear and trembling after careful, prayerful consideration and with a genuine sense of regret, regret at having been forced, by whatever commitments or exigencies one may cite, to refuse one of God's most mysterious and gracious gifts.

For is it not a part of love, at least love that calls itself Christian, that it forever longs to extend itself, reproduce itself, materialize itself, incarnate itself into the world? The doctrine of Incarnation is an affirmation that God could completely love the world only by bearing a child forth into the world. Such incarnating love becomes a paradigm for human love.

I can say it no better than a colleague of mine recently.

Upon hearing that he and his wife were expecting their first baby, I congratulated him by saying something like, "Well, you two are in for some major changes, I suppose."

"Changes?" he replied. "You couldn't dream of how many changes we're having to make. My whole life is being rearranged by a person I haven't even met yet!"

Then, in a more reflective mood, he said, "You know, *I never really knew how selfish I was.* Not materially selfish, just self-centered, self-directed. I had everything all planned out, running my life just fine, my wife and I proceeding down our separate tracks. Then this baby. There's no telling what we will be learning next."

There is no telling. For nothing so disrupts our tidy futures, nothing so clearly mirrors our human best and our demonic worst, nothing so demands from us, humbles us, or gives to us as does the blessed burden of a child. Like all God's gifts, the blessing of children is also a burden. But like all God's vocations, children are burdens that can be blessings. And there are more blessings in store for us, along with a number of surprises, when we dare to remain open and faithful to all God's gifts—especially the gift of children.

Whenever we dare to receive this burden of fragile dependent, threatening, disrupting new life, we receive more than we know. We receive this weak little one as we, weak little ones, have been received. And so Jesus, that lover of little ones, reminds us, "Whoever receives one such child in my name receives me; and whoever receives me, receives not me but him who sent me" (Mark 9:37).

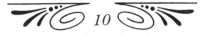

10

"Let Us Offer Ourselves and Our Gifts to God"

*O*ne of my most vivid memories of how difficult ethics can be occurred while I was in seminary. The Black Panthers, a radical activist group of the late 1960s and early 1970s, were on trial in the New Haven Courthouse. Local police saw the Panthers as a violent, revolutionary menace. Many others viewed the Panthers as an earnest, victimized group whose efforts for social justice were misunderstood and unfairly condemned by unjust city authorities.

A number of New Haven Panthers had been jailed and charged with the murder of a police informant. Many of us Yale students were concerned that the Panthers might be judged unfairly. The president of Yale publically stated his doubts that the accused could get a fair trial. Many in the black community saw the trial as yet another example of police harrassment of black people. Tensions mounted. National Guard troops were called in to quell disturbances. We went to class amidst apocalyptic scenes of armed troops, shouting protestors, tear gas, and steadily building anger on both sides.

At the divinity school, we were in a quandary. What should we do? We wanted to insure that justice was done. We wanted to show our commitment to the needs of the black community. So one night, at the peak of the crisis, we had a general meeting in the Divinity School Commons. A demonstration was to take place in front of the courthouse the next day. There might be violence, with edgy troops and angry protestors confronting each other (the Kent State tragedy had taken place a few months before). But after much discussion, we decided that we must make a witness at the courthouse. We would show people that we were unafraid of the possible consequences. The next day we would move *enmasse* to the New Haven Green where we would courageously join the protest—come what may.

At that moment the doors to the commons burst open. Two uniformed Black Panthers charged into the room and took over the meeting.

"Who do you white honkies think you are?" one Panther asked. "Where were you when we needed you? Now that we have taken things in our own hands, here you come wanting to get on board."

"You don't fool us," said the other "You don't care about us. All you want is to soothe your guilty white consciences by parading tomorrow in front of the cameras. Stay home! We don't want you."

They left as quickly as they had come, leaving the crestfallen seminarians in despair. To have at last summoned the courage to act, only to be told that they did not want us, left us in confusion. What should we do? If we go down to the courthouse we are trying to work out our white guilt through meaningless token gestures. If we do not go, we are cowards and racists.

The next day, in a half-empty classroom, we asked our professor what we should do. Some students had gone to the courthouse to make their protest. Some had gone to Vermont to hike. Some of us had stumbled to class, perhaps hoping that a good lecture on biblical theology would put the matter out of our minds. "What are we supposed to do? We're damned if we do, and damned if we don't," one person complained.

"No, you are wrong," Dr. Childs responded.

"You're a Christian. Because you are a Christian you know that you are forgiven if you do and forgiven if you don't. Who can say all the reasons that you may or may not act in this situation? God knows. Your job is not to make yourself righteous. Only God can do that. Luther says, sin boldly. Boldly offer yourself and all your mixed motives and wrong reasons to God. Only that can save you from self-serving acts or paralyzing fear."

In those occasions in life when we are faced with a "damned if we do, damned if we don't" dilemma, whether we do or don't, let us claim our decisions and our actions as offering to God. We do not know all the mixed, questionable motives that may lie behind our actions. We are not called to know everything or to justify ourselves. Fortunately, we are called to lay ourselves and our actions upon the altar. It is only there, as we and our actions are received, blessed, broken, and used by God in God's work that we can speak of good deeds. A Christian is required only to render to God and to God's creation the daily service of oblation, offering.

Here, at the end of our exploration into worship and ethics, let us be explicit about what we have implied throughout these pages. *A Christian's worship and ethics are best understood as the Christian's continual self-giving to the God who has given so continuously and selflessly to us.*

Offerimus

In the early church, bread and wine were offered at the Eucharist, along with an offering for widows, orphans, and others in need in the congregation. Justin Martyr (early second century) is the first to give explicit reference to the offertory: "Then bread and a cup of water mingled with wine are presented to the president of the brethren. Taking them, he sends up praise and glory to the Father of all, through the name of the Son and Holy Spirit, and offers thanksgiving at some length that we have been deemed worthy to receive these things at His hand."[1] Hippolytus (A.D. 200) describes how the deacons collected the people's gifts (often including not only bread and wine but also olives, cheese, honey, milk, and other food) and brought them to the table to be blessed. "To him [the bishop] let the deacons bring the oblation and he with all the presbyters laying his hand on the oblation shall say giving thanks: . . ."[2] While the whole Eucharist was an offering, a gift to God in thanksgiving for the gifts God has given to us, the offertory made this explicit. From the ordinary stuff of everyday life these gifts were received and prepared, prayed over and distributed to the faithful as a visible sign of the self-giving of God. No reward for donors was expected. The gifts were an overflowing of gratitude. Leftovers were given to the needy. Oblation was the fitting response to the oblation of God in Jesus Christ and fitting service to God and God's poor. How utterly mundane and materialistic was the worship of the early church, how willing to consecrate and claim the ordinary and the everyday. Irenaeus made bitter argument with those gnostics who sought to spiritualize the Christian material offering out of existence. He saw how essential it was to root the offering to everyday life, how it expressed an incarnational faith.

The offertory procession was a prominent part of early medieval worship. In this solemn parade, the faithful brought their gifts forward. The offering was received by the celebrant, laid upon the altar, and then blessed. By the late Middle Ages, the offertory procession was gone. Now, only the priest was worthy to offer the gifts. Increasing clericalism and sacerdotalism had taken the offering out of the hands of the laity and given it exclusively to the clergy. This was a disastrous loss of an essential linkage of worship and life. Holy bread offered by holy hands removed the Eucharist from the daily experience of the faithful and removed the faithful from their rightful place in the making of thanksgiving to God.

Protestant reformers rejected the description of the Eucharist as an *oblatio*, "an oblation," on the grounds that it denigrated the uniqueness of Christ's offering on the cross. Their objection was based, in part, on widespread misunderstandings of the Mass as an offering of the church to God, and in part, on their reaction against medieval clerical sacerdotalism. How presumptuous of us, the reformers thought, to presume that we unworthy humans can offer anything that in any way adds to or enhances Christ's all-sufficient offering of himself upon the cross. As Cranmer's service said, on the cross Christ made "by the one offering of himself, a full, perfect, and sufficient sacrifice for the sins of the whole world." Ironically, in their suppression of the offertory, the reformers were promoting late medieval Roman scholasticism even as they were opposing it. A prominent theme of late medieval piety was our sin and our unworthiness to come before this holy and righteous God with our pitiful praise.[3]

Some reformers were willing to apply "sacrifice," with qualifications, to the dispositions of the worshipers. Here is Cranmer's prayer:

> O Lord, our heavenly Father, we, thy humble servants, desire thy fatherly goodness mercifully to accept this our sacrifice of praise and thanksgiving; most humbly beseeching thee to grant, that, by the merits and death of thy Son Jesus Christ, and through faith in his blood, we and thy whole Church may obtain forgiveness of our sins, and all other benefits of his passion.
>
> And here we offer and present unto thee, O Lord, ourselves, our soul and bodies, to be a reasonable, holy, and lively sacrifice unto thee.[4]

While Cranmer spoke of our "sacrifice of praise and thanksgiving," he was careful to qualify this with firm and frequent reiteration of our basic unworthiness when compared to the worthiness of the Lamb which was slain. "And although we be unworthy, through our manifold sins, to offer unto thee any sacrifice, yet we beseech thee to accept this our bounden duty and service, not weighing our merits, but pardoning our offenses."

In order to give liturgical expression to his doctrine of justification by grace through faith, Luther was adamant in his refusal to speak of the Lord's Supper as a *sacrificium* (humanity's gift to God). Instead Luther exclusively stressed the Eucharist as a *testamentum* (God's gift to humanity). In other words, the action was mostly one way, God offering to us. The path to God was faith, not works, including our work of offering in the Eucharist.

As often happens in reform movements, reaction to abuses produced overreaction. In deleting the offertory or in "spiritualizing" it (making it more an offering of our hearts and minds than an offering of the fruits of our labors) reformed liturgies cheated their participants out of a full liturgical expression of faith. While classical reformers like Luther and Calvin were able to maintain the importance of human self-giving as appropriate response to divine self-giving, more radical groups like the quietists, suspected all gestures and deeds in worship or in life as an attempt to achieve salvation by works rather than by faith. Only the securely and consciously regenerate dare attempt good works.

The deletion, psychologizing, or understating of the offertory implicitly raised the question What, if anything, does God expect of humanity? This is particularly strange in light of some scripture passages dear to the reformers. For instance, Ephesians 2:8-9 was a favorite text of the Reformation, particularly its Lutheran wing: "For by grace you have been saved through faith; and this is not your own doing, it is the gift of God—not because of works, lest any man should boast." But the passage does not stop with a mere condemnation of works. The next verse: "For we are his workmanship, created in Christ Jesus for good works, which God prepared beforehand, that we should walk in them" (v. 10).

We are made new creations in Jesus Christ "for good works," so that we should learn to "walk" in these acts. The same can be said of I Peter, a favorite baptismal text used to support the priesthood of believers argument. "But you are a chosen race, a royal priesthood, a holy nation, God's own people, that you may declare the wonderful deeds of him who called you out of darkness into his marvelous light" (2:9).

The conjunction "that" (*propos*) here means "in order that." All these works have been done for us in order that we might join in the works of God.

In their attempt to embody the doctrine of justification by faith in their liturgies, it is unfortunate that the reformers did not have a corresponding liturgical embodiment of the doctrine of sanctification, perhaps in the offertory. This would have strengthened their liturgies and might have checked such theological and liturgical extremism as occurred later among the quietists.

The eucharistic liturgies of the reformers deleted offertory ceremonial. Cranmer eventually directed that the bread and wine should be placed upon the table before the service. Alms should then be collected without recognition or fanfare.[5]

The deletion or de-emphasis of the offertory in reformation liturgies contributed to the ever-present danger of divorcing Sunday liturgy from daily life. It gave the faithful the erroneous impression that Christian worship is mostly a "spiritual" affair from which the material is carefully excluded. How strange that the reformers' stress upon a Christian's daily work as divine vocation found little expression in Sunday worship. How unfortunate that a liturgical reform movement, which intended to give the laity greater involvement in liturgy, overlooked the central, historic liturgical action by which the laity participated.

Our contemporary padded offering plates and the restrained, almost embarrassed, way we deal with money in worship is the heritage of a liturgical tradition that has lost the once powerful gesture of offering.

Fortunately, new eucharistic liturgies have recovered the offertory. It comes after the scripture, the sermon, and the prayers of intercession. If the offertory occurs before the sermon, it makes a poor image, as if our giving is the admission fee before God will give to us. When placed after the reading and exposition of the Word, the offertory links the liturgy of the word with the liturgy of the table. The offertory is claimed as a fitting response to the proclamation of the word, the ministry of the faithful as they join with the celebrant in his or her ministry at the table.

"As a forgiven and reconciled people, let us offer ourselves and our gifts to God," says the celebrant as the people enter the offertory in the United Methodist Alternate Service of the Lord's Supper. Then, in the prayer of thanksgiving in that service, the gifts are blessed using the words,

> We experience anew, most merciful God,
> the suffering and death,
> the resurrection and ascension of your Son,
> asking you to accept
> this our sacrifice of praise and thanksgiving
> which we offer
> in union with Christ's offering for us,
>
> Send the power of your Holy Spirit on us,
> gathered here out of love for you,
> and on these gifts.
> May the Spirit help us know
> in the breaking of this bread
> and the drinking of this wine
> the presence of Christ
> who gave his body and blood for all.
> And may the Spirit make us one with Christ,
> one with each other,
> and one in service to all the world.[6]

As a family in the congregation brings a loaf of homebaked bread and a pitcher of wine forward, joined by those who have collected the offering, no one need be told that this is the oblation of God's people; no one needs a theological lecture on the Eucharist as our thanksgiving to God for God's gifts to us. The oblation is visible in the acts of the faithful.

Offerimus, "Let us offer," is the invitation to joyful participation both in Christian worship and in Christian life.

An Ethic of Gratitude

The offertory in Sunday worship is a paradigm, a visible enactment of the basis of Christian ethics. In the offering, we show that God's gifts call forth response. We love because God first loved us. As the German language expresses it, every *Gabe* ("gift") entails an *Aufgabe* ("task, assignment"). Grace and gratitude are linguistically and theologically related. God's *charis* evokes our *eucharistia*. "Freely you have received, freely give" is more than a hackneyed announcement of the offertory. From this liturgical affirmation flows our ethical motivation. This is the imperative grounded in the Christian indicative.

So James Gustafson declares that gratitude,

> is at the heart of religious morality in the Western world. When religious morality has taken the forms of precise determinations in laws and rules, this has been done to spell out what a thankful community ought to do. When it has been taught in terms of spontaneous deeds of loving service, this too has been understood to stem from gratitude. God has been good to human persons and communities; in thankfulness to him we have reason enough to seek the well-being of others, to honor their rights, to fulfill our natural duties and obligations to them. In thankfulness we are moved to do so. This theme is central in the morality and ethics of both Judaism and Christianity. . . . God has done good things for us; in thankfulness we are to "go and do likewise."[7]

Gratitude arises out of our experience of God as a trustworthy and beneficent creator, sustainer, and redeemer of the world. Gratitude engenders a reason for being moral and an empowering of the will to act in complement to God's goodness toward humanity.

Admittedly, the beneficence of God is only partially confirmed in our everyday experience. If we are honest, we must admit that the hard times of life, the disasters which befall us, and the misery of existence for many people mock a facile affirmation of God's goodness. Everyday experience only partially confirms that God is good or that gratitude is the natural response of the creature to the Creator. While many may be able to affirm the grace and goodness of God in their lives, sometimes their affirmations can only be spoken by denying the hard facts of life, which may lead many of their less fortunate brothers and sisters to doubt the beneficence of God.

The ability to affirm that God is good is a gift of faith. Certitude in the goodness of God may arise more out of faith in the testimony of our tradition than out of our personal experiences. To be part of the Christian community is to be able to affirm, sometimes all experiential evidence to the contrary, that, "If God is for us, who is against us? He who did not spare his own Son but gave him up for us all, will he not also give us all things with him?" (Rom. 8:31b-32).

Even though our occasions for gratitude and thanksgiving may not occur as often as we might like, they do seem to come frequently enough to keep Christians singing. Life can be tough. But most of the time, most of us are grateful for life itself, regardless of our circumstances. Whether in nature or in human society, we all live our lives as debtors, receiving more than we earn or deserve, much more than we contribute to society or life. We need not resort to cheap religious rhetoric to find something in our lives that elicits some measure of *eucharistia*.

The Protestant reformers grounded their ethics in gratitude—making all the more tragic their inability or unwillingness to recover the offertory in their liturgies. They believed that good works were the fruit of faith. Cranmer's prayer of consecration sees Christ as God's supreme gift.

> Almighty God oure heauenly father, whiche of thy tender mercye dyddest geue thine onely sonne Jesus Christ, to suffre death upon the crosse for our redempcion, who made there (by hys one oblacion of hymselfe once offered, a full, perfecte and sufficiente sacrifice, oblacion, and satisfaccion for the synnes of the whole worlde: and dyd institute, and in hys holye Gospell commaunde us, to continue a perpetuall memorye of that his precious death.[8]

But like other reformation liturgies, Cranmer's prayer focuses on only one aspect of the oblation of Christ—his self-giving on the cross. Early Christian prayers, like that of Hippolytus, show that the gifts of God in Christ were many: creation, the exodus, the prophets.[9] The continual self-giving of Christ involved many acts of grace before and after the cross. These were brought to their summit in his oblation on Calvary. Jesus only did on the cross what he did throughout his ministry—give himself to God and to those God loved.

As Cranmer's liturgy said, now we are to be a "reasonable, holy, and lively sacrifice" to God. While we can in no way add to Christ's act of atonement, we do signify its effectiveness as we offer ourselves to God in response to God's continuing self-giving to the world. "I appeal to you therefore, brethren, by the mercies of God, to present your bodies as a living sacrifice, holy and acceptable to God, which is your spiritual worship" (Rom. 12:1-2).

The sacrifice of Christ, his act of total self-giving on the cross, establishes the pattern for our self-giving in the offertory or in daily life. We are freed, by his oblation, to offer ourselves and our gifts to God, because, without his oblation, our human offering would be so puny and inconsequential that we would be led either to despair over our ineffectiveness or to deluded claims of our effectiveness. But "effectiveness" is not the point. The point is that we extravagantly, unreservedly give ourselves in carefree response to the extravagant self-giving of Christ. We co-operate with the graciousness of God. We are not forced, in our ethics, to be effective or successful; we are asked to be gracious. We are invited to give. And one of the main things we give up is our selfish claim to be the chief actors in the drama of justice and the chief fabricators of what is right and good.

"Don't you ever get discouraged by your lack of success?" a reporter asked Mother Teresa of Calcutta.

"No," she replied, "because God has called me, not to be successful, but to be faithful."

Anything less than carefree gratitude is never quite enough so far as responsiveness to God is concerned. Anything less has a way of being self-aggrandizing, calculating, over-scrupulous, or smug. All we are to do is to be a living sacrifice.

We must take care in interpreting that word "sacrifice." In our speech, it has come to mean "giving up something of value." We speak of someone's "making a sacrifice," often implying that the person has given up something with the hope of obtaining something better.

But in the biblical sense, "sacrifice" had a different connotation. In the ancient world, a sacrifice was a feast, a joyous celebration between gods and the people. The death of a victim was not the chief focus; an animal had to be slaughtered to provide the meal, but its death had no special significance. In the Old Testament, sacrifice was a joyous feast in which the people gave God gifts from some of the bountiful gifts which God had given them. A sacrifice was a gift, not in the sense of giving up something, but in the sense of a spontaneous outpouring of gratitude from the fruits of God's graciousness.

> We give thee but thine own,
> Whate'er the gift may be:
> All that we have is thine alone,
> A trust, O Lord, from thee.[10]

And yet, sacrifice does entail cost. The sacrifice of Christ on the cross, his self-giving unto death, his oblation, was costly. Focus upon that complete self-giving of God in Christ often moves Christians to complete self-giving of themselves. Isaac Watts expressed it in his familiar hymn.

> When I survey the wondrous cross
> On which the Prince of Glory died,
> My richest gain I count but loss,
> And pour contempt on all my pride. . . .
>
> Were the whole realm of nature mine,
> That were an offering far too small;
> Love so amazing, so divine,
> Demands my soul, my life, my all.[11]

The fifth section of John and Charles Wesley's *Hymns on the Lord's Supper* was entitled, "Concerning the sacrifice of our persons." The offering of our selves to Christ, in response to his offering on the cross, is to be "sacrificial"—it will resemble his offering in its extravagance, its abandonment of the self, and its overflowing graciousness.

It is interesting, in this matter of offering, that when we speak of the depths and heights of sacrifice, familiar hymns come to mind. Perhaps human language cannot speak of Christ's oblation and the response of Christians without resorting to poetry, without our speech becoming liturgical, even doxological.

The image of ethics as offering must be pushed even further. We are not merely to do good works for and with God. The gospel demands more. We are to become the good work of God. The affirmation, "You are God's temple," (I Cor. 3:16) can be made because of the more sweeping claim that, "all are yours; and you are Christ's; and Christ is God's" (vv. 22-23). "Imitate what you handle," says the bishop to the new priest in the Roman Catholic Ordinal.[12] In giving, we become like what we give. In the continual offering up of ourselves and our gifts, we become, to use an old word, "transubstantiated" into the Body of Christ. Every time we offer a gift at the altar or offer our works of loving service in the world, we are not simply doing what God wants us to do; we are submitting ourselves to be remade in God's image. Barth says that casuistry in ethics is destructive because ethics means, "not only to choose and realize this or that, but to choose and realize oneself in this or that. So, then, an action done in obedience to God cannot consist only in carrying out something that God wishes, but *in man's offering himself to God in so doing*" (emphasis mine).[13]

Thus we return to where we began—with the ethics of character. In the offertory, in the weekly enactment of the pattern for Christian self-giving, we form and confirm who we are and how we are to live in the world. This gives shape and character to the world as something offered to the glory of God. Here we begin to envision those patterns of human institutional relations that show forth this glory. Here we start seeing ourselves as givers, as those who have been graciously invited to join God's feast at the Lord's table and then to join in God's work in the world. The mechanic who

brings the offering plate to the altar on Sunday morning as
the Doxology is sung, as he stands there, does he start to see
himself as part of God's work? Does he begin to look at his
Monday through Saturday labors at the garage in a new
light? Is his labor redeemed, claimed for the glory of God in
this moment of offering? Who can say? And yet, if this man
or his work is to be redeemed, sanctified, consecrated, and if
his steps are to fit into the beat of the holy procession of
God's givers to the altar, it must occur here.

An Episcopal priest told me of a man in his church who
insisted on purchasing the wine for the Eucharist each
Sunday. The man was a recovered alcoholic. When asked
why it was important for him to buy the communion wine,
the man replied, "I was possessed by that demon for twenty
years. It controlled me. Now, when I go into the liquor store,
purchase the wine, walk out, and put it in the sacristy at
church, I think, 'That wine is not evil. It's the abuse of it
that's evil. That wine will be taken up to the altar, blessed,
and poured for the church. It will be holy. That destructive
stuff will be tamed, blessed, made holy. That wine is me.'"

Such a testimony helps to explain the extravagant
liturgical language of Ephesians 5:1-2: "Therefore be
imitators of God, as beloved children. And walk in love, as
Christ loved us and gave himself up for us, a fragrant
offering and sacrifice to God."

Leitourgia as Eucharistia

In moments of ethical uncertainty or difficulty, such as I
experienced that week in New Haven, we are driven back to
the recognition that our ethics is a liturgical matter. The
surgeon facing a life or death decision at the operating table,
the couple whose married life has become a tragedy, the
person deciding whether or not to participate in a political
revolution, the parents wondering how to respond to their
severely retarded child—any Christian action on these
occasions will have the quality of oblation, a prayer ending
with a doxology. We are not forced to self-sustain
righteousness. Our actions are not the only actions. In

offering ourselves and our gifts to God our acts and lives are graciously fitted into a larger pattern, woven into the fabric of God's ceaseless involvement in human history. We lay it all upon the altar, confident that what we give will be blessed and used, that somehow, through God's mysterious action, our few loaves and fishes will be enough.

Simply Assisting God

I am a humble artist
moulding my earthly clod,
adding my labour to nature's
simply assisting God.

Not that my effort is needed;
yet somehow, I understand,
my maker has willed it that I too should have
unmoulded clay in my hand.[14]

Not only the offering on Sunday morning, but many other acts of worship are oblational. The church traditionally believed that the adequacy of all worship should be measured by how well it conforms to the eucharistic pattern of self-giving in the Lord's Supper.

The whole Eucharist is an oblational activity, the supreme liturgical endeavor that enlightens our lives as offering. Here the material is lifted up and called holy. Here the daily stuff of bread and wine is offered. Here we are drawn into the action by which we become who we are called to be. Augustine beckoned the faithful to offer themselves at the Lord's table: "If, then, you are Christ's body and his members, it is your own mystery which is placed on the Lord's table; it is your own mystery which you receive. It is to what you are that you reply Amen, and by replying subscribe."[15]

Baptism begins the offertory movement. God gives us life. Now, in this initial act of self-giving, we get our first taste of what it means to offer oneself to God. In that first surrender and sacrifice, we do not, cannot know all that will be asked of us. In later acts of baptismal renewal and confirmation, we have opportunities to renew or remember our initial offering of ourselves to God and to grow into its meaning.

Hippolytus tells us in his *Apostolic Tradition* that early Christians were allowed to offer gifts at the Eucharist only after they had been baptized. The implication being that one is able to offer gifts at the Lord's table only after offering the self in baptism.

Baptism also reminds us that offering oneself to God can be a costly, sometimes painful, sacrificial, always life-changing experience. We offer ourselves unreservedly to God with the knowledge that God will take us, transform us, and use us for divine purposes. An offertory can be dangerous and expensive.

As we noted earlier, the sermon is oblational in a number of ways. It is the preacher's offering of the self and his or her homiletical efforts. The sermon involves the offering by the preacher of the people's doubts, questions, and present dilemmas before the light of God's Word. The sermon is oblational in those rare moments when the preacher unconditionally offers him or herself in service to the Word, those all too rare sermons when the congregation realizes that it is hearing one who is bringing them close to the truth—come what may. When the sermon is the preacher's production rather than the preacher's offering, the congregation usually misses an opportunity to hear their pastoral leader humbly standing under the power and burden of the text. They become the victims of homiletical vanity and presumption rather than witnesses that, even in times so out of joint as these, amid people so unfaithful, with preachers as unskilled as this one, there is a word.

There is also grace for us preachers. The gift of proclamation is response to the gift of the Word. Our response need not be perfect. Indeed, when sermons try to be perfect, (as in any presumptuous human work), they lose their oblational quality. We need not be flawless or successful. We need only be faithful. We need not present perfect gifts, only the honest labor of our hands. On the altar of God, this is enough. God can use even this.

I suggested in chapter 8 that, in the marriage service, a

man and a woman offer themselves unreservedly, unconditionally to one another in their promises. Then these
promises are offered to God, in the belief that the union of
this man and woman parallels and complements the uniting
work that God is doing throughout the world.

Weddings are a conglomerate of many things. Here the
fleshly and the spiritual, *eros* and *agape,* pagan and Christian
are all mixed together. Mere romantic infatuation may have
brought this man and woman together. The church wants
more commitment than that, but at least this may be the
beginning. This mix of motives, feelings, reservations, and
doubts must be offered by bride and groom, parents,
friends, and church at the wedding, given to God, without
whom human union would be impossible.

Chapter 9 affirmed children as gifts offered by God to
parents and the church. We do not own them or wholly
create them. Children come to us as one of the blessings of
marriage, as gifts. They come with certain givens over which
we have little control. So parents need not feel guilty when
children do not measure up to parental ideals for human
beings. Because they are gifts, we can offer them back to
God without guilt or embarrassment. Their value is hid with
God in Christ. Parents are not asked to be perfect. They are
asked to be receptive. Receptivity to the surprises and
unknowing each child brings, is what God asks in this gift or
any other.

Whether it be the worship of God in sermons, marriage,
the Eucharist, or hymns, the true test of our worship is how
well we respond to the self-giving of God through our giving
of ourselves. The sincerity of our thankfulness in worship
will be judged by whether or not we show forth that
thankfulness in our self-giving to others. God asks us only to
do in our ethics what we do in our worship, until our whole
life is one continuous act of eucharistia.

And so it was said that if you are "offering your gift at the
altar, and there remember that your brother has something
against you, leave your gift there before the altar and go;
first be reconciled to your brother, and then come and offer
your gift" (Matt. 5:23-24). God needs no self-offering from

us in worship which is not complemented by our self-offering to our brothers and sisters in our work.

In the week-in-week-out rhythm of prayer and praise, in the daily rhythm of our acts and decisions, let us offer ourselves and our gifts to God. Let us come before God with songs and shouts of praise, with works of mercy and love, that the ancient word might be fulfilled in us today. "Let us continually offer up a sacrifice of praise to God, that is, the fruit of lips that acknowledge his name. Do not neglect to do good and to share what you have, for such sacrifices are pleasing to God" (Heb. 13:15-16).

Notes

Preface

1. I am thinking of J. C. Hoekendijk, *The Church Inside Out* (Philadelphia: The Westminster Press, 1964); and Harvey Cox, *The Secular City* (New York: The Macmillan Co., 1965).
2. *Worship as Pastoral Care* (Nashville: Abingdon, 1979); and John H. Westerhoff and William H. Willimon, *Liturgy and Learning Through the Life Cycle* (New York: The Seabury Press, 1980).

Chapter 1

1. Massey Shepherd, "Liturgy and Mission," in F. S. Collier, ed., *Liturgy Is Mission* (New York: The Seabury Press, 1964), p. 40.
2. Constitution on the Sacred Liturgy *(Constitution de Sacra Liturgia)* No. 10.
3. Daniel Berrigan, S.J., *The Catholic Worker,* December 1976, p. 4.
4. See the Introduction to Peter Brunner, *Worship in the Name of Jesus,* trans. M. H. Bertram (St. Louis: Concordia Publishing House, 1968).

Chapter 2

1. Albert C. Outler, *Psychotherapy and the Christian Message* (New York: Harper & Brothers, 1954), p. 196.
2. James M. Gustafson, "Christian Ethics in America," in *Christian Ethics and the Community* (Philadelphia: Pilgrim Press,

1971), pp. 23-82; and "Christian Ethics," in Paul Ramsey, ed., *Religion* (Englewood Cliffs, N.J.: Prentice-Hall, 1965), p. 287.

3. We can distinguish several methodological orientations currently in use in the discipline of Christian ethics—all of which are used somewhere in this study: (1) Ethics that uses the methods of philosophy; either using ontology, inquiring into the moral significance of the nature of God, or by using linguistic analysis to clarify the function of moral language. (2) Ethics treated as a branch of systematic theology, beginning with doctrinal affirmations, deriving moral norms from these doctrines. (3) Or ethics that begins more empirically and analytically; reflecting on the nature of the moral life; how we are and become moral creatures. The social sciences are often enlisted when ethics is done by this method. James M. Gustafson, "Christian Ethics and Social Polity," in Paul Ramsey, ed., *Faith and Ethics: The Theology of H. Richard Niebuhr* (New York: Harper & Brothers, 1958), pp. 124ff.

4. Martin Luther, "A Treatise on Christian Liberty," in *Three Treatises* (Philadelphia: Fortress Press, 1943), p. 251.

5. See Calvin's remarks on "the order of right teaching" in John Calvin, *Institutes of the Christian Religion,* John T. McNeil, ed. (Philadelphia: The Westminster Press, 1960), I, 1, pars. 1, 3. See James Gustafson's, *Protestant and Roman Catholic Ethics* (Chicago: University of Chicago Press, 1978) for a comparison of Catholic and Protestant ethics.

6. Bruce C. Birch and Larry L. Rasmussen, *Bible and Ethics in the Christian Life* (Minneapolis: Augsburg Publishing House, 1976).

7. Joseph Fletcher, *Situation Ethics: The New Morality* (Philadelphia: The Westminster Press, 1966), and *Moral Responsibility* (Philadelphia: The Westminster Press, 1967).

8. Paul L. Lehmann, *Ethics in a Christian Context* (New York: Harper & Row, 1963), p. 138.

9. See James T. Laney, "A Critique of Radical Contextualist Ethics" (Ph.D. diss., Yale University, 1966). Modern Christian ethics' emphasis on individualized, heroic decision is a reflection of modern humanity's preoccupation with man as actor and self-creator *(homo fabricator)*. From this rather Pelagian point of view, the Christian moral life is seen as right decision, a decision which can arise from the essential goodness and courage within ourselves. James Sellars' *Theological Ethics* (New York: The Macmillan Co., 1969)

arises from this essentially Pelagian position. Contemporary stress on "man the maker and decider" has its philosophical roots in Kant: "The good will is not good because of what it effects or accomplishes or because of its adequacy to achieve some proposed end, it is only good because of its willing, i.e., it is good of itself." Immanuel Kant, *Foundations of the Metaphysics of Morals,* trans. Lewis White Beck (New York: Bobbs-Merrill Co., 1962), p. 54.

"You are the sum of your choices," claimed Wayne Dyer in his popular *Your Erroneous Zones* (New York: Avon Books, 1977), p. 241. Existentialists, Mazlowvians, and Rogerians isolated the self into private consciousness, apart from the world. Rather than expanding it, the human potential movement shrunk the self.

10. Lehmann, p. 45, 72, 74.
11. Among Protestant ethicists, Paul Ramsey is probably the best representative of those who argue for the upholding of principles in the situation-versus-principles debate. Ramsey argues that love is sentimentalized and emptied of content when it is not "imprincipled." Paul Ramsey, *Deeds and Rules in Christian Ethics* (New York: Charles Scribner's Sons, 1967). However, in focusing on principles and norms, Ramsey tends to overlook the dynamics of the continuing, multifaceted formation of the moral self. I hope to focus on the liturgical context, not simply as a source for Christian principles, but as a context for Christian formation; a formation that is often subconscious and nonrational rather than merely the result of rational reflection upon the relevance of Christian principles.
12. James M. Gustafson, "Context Versus Principles: A Misplaced Debate in Christian Ethics," Martin E. Marty and Dean G. Peerman, eds., *New Theology No. 3* (New York: The Macmillan Co., 1966).
13. For Barth's ethical thought see, Karl Barth, *Church Dogmatics,* ed. G. W. Bromiley and T. F. Torrance (Edinburgh: T. & T. Clark, 1956–62), I, 2, pp. 362ff., 782ff.; II, 2, pp. 509ff.; III, 4, pp. 3ff. See James M. Gustafson's *Christ and the Moral Life* (New York: Harper & Row, 1968) for what I believe to be the best treatment of Barth's ethics.
14. Rudolph Bultmann, *Existence and Faith,* trans. and ed. Schubert M. Ogden (New York: Meridian Books, 1960), p. 182.

Existentialist ethics eschews principles, traditions, and

community in order to keep all ethical options open. Ironically, the opposite is achieved. Without any meaningful external basis for decisions, we are drawn ever more narrowly into ourselves. For a sociologist's view of the paradoxical limitations of our modern "freedom," see Daniel Yankelovich, *New Rules* (New York: Random House, 1981), chs. 5 and 8.

15. Aristotle, *Nicomachean Ethics,* trans. Martin Ostwald (New York: Bobbs-Merrill Co., 1962) 1179625-26, p. 296.

16. Gustafson delineates two basic perspectives with which Christian ethics has viewed the moral self. One perspective, shared by such thinkers as Schleiermacher, Bushnell, and, I think, Gustafson himself, says the self "in its action *expresses the personal history that it has accumulated* through its past experiences and associations." The second perspective, shared by Kant, Barth, and existentialists like Bultmann, says the self "in its action is a *free self undetermined* by its phenomenal history, facing an imperative . . . an open present and future, and acting out of this freedom to determine the future." James M. Gustafson, *Christ and the Moral Life,* p. 93. The ethics of character comes out of the first perspective.

17. The major sources for this new attention to moral formation and character are: James M. Gustafson, *Christian Ethics and the Community* (Philadelphia: United Church Press, 1971) and *Can Ethics Be Christian?* (Chicago: University of Chicago Press, 1975); Stanley Hauerwas, *Character and the Christian Life: A Study in Theological Ethics* (San Antonio: Trinity University Press, 1975); and David Bailey Harned, *Faith and Virtue* (Philadelphia: Pilgrim Press, 1973), J. W. McClendon, *Biography As Theology* (Nashville: Abingdon Press, 1974), ch. 1.

18. See Peter Berger and Thomas Luckmann, *The Social Construction of Reality* (Garden City, N.Y.: Doubleday & Co., 1966).

19. John Wesley, "Sermon on the Mount—IV," *Sermons on Several Occasions* (London: Epworth Press, 1956), p. 237.

20. James B. Nelson, *Moral Nexus; Ethics of Christian Identity and Community* (Philadelphia: The Westminster Press, 1971), p. 26. While claiming that the church is the "Moral Nexus," Nelson fails (as do Hauerwas and Gustafson, by the way) to refer to the liturgy as part of that nexus.

21. R. H. Tawney, *Religion and the Rise of Capitalism* (London: J. Murray, 1966), pp. 227-30. Tawney describes the ethical

result of the Puritan's individualized quest for salvation. "When earthly props have been cast down, the soul stands erect in the presence of God . . . first the spirit burns brightly on the hearth; but through the windows of his soul the Puritan, unless a poet or a saint, looks on a landscape touched by no breath of spring . . . a wilderness to be subdued with aching limbs beneath solitary stars. . . . Those who seek God in isolation from their fellow men, unless armed for the perils of the quest, are apt to find, not God, but a devil, whose countenance bears an embarrassing resemblance to their own. The moral self-sufficiency of the Puritan nerved his will, but it corroded his sense of social solidarity."

Whether or not Tawney described the actual life of historical Puritans, he described the moral and spiritual results of any type of spiritual isolationism that idealizes autonomy and minimizes community.

22. In passing we might note the influential work of psychologist Lawrence Kohlberg who has proposed a theory of moral development based upon reasons people give for behaving in particular ways. Kohlberg identifies three levels of moral development, each consisting of two stages. While Kohlberg does not claim that his theory is grounded in a Christian perspective, some Christian educators and ethicists have been attracted to it. I regard Kohlberg's theory as an inadequate description of Christian moral development for two reasons. First, conceiving the moral life as a series of stages tends to portray our moral selves as more orderly and coherent than they are in real life. Second, Kohlberg defines the final stage in moral development as an autonomous ethical self, a free agent who is liberated, not only from the conventions of society, but also from traditions within the community. I see this as antithetical to Christian commitments and a spurious attempt to give empirical justification to the liberal myth of the autonomous individual. See "Stages of Moral Development as a Basis for Moral Education" in C. M. Beck, B. S. Brittenden, and E. V. Sullivan, eds., *Moral Education: Interdisciplinary Approaches* (Toronto: University of Toronto Press, 1971), pp. 86-92 for a critical examination of Kohlberg's theory; also Stanley Hauerwas, *A Community of Character: Toward a Constructive Christian Social Ethic* (Notre Dame, Ind.: University of Notre Dame Press, 1981), pp. 129-52; and Craig Dykstra, *Vision and Character* (New York: Paulist Press, 1981), ch. 1.

23. James M. Gustafson, *The Church as Moral Decision-Maker* (Philadelphia: Pilgrim Press, 1970.

24. Jonathan Edwards, *Treatise Concerning the Religious Affections,* ed. John E. Smith (New Haven: Yale University Press, 1959), p. 118. Edwards set the course for a peculiarly American religious concern: the definition of and examination of religious emotions. This decidedly "psychological" emphasis of Edwards is carried on in William James' *Varieties of Religious Experience* and, more recently, Don E. Saliers, *The Soul in Paraphrase* (New York: The Seabury Press, 1980) and Richard R. Niebuhr's *Experiential Religion* (New York: Harper & Row, 1972).

25. See Harold H. Titus and Morris Kenton, *Ethics for Today* (New York: American Book Company, 1966), pp. 280-81.

26. Iris Murdoch attempted to shift the focus of attention in ethics from choice to vision in her "Vision and Choice in Morality," in Ian T. Ramsey, ed., *Christian Ethics and Contemporary Philosophy Sovereignty of Good* (London: Routledge & Kegan Paul, 1970). "I can only choose within the world I can *see,*" Murdoch told the glorifiers of choice, p. 37. Dykstra contrasts "juridical ethics" of judgment and choice with "visional ethics." *Vision and Character,* chs. 1 and 2.

27. "The word 'perspective' is drawn from the sphere of its normal usage, that is, visual experience, and suggests that the point from which things are seen and observed determines what is seen and what is not seen, which aspects of what is seen are outstanding, which are shadowed and which are clear. . . . Perspective is used to refer to the state of the observing subject; to his preferences for certain things, to his fundamental vocabulary for describing and evaluating what he observes, his criteria for rational judgment, and his values that determine his affective responses. Sometimes the word 'understanding' has been used to cover these things, and this is fitting and proper if it is used in such a way that the affections are included together with the intellect." Gustafson, *Christ and the Moral Life,* p. 242.

28. See chapter 2 of Stuart Hampshire's *Thought and Action* (New York: Viking Press, 1960).

29. Gustafson, *Christ and the Moral Life,* p. 264. Jürgen Moltmann's *Theology of Hope* (New York: Harper & Row, 1967) and, more recently, *Hope and Planning* (New York: Harper & Row, 1971) speaks of eschatological hope as an

attitude or disposition, a kind of vision, that grasps the Christian. But his futuristic "hope" lacks specific content because Moltmann isolates a Christian's hope from the specifics of Christian tradition and other Christian virtues or motivating factors. By reducing everything to "hope," Moltmann suffers from some of the same reductionism of the ethicists who reduce all Christian action to "love." His "hope," in its lack of content and context, is an insufficient basis for ethics. I think a similar criticism could be made of those theologians who speak of Christian vision and intention as "liberation." We must be critical of any ethics that attempts to reduce the Christian ethical endeavor to one overarching principle. The criticism arises because: (1) The Christian moral life is a complex of many virtues, principles, motivating factors, visions, and theological commitments, and (2) In order to have a single, overarching principle for Christian action, one must devise a principle so amorphorous and general (i.e., "love," "hope," "liberation") that one can easily give it any content one wishes. God no longer defines "liberation." Rather, our vague notions of "liberation" define God. My assumption is that the Christian's vision must be rooted in the tradition, principles, scripture, revelation, community, and worship of the church—or else it is a dangerously myopic vision that is limited by my merely parochial, merely contemporary, merely personal view of what ought to be. For example, in *To Change the World*, Rosemary Radford Ruether caricatures Jesus as a "radical social iconoclast" who is more "proleptic than final," more "paradigmatic than exclusivistic" for contemporary believers. By emptying Christianity of its narrative and historical content, Ruether is free to change the world unhindered by the specifics of the gospel (New York: Crossroads Press, 1982).

30. Stanley Hauerwas, *Vision and Virtue: Essays in Christian Ethical Reflection* (Notre Dame, Ind.: Fides/Clarentian, 1974), p. 2.

31. Lehmann notes that "Ethos" is derived from the Greek verb *eiotha* meaning "to be accustomed to." In its noun form it meant "dwelling" or "stall," an accustomed place which gives stability and security to a person's existence. "Ethos" therefore denotes that discernable, patterned context that gives necessary stability and security to a person's moral life—all the principles, rules, virtues, and visions the community offers the

individual. Paul Lehmann, in John A. Hutchison, ed., *Christian Faith and Social Action* (New York: Charles Scribner's Sons, 1953), p. 28.

32. Gustafson, *Christ and the Moral Life*, p. 257; and also "The Eclipse of Sin," *Motive*, 25 (March 1965), 4-8. Hauerwas says, "In the name of a more humane ethic, contemporary Christian ethics downgrades principles, rules, criteria, and institutions; this move is ironical since it is just such objective realities which enable us to be humane." *Vision and Virtue*, p. 106.

33. I therefore disagree with Earl Brill. "If Christians find themselves isolated in their advocacy of a moral position, it may be that the entire society has lapsed into an inhuman barbarism. It is more likely, however, that the Christians are merely in error." *The Christian Moral Vision* (New York: The Seabury Press, 1979), p. 9. Jack Sanders can say "Jesus does not provide a valid ethic for today," because Sanders is looking for an ethic for non-disciples. *Ethics in the New Testament: Change and Development* (Philadelphia: Fortress Press, 1975), p. 29.

34. Philip P. Hallie, *Lest Innocent Blood Be Shed: The Story of the Village of Le Chambon and How Goodness Happened There* (New York: Harper & Row, 1980).

35. And so Don Saliers calls worship a characterizing activity. "It takes time and place and people. When worship occurs, people are characterized, given their life and the fundamental location and orientation in the world. Worship characterizes human beings who recall and give expression to a story about the world." "Liturgy and Ethics: Some New Beginnings," in *The Journal of Religious Ethics* (1979), 175. As Hauerwas says, "The great social task of the church is to become a community where symbolic discourse is used and embraced in ritual and practice because of its assurance that God had indeed redeemed the world in Jesus Christ." *Vision and Virtue*, p. 8.

Chapter 3

1. *Motu proprio*, 1903. The phrase is repeated in Pius XII's *Mediator Dei* (1947) though reversed to speak first of the sanctification of man and then the glorification of God. See James White, *Introduction to Christian Worship* (Nashville: Abingdon, 1980), p. 20.

2. William Temple, *The Hope of a New World* (New York: The Macmillan Co., 1943), p. 26.

> A more subtle but no less important instrument for moral development is the worship of the church. Regular participation in the hearing of the Word and reception of the sacrament contributes to moral formation. Even when ethical issues are not directly addressed in worship we meet a Lord who loves us and who calls us out of our preoccupation with self. In worship we identify and acknowledge our moral failures, we offer up our moral dilemmas, we receive forgiveness of our sins and offenses. In worship we hear the call to share God's love with all of his children and we are sent forth to serve in the cause of freedom, justice, and peace. Worship creates a context that contrasts sharply with the aggressive, competitive, and self-centered ethos of contemporary society.

Earl Brill, *The Christian Moral Vision* (New York: The Seabury Press, 1979), p. 215.

3. Paul W. Hoon, *The Integrity of Worship* (Nashville: Abingdon, 1971), pp. 30-31.

4. See Jacques Ellul's opening chapter on deceitful prayer in his *Prayer and Modern Man*, trans. C. E. Hopkin (New York: The Seabury Press, 1973).

5. Karl Barth, *Church Dogmatics*, I, 2, pp. 280-361. See also James F. Gustafson, *Ethics from a Theocentric Perspective: Theology and Ethics* (Chicago: University of Chicago Press, 1981), pp. 293-99.

6. Edward Norbeck, *Religion in Primitive Society* (New York: Harper & Row, 1961), pp. 138ff.

7. Edward Shils, "Ritual and Crisis," in Donald R. Cutler, ed., *The Religious Situation: 1968* (Boston: Beacon Press), p. 736. Of course, rituals can be dysfunctional as well as functional, keeping us from reality rather than aiding us in approaching reality.

8. Victor W. Turner, *The Ritual Process: Structure and Anti-Structure* (Chicago: Aldine Publishing Co., 1969).

9. Erik Erikson, *Toys and Reasons* (New York: W. W. Norton & Co., 1977), pp. 43-44.

10. William H. Willimon, *Worship as Pastoral Care* (Nashville: Abingdon, 1979), p. 178.

11. J. Bronowski, *The Identity of Man* (Garden City, N.Y.: The Natural History Press, 1971), p. 135.

12. John Dewey, *Theory of the Moral Life* (New York: Holt, Rinehart and Winston, 1966), p. 135. Throughout this study on liturgy and ethics there is the implicit assumption that ethics is more than mere rational reflection on Christian behavior. Our

character is the sum of emotional and rational factors. The liturgy is one of those factors. Worship is an emotional activity. The word "emotional" means, in its Latin root, literally "to move out." To say that ethics and worship are emotive is to indicate that they help us to move out of ourselves into a larger reality. Too often, "emotional" carries the connotation of being locked in some inner world of feeling. The emotive power of the symbols and metaphors of the faith evoke emotions which, rather than locking us in, open doors and introduce us to dimensions of reality we would otherwise have missed. Such moving out and opening up is essential to creative decision-making Christian living.

Don Saliers' *Soul in Paraphrase* is an excellent attempt to reclaim the centrality of the religious affections as a concern for Christian life.

13. Jonathan Z. Smith, "The Influence of Symbols upon Social Change: A Place on Which to Stand," in James Shaughnessy, ed., *The Roots of Ritual* (Grand Rapids, Michigan: Wm. B. Eerdmans Publishing Co., 1973).

14. J. C. Hoekendijk, trans. Isaac C. Rottenberg, *The Church Inside Out,* p. 54.

15. Valyi Nagy, Ervin and Heinrich Ott, *The Church as Dialogue,* trans. Reinhard Ulrich (Philadelphia: Pilgrim Press, 1969), p. 56.

16. *Constitution on the Sacred Liturgy,* # 2.

17. George A. Lindbeck, *The Future of Roman Catholic Theology* (Philadelphia: Fortress Press, 1970), pp. 50, 55.

Jürgen Moltmann has characterized our current problem as the "Identity-Involvement Dilemma." When the church becomes preoccupied with its identity, it becomes a religious club, removed from the struggles of the world. On the other hand, when the church involves itself in social and political struggle, it tends to get swallowed up by secular movements and lose its identity as the church. The blend which results is what Moltmann calls chamelion theology—adapting to blend with the secular surroundings. The separation of identity from involvement is a major problem for the church, in our time. "Christian Theology Today," *New World Outlook,* 62 (1972), pp. 483-90.

David Kelsey says, "The activities . . . of a Christian worshiping community should all be ordered to one end, viz., shaping the identities of its members. . . ." "The Bible and Christian Theology," *Journal of the American Academy of Religion,* 48 (1980) 387.

18. Paul Ramsey, "Kant's Moral Theology or a Religious Ethics?" in H. Tristram Englehardt, Jr. and Daniel Callahan, eds., *Knowledge, Value and Belief* (Hastings-on-Hudson, N.Y.: Institutes of Society, Ethics, and the Life Sciences, 1977), p. 66.

19. Bronowski, *Identity of Man,* p. 35.

Obviously, in my stress on the church and its liturgy as the primary locus of moral formation, I am in agreement with James B. Nelson who says, in criticizing contemporary Christian ethics: "A serious shortcoming in most Protestant Christian ethics has been its tendency to speak of God's gratitude-eliciting work in ways which imply that the church is quite incidental to the process . . . a relational theology and ethics must recapture, but in a new and broad way, the Roman Catholic and Reformation Protestant claim *extra ecclesiam nulla salus*—outside the church there is no salvation." *Moral Nexus* (Philadelphia: The Westminster Press, 1971), p. 44.

20. Martin Heidegger, *Being and Time* (London: SCM Press, 1962), pp. 91-148.

21. Having spoken of liturgical architecture as having power to form and to express our vision, I cannot leave these comments on the blurring of Christian symbols and metaphors without quoting the devastatingly funny indictment of contemporary, liberal ecclesiastical architectural and theological enculturation in Peter De Vries' *The Mackerel Plaza* (New York: Popular Library, 1977), pp. 8-9:

> Our church is, I believe, the first split-level church in America. It has five rooms and two baths downstairs—dining area, kitchen and three parlors for committee and group meetings—with a crawl space behind the furnace ending in the hillside into which the structure is built. Upstairs is one huge all-purpose interior, divisible into different-sized components by means of sliding walls and convertible into an auditorium for putting on plays, a gymnasium for athletics, and a ballroom for dances. There is a small worship area at one end. This has a platform cantilevered on both sides, with a free-form pulpit designed by Noguchi. It consists of a slab of marble set on four legs of four delicately differing fruitwoods, to symbolize the four Gospels, and their failure to harmonize. Behind it dangles a large multi-colored mobile, its interdenominational parts swaying, as one might fancy, in perpetual reminder of the Pauline stricture against those "blown by every wind of doctrine." In

back of this building is a newly erected clinic, with medical and neuropsychiatric wings, both indefinitely expandable. Thus People's Liberal is a church designed to meet the needs of today, and to serve the whole man. This includes the worship of a God free of outmoded theological definitions and palatable to a mind come of age in the era of Relativity.

22. E. R. Dodds, *Pagan and Christian in an Age of Anxiety* (Cambridge: Cambridge University Press, 1965).

23. James F. White, "The Words of Worship: Beyond Liturgical Sexism," *Christian Century*, December 13, 1978, pp. 1202-6.

24. As Suzanne Langer says, "Man can adapt himself somehow to anything his imagination can cope with; but he cannot deal with chaos. . . . Therefore our most important assets are always the symbols for our general orientation in nature, on the earth, in society and in what we are doing: the symbols of our *Weltanschauung* and *Lebenanschauung*." *Philosophy in a New Key*, 4th ed. (Cambridge: Harvard University Press, 1960), p. 287. See also Dykstra, *Vision and Character*, ch. 3.

25. In this matter of Christian metaphor and language, Hauerwas says, "The task of Christian ethics is to help keep the grammar of the language of faith pure." *Character and the Christian Life*, p. 233.

26. Bronowski, *Identity of Man*, p. 64.

27. Bronowski notes that human action can arise from two kinds of resolve: (1) We rationally assess the consequences of optional actions and decide, in light of the evidence, to do something in a certain way: I do not hit my neighbor because he will hit me back. This he calls, *Formal Knowledge*. (2) I decide to do something because of my *Knowledge of Myself*, seeing myself in another and, through this vision, seeing both myself and the other: I do not hit my neighbor because he is a fellow human being and one of my God's children. Suggested by *Identity of Man*, p. 24.

28. Iris Murdoch, *The Sovereignty of Good* (New York: Schocken Books, 1971), pp. 86-87. See S. Dennis Ford's criticism and modification of Murdoch in "The Moralist: As Chooser, As Artist, As Critic" *Religion in Life* (1979), pp. 413-24. See also Peter A. Bertocci and R. M. Millard, *Personality and the Good* (New York: David McKay Co., 1963), p. 352, 494-95.

29. Hauerwas, *Vision and Virtue*, p. 40.

30. Dykstra says, "The moral world is a world of mystery. Rather than a world of problems. People are mysteries, and being

moral means treating them as such." *Vision and Character,* p. 36. Our moralizing does us great disservice when it seeks to reduce the ambiguity of our ethical existence. The best that ethics can do is to analyze the richness and multiplicity of our ethical life, perhaps deepen and enrich our metaphors and symbols. As Hauerwas says,

> The moral life does not consist just in making one right decision after another; it is the progressive attempt to widen and clarify our vision of reality. . . . Because contemporary Christian ethicists have assumed that 'the ethical' primarily concerns action and decision, they have found little moral significance in basic affirmations about God, Christ, grace, and sanctification. . . . Being a Christian involves more than just making certain decisions; it is a way of attending to the world. It is learning "to see" the world under the mode of the divine. . . . A Christian does not simply "believe" certain propositions about God; he learns to attend to reality through them. This learning requires training of our attention by constantly juxtaposing our experience with our vision. . . . The problem is to become as we see. *Vision and Virtue,* pp. 44-46.

31. Hauerwas, *Ibid.,* p. 20.
32. Kenneth E. Kirk, *The Vision of God* (London: Longmans Green, 1934), p. 1.
33. John Fry, in *The Immobilized Christian* (Philadelphia: The Westminster Press, 1963) has a brilliant phenomenological analysis of how ethics are unconsciously shaped and conditioned prior to our rational reflection on them. This unconscious social influence upon Christian ethics has been noted before, but by a theologian who has not been in vogue for some time. Horace Bushnell spoke of certain influences upon morality through which "men are ever touching unconsciously the springs of motion in each other; . . ." and said we need "a more thorough appreciation of the relative importance of that kind of influence or beneficence which is insensibly exerted." "Unconscious Influence," in *Sermons for the New Life* (New York: Charles Scribner's Sons, 1907), p. 186.
34. Bernard Häring, *The Sacraments in a Secular Age* (Slough: St. Paul Publications, 1976). "Prayer consists of attention . . . the orientation of all the attention of which the soul is capable toward God." Simone Weil, *Waiting for God,* trans. E. Craufurd (New York: Harper & Row, 1973), p. 105.
35. So John Macquarrie says, "the greatest obstacle in the way of our realizing the presence of God [in worship] . . . [is that] our

horizons have been narrowed to considerations of production and consumption, our idea of the good life is built around the advertisements in the glossy magazines, and the only possible result of this unspirituality is an impaired vision." *Paths in Spirituality* (New York: Harper & Row, 1972), p. 124. In his book on ethics and pastoral care, Don S. Browning notes that one of the ways worship facilitates moral formation is, "by imparting the moral vision which is the substance of the Christian faith." *The Moral Context of Pastoral Care* (Philadelphia: The Westminster Press, 1976), p. 102.

36. Alfred North Whitehead, *Science and the Modern World* (New York: The Macmillan Co., 1926), pp. 274-76.

37. Geoffrey Wainwright, *Doxology* (New York: Oxford University Press, 1980), p. 3.

38. Murdoch, *Sovereignty of Good*, pp. 55-56.

"One's loves govern one's intentions, . . . the moral life consists in the right ordering and directing of one's loves." James F. Gustafson, *Can Ethics Be Christian?* (Chicago: University of Chicago Press, 1975), p. 75.

Richard R. Niebuhr says, "It is not sufficient to conceive of faithful man in the world as a rational soul, nor even as a rational being whose dignity lies in choosing and willing. He is also an affectional being whose thinking and willing are themselves always qualified by a specific affection or resonance that pervades the whole person-world polarity." *Experiential Religion* (New York: Harper & Row, 1972), p. 45.

39. John Macquarrie has described worship as "concentration," the recollecting or gathering of the self in a focal experience of encounter that is a compelling, formative center. *Principles of Christian Theology* (London: SCM Press, 1966), p. 434. Worship is thus a dialectical experience of concentration through consolidation and attentiveness to the "givens" of the faith and expansive envisioning through ecstatic attentiveness to the visions and dreams of the faith.

40. Hauerwas, *Vision and Virtue*, p. 194.

Worship is the "enactment of the core dynamics of the Christian life . . . its central and focusing activity. It is paradigmatic for all the rest of the Christian life." Dykstra, *Vision and Character*, p. 106.

41. Kirk, *The Vision of God*, p. 108.

42. A phrase suggested by Karl Barth's discussion of tradition in *Church Dogmatics*, IV, p. 705.

43. Of course, the Bible itself is one of the traditions that worship constantly keeps before us. For more on this matter, see my *The Bible and Worship: The Sustaining Presence* (Valley Forge, Pa.: Judson Press, 1981).

44. G. K. Chesterton, *Orthodoxy* (New York: Dodd, Mead, 1952), p. 85, as quoted in Nelson, *Moral Nexus,* p. 39.

    Theologies of Liberation have not missed the revolutionary power of tradition. Justo and Catherine Gonzalez say that,

    the conservative character of the liturgy can also be its greatest value, . . . The preacher of liberation may be tempted to avoid as much of the traditional liturgy as possible and concentrate only on contemporary issues. Such an avoidance is neither necessary nor useful. In fact, the more it can be shown that what is being emphasized by liberation theology is at the heart of the gospel, especially as it was understood in the earliest time of the church's history . . . the more helpful it will be to the congregation. . . . To be a preacher of liberation can make one also the rediscoverer of some of the greatness of the liturgical tradition. *Liberation Preaching* (Nashville: Abingdon, 1980), pp. 104-7.

Chapter 4

1. Barth, *Church Dogmatics,* trans. A. T. Mackay, *et al.,* III, pp. 17, 18, 22, 25.

2. Ramsey, "Liturgy and Ethics," p. 143.

3. H. Richard Niebuhr, *The Responsible Self* (New York: Harper & Row, 1963), p. 63. Niebuhr speaks of ethics as "the understanding of ourselves as responsive beings, who in all our actions answer to action upon us in accordance with our interpretation of such action" (p. 57). Unfortunately, "the responsible self" is a rather neutral being who responds out of a vague context of the general Christian heritage. Response to a given situation, in Niebuhr's ethics, seems to outweigh response to a specifically Christan ethos. I see the Christian as responding to a specific story, a discernible ethos, a particular relationship with God in Jesus Christ.

4. Stanley Hauerwas, *Vision and Virtue,* p. 115. Jonathan Edwards speaks of sin as "contractedness," "like some powerful astringent," the opposite of the expansive function of worship. Jonathan Edwards, *Charity and Its Fruits* (Edinburgh: Banner of Truth Trust, 1969), pp. 157-58.

5. James Gustafson, "Patterns of Christian Social Action," *Theology Today,* 18 (July 1961) 171.

6. Kirk, *The Vision of God,* p. 46.

7. "The moral ideal for Christians lies not in a code, nor in a social order. It lies in a life where love of God and man is the spring of every thought and word and action." T. W. Manson, *The Teaching of Jesus* (Cambridge: 1932), p. 312.

8. Murdoch, *The Sovereignty of Good,* p. 103.

> It is not precisely by trying to make ourselves into good men that we become good men. It is not by careful cultivation of our characters in the light of an ideal that the finest character is actually formed. That purely moralistic method is apt to lead either to manifest failure or, . . . to a self-righteous pride, which is really the worst failure of all. . . . The true saints have followed a different way. Instead of concentrating on their own character, they have been God-centered. They have been less conscious of themselves than God, less conscious of an ethic or an idea than the love of God, which called out the response of their faith and love. . . . looking back, they have regularly confessed that what ever good was in their lives was not their own achievement but was due to divine grace.

> D. M. Braillie, *The Theology of the Sacraments* (New York: Charles Scribner's Sons, 1957), pp. 136-37.

> The human problem, says Gabriel Marcel, is "the illusion of moral egocentricity," our innate tendency to organize the whole world around ourselves. The answer to this problem is liturgial before it is ethical. *Homo Viator,* trans. E. Craufurd (New York: Harper & Row, 1962), p. 19.

9. Gustafson, *Can Ethics Be Christian?,* pp. 79-80.

10. Murdoch, p. 59. "Ethical theory is not meant to provide man with a program the implementation of which would be life's goal. Nor is it meant to present man with principles to be interpreted, applied, and put into practice. . . . Ethics exists to remind man of his confrontations with God, who is the light illuminating all his actions." Karl Barth, *The Humanity of God,* trans. Thomas Weiser (Richmond: John Knox, 1963), p. 86. "Sin is occasioned precisely by the fact that man refuses to admit his 'creatureliness.'" Reinhold Niebuhr, *The Nature and Destiny of Man* (New York: Charles Scribner's Sons, 1964), vol. 1, p. 16.

11. Murdoch, p. 40.

> "Nothing erodes the public morality so much as the acquiescence in what is expedient when what is true is unpalatable." Bronowski, *Identity of Man,* p. 110.

12. Murdoch, p. 44.

> "A friend once wrote Turgenev: 'It seems to me to put

one's self in the second place is the whole significance of life.'
To which Turgenev replied: 'It seems to me that to discover
what to put before one's self, in the first place, is the whole
problem of life.'" John C. Schroeder, "A Deeper Social
Gospel," *The Christian Century,* July 26, 1939.

13. See note 1.
14. Reinhold Niebuhr, "Sects and Churches," *The Christian
    Century,* July 3, 1935.
15. *Ibid.,* "The Weakness of Common Worship in American
    Protestantism," *Christianity and Crisis,* May 28, 1951.
16. Macquarrie, *Principles of Christian Theology,* pp. 259-62.
17. H. Richard Niebuhr's classic criticism of a complacent, liberal
    theology and church: "A God without wrath brought men
    without sin into a kingdom without judgment through the
    ministrations of a Christ without a cross" (p. 193). "To be
    reconciled to God now meant to be reconciled to the
    established customs of a more or less Christianized society"
    (p. 181). *The Kingdom of God in America* (Chicago: Willett, Clark,
    and Company, 1937), p. 193. See Leonard I. Sweet, "Not All
    Cats Are Gray: Beyond Liberalism's Uncertain Faith," *The
    Christian Century,* June 23-30, 1982.
18. While I concede the continuing validity of the church in its
    "mainline" forms, the "public church" as Martin E. Marty calls
    it, and I agree with Marty's assessment of the public church's
    contributions toward the betterment of American life, Marty
    underestimates the gravity of the present situation and the
    public church's difficulties in being the church. Martin E.
    Marty, *The Public Church* (New York: Crossroad Press, 1981).
    See Alasdair MacIntyre's criticism of liberal Christian ethics in
    Secularization and Moral Change (London: Oxford University
    Press, 1967).
19. Hans Conzelman, *An Outline of the Theology of the New Testament*
    (New York: Harper & Row, 1969), p. 63.

Chapter 5

1. The question of the possible precedents for John's baptism of
   repentance has occupied scholars for some time. Behind his
   baptism lies a long history of the use of water in the religion of
   Israel (see Lev. 15:5, 17:15, e.g.). Members of the sect at
   Qumran, John's contemporaries, saw their repeated lustra-
   tions as a means of moral and religious cleansing, as a means of
   preparing the Way of the Lord. See G. R. Beasley-Murray,

Baptism in the New Testament (London: Macmillan, 1963), pp. 39-40 for a discussion of antecedents. My own view is that John needed no other precedents than the obvious and universally exploited ritual possibilities of water and washing.

2. I suspect that later defenders of paedobaptism have a vested interest in getting as many baptismal themes as possible, besides repentance, into an account of baptism. I personally believe that the baptism of the children of Christian parents can be defended as a legitimate pastoral modification of the norm of adult baptism. But it need not be defended by recourse to Augustine's emphasis on original sin, to Luther's notions of incipient infant faith, to Calvin's inheritors of the covenant theme, or (more to the point of present practice) to fuzzy affirmations about the essential cheapness of divine grace. See Laurence H. Stookey, *Baptism: Christ's Act in the Church* (Nashville: Abingdon, 1982) for a good contemporary defense of infant baptism.

3. Beasley-Murray, *Baptism*, p. 72.

4. I use as the basis for my interpretation Robert W. Jenson, "The Mandate and Promise of Baptism," *Interpretation* (July, 1970), and N. Gaumann, *Taufe und Ethik: Studien zu Romer 6* (Munich: Kaiser Verlag, 1967).

5. Albert Schweitzer, *The Mysticism of Paul the Apostle*, trans. W. Montgomery, 2nd ed. (London: Adam & Charles Black, 1953).

6. Martin Dibelius, *From Tradition to Gospel*, trans. B. O. Woolf (London: Nicholson & Watson, 1934), pp. 238-39.

7. The Pauline Epistles and I Peter are at one in this:

> Baptism is not merely turning over a new leaf—it is death and resurrection. . . . As soon as Baptism is treated as chiefly a cleansing, the tendency is to interpret it as a cleansing from past sins, with the corollary that thereafter the baptized must keep himself clean. But as long as membership in Christ is treated as new life—as the bringing of a person through death into a new relationship and an entirely new mode of existence—the supernatural, wholly divine agency is more prominent. The "indicative," the statement, that we have died and been buried with Christ and are now alive in Him, is a more potent one than the statement that we were once washed. "Become what you are!" is a more deeply Christian imperative than "Keep yourself clean!"

C. F. D. Moule, *Worship in the New Testament* (Richmond: John Knox Press, 1957), p. 57.

8. R. C. Tannehill, *Dying and Rising with Christ* (Berlin: Topelmann, 1966), p. 1.

9. The radical anabaptists illustrate the assertion that one cannot think of the church without thinking of baptism.

10. See E. Jungel, "Zur Kritik des sacramentalen Verstandnisses der Taufe," in F. Viering, ed., *Zu Karl Barths Lehre von der Taufe* (Gutersloh: Mohn, 1971), pp. 25-43.

11. Wainwright, *Doxology*, p. 132.

> The Baptism of every infant should be a renewed Baptism for every adult present. . . . They should examine themselves how far they have kept the faith for which they were claimed. . . . Baptism does not merely concern the child or parents. . . . It is . . . principally for the church. . . . It revives by faith its sense of the new and eternal life of forgiveness.

P. T. Forsyth, *The Church And the Sacraments* (London: Longmans, Green, and Co., 1917), pp. 181-82. See Regis Duffy, *Real Presence: Worship, Sacraments and Commitment* (New York: Harper & Row, 1982), ch. 5.

12. Gradually, a system of penance developed in an attempt by the church to deal pastorally with the reality of postbaptismal sin. This ministry of reconciliation was seen as an attempt to call penitents back to the abiding reality of their baptism, to renew their vision and restore their faith in the baptismal promises—so that they might begin again the journey of living out the meaning of their baptism. See J. D. Crichton, *The Ministry of Reconciliation: A Commentary on the "Ordo Paenitentiae,"* (London: Chapman, 1974). New services of baptismal renewal can have much the same effect. See chapter 7 of my *Worship as Pastoral Care*.

13. R. Martin, *Carmen Christi* (Cambridge: Cambridge University Press, 1967).

14. After declaring that the baptized are slaves of God (Rom. 6:16-19), Paul switches to the metaphor of sonship, those who cry "Abba! Father!" (Rom. 8:15-17; cf. Gal. 4:6-7). Sonship implies our free cooperation with God—not forced labor. We are *filii in Filio* (Gal. 3:26-27; 4:4-6). But children of God are to walk in the Spirit of God (Rom. 8:14; cf. Gal. 5:16, 25). We are to be children of God who act in conformity with the actions of God's Son. Obedience is expected of the baptismal sons and daughters no less than the servants.

15. Leander E. Keck, *Paul and His Letters* (Philadelphia: Fortress Press, 1979), pp. 45-46.

16. Aidan Kavanaugh, *The Shape of Baptism: The Rite of Christian Initiation* (New York: Pueblo Publishing Company, 1978), p. 58.

17. Tannehill (*op. cit.*) argues that Hellenistic Christians tended to understand baptism in the manner of the pagan mysteries. They interpreted the death-life metaphors of baptism exclusively in the present tense, thinking that their resurrection had already taken place. Romans 6, then, shows Paul attacking the simple parallelism, "Christ has risen" and "I have risen." He keeps the believer's resurrection in the future tense (Rom. 6:8), the unfinished death-life work in the subjunctive mood (v. 4).

    A similar thought process is shown in Colossians 2 and 3 where our death/resurrection in baptism (3:1) is qualified by "not yet" (3:4) and by ethical exhortation (3:5ff.). The ethical exhortation keeps the baptismal experience grounded in the facts of human history rather than floating off into the ethereal realm of the enthusiast who seeks to bypass the cross on the way to glory.

18. Kavanaugh, *The Shape of Baptism*, p. 159.

19. Thus conversion is a major theme of liberation theologians:

    > Our conversion process is affected by the socioeconomic, political, cultural, and human environment in which it occurs. Without a change in these structures, there is no authentic conversion. We have to break with our mental categories, with the way we relate to others, with our way of identifying with the Lord, with our cultural milieu, with our social class, in other words, with all that can stand in the way of a real, profound solidarity with those who suffer. . . . Only thus, and not through purely interior and spiritual attitudes, will the "new person" arise from the ashes of "old."

    Gutiérrez, *A Theology of Liberation*, p. 205. See also Stookey, *Baptism*, pp. 37-40.

20. "Thanksgiving Over the Water," from the service of Holy Baptism, *The Book of Common Prayer* (New York: The Church Hymnal Corporation, 1977), pp. 306-7.

Chapter 6

1. Conzelmann says the Corinthian perversion arose,

    > . . . because the Corinthians were crude sacramentalists (along the lines of the mystery religions). They thought that sacramental food worked as a substance. Each ate it for himself. This pneumatic individualism destroyed fellowship. Paul does not appeal to the Corinthians to recognize the sacramental significance of the consecrated food—they do that already. They should rather understand that the sacrament takes place in the context of the church and is thus to be actualized by the realization of their

community. *An Outline of the Theology of the New Testament*, trans. by John Bowden (New York: Harper & Row, 1969), pp. 52-53.

See also Oscar Cullmann and F. J. Leenhardt, *Essays on the Lord's Supper* (London: Lutterworth Press, 1958), p. 5-23; Willi Marxsen, *The Lord's Supper as a Christological Problem* (Philadelphia: Fortress Press, 1970), pp. 11-14, and Duffy, *Real Presence*, pp. 4-28, 133-55. Paul's concern was "not that the Corinthians are profaning a holy rite but that they are fragmenting a holy society." W. Orr and J. Walther, *I Corinthians* (Garden City, N.Y.: Doubleday & Co., 1976), p. 269.

2. John Wesley, "The Duty of Constant Communion," Sermon CI, p. 148.

3. John Wesley, *Forty-Four Sermons* (London: Epworth Press, 1944), p. 523.

4. It is in a combination of these [inward orientation and outward expression] that he [Wesley] sees sanctity. Entire sanctification becomes a perfecting of the personality . . . to Wesley, perfection is not only perfection in actual acts; it embraces as well the whole disposition which lies behind them, the soul with all its tempers. He sees perfection as perfection in obedience too, but this is an expression of the inward perfection of the individual personality or character. . . . Thus to Wesley perfection means the perfected and harmonious personality.

Harold Lindstrom, *Wesley and Sanctification* (Nashville: Abingdon Press, 1946), pp. 158-59.

In his writing on ethics, Barth defines santification in this way:

Sanctifying . . . is, in the language of the Bible, very generally an action in which someone or something is lifted out of the secularity of the surrounding world and his or its own previous existence, dedicated to the service of God (often cultically), and made worthy and suitable for this purpose. Sanctification means the separation, claiming, commandeering, and preparation of a person, place or object with a view to this higher purpose destined for them. *The Christian Life*, trans. G. W. Bromiley (Grand Rapids, Michigan: Wm. B. Eerdman's Publishing Co, 1981), p. 157.

5. From Bard Thompson, *Liturgies of the Western Church* (New York: World Publishing Co., 1961), pp. 277-78.

6. *Ibid.*, p. 281.

7. In post–World War II theology's attempt to recover the primal emphasis on justification, it neglected sanctification. In an instant-gratification, youth-infatuated, push-button society, we lost sight of the Christian faith as something that requires

long-term struggle and work, "going on to perfection," as Wesley might say. John Macquarrie reminds us:

> The Christian life, with its demand for self-giving love and for continual growth in likeness to Christ, lays a fundamental and extremely difficult demand upon those who embark upon it. Saints who have spent a lifetime in learning, growing and developing, still bemoan their lack of proficiency in following the Christian way. . . . we hear of sudden conversions, but we usually find that these have been preparing over a considerable time in the minds of the people concerned; . . . such people do not attain to complete and mature Christian character the moment after conversion.
>
> There are no short cuts from faith (the conviction that Christ is Lord and is love sovereign) to life (the acting out of this faith in daily deeds of self-giving love). On the contrary, this is for most people a long and arduous way. . . . Worship, both in its corporate exercise and in whatever other acts may be appropriate to each individual, is the discipline leading from faith to action. It is the process by which the disciple is formed and becomes increasingly mature in the Christian religion. . . .
>
> True worship is . . . work which issues in the most valuable results. . . . it is *creative* work. It is creating persons of spiritual depth, and through them the creative Spirit will reach out further still. *Paths in Spirituality* pp. 16-18.

See also Richard Foster, *Celebration of Discipline* (New York: Harper & Row, 1978), and Gustafson's use of "piety" in *Ethics from a Theocentric Perspective*, p. 201.

8. Jürgen Moltmann, *The Church and the Power of the Spirit* (New York: Harper & Row, 1977), p. 258.

9. Unfortunately, the peace eventually degenerated into a schematic, stylized gesture. In the Eastern church it was reduced to a greeting between the priest and congregation before the eucharistic prayer. In the West, it became a mere accolade exchanged by the ministers before communion. Fortunately, modern liturgical innovation has attempted (with varying degrees of success) to reintroduce the peace as an act of the whole congregation. This is an essential connection between worship and ethics, a "ritual hinge between social ethics and common praise."

Wainwright, *Doxology*, p. 143.

10. Thompson, *Liturgies*, p. 9. In our earliest complete account of a Christian eucharist, note the explicit ethically formative or ethically active aspects of this celebration:

> The rich among us come to the aid of the poor, and we always stay together. . . . On the day which is called Sunday, all who live in the cities or in the countryside gather together in one place. And the memoirs of the apostles or the writings of the prophets are read as long as there is time. Then, when the reader has finished, the president, in a discourse, admonishes and invites the people to

practice these examples of virtue. Then we all stand up together and offer prayers. And, as we mentioned before, when we have finished the prayer, bread is presented, and wine with water; the president likewise offers up prayers and thanksgivings according to his ability, and the people assent by saying, Amen. The elements which have been "eucharistized" are distributed and received by each one; and they are sent to the absent by the deacons. Those who are prosperous, as they wish, contribute what each one deems appropriate; and the collection is deposited with the president; and he takes care of the orphans and widows, and those who are needy because of sickness or other cause, and the captives, and the strangers who sojourn amongst us—in brief he is the curate of all who are in need.

11. *We Gather Together*, Supplemental Worship Resources 10 (Nashville: The United Methodist Publishing House, 1980), p. 10. See George Webber's account of the celebration of the Lord's Supper in East Harlem Protestant Parish in M. J. Taylor, ed., *Liturgical Renewal in the Christian Churches* (Baltimore: Helicon, 1967), Webber says of their communion,

> The whole family eats together, remembering that we are united again to Christ and to one another and are given the food of life that we might enter into God's work. Here is truly a sign of the truth of the Gospel that in Christ there is neither rich nor poor, male nor female, bond or free, Puerto Rican, Negro, white—that transcends all human barriers. (pp. 66-67)

12. Robert Hovda, "The Ethical Demands of the Eucharist—Reflections on the Context of Celebration," *Living Worship*, August-September, 1978.

13. The radical reformer Zwingli, whatever his limitations as a eucharistic theologian, should at least be given credit for his early recovery of the meal at the Lord's Supper as a principal expression of the love and communion of Christians with explicit ethical connotations. See A. C. Cochrane, *Eating and Drinking with Jesus: An Ethical and Biblical Inquiry* (Philadelphia: The Westminster Press, 1974).

14. Joachim Jeremias, *The Eucharistic Words of Jesus* (Philadelphia: Fortress Press, 1966), pp. 179-82, 225-31.

15. The celebration of the risen Christ by the assembly of believers is one of the most effective political actions that men can perform in this world—if it is true that this celebration, by contesting any power system which oppresses mankind, proclaims, stirs up and inaugurates a new order in the created world.

Gonzalez and Gonzalez, *Liberation Preaching: The Pulpit and the Oppressed,* p. 70.

Neill Q. Hamilton divides American Protestants into the

liberal "Public Party Protestants" who often neglect the formation of the church and try to impose watered-down notions of justice on society at large, and the evangelical "Private Party Protestants" who neglect justice in the church and confine ethics to private, personal concerns, *Recovery of the Protestant Adventure* (New York: The Seabury Press, 1981), pp. 179ff. In the church, "reform begins at home," p. 208.

16. Stanley Hauerwas, *Truthfulness and Tragedy* (Notre Dame, Ind.: University of Notre Dame Press, 1977), pp. 142-43. Mark Searle argues,

> The justice of God presented in the liturgy is anything but an abstraction, for the liturgy of the Church sacramentalizes the presence of Christ, the Just One. For that reason, and for that reason alone, we can say that the liturgy not only proclaims the justice of the Kingdom of God as something to be done but actually renders it present, not as an achievement of ours but as a gift of God. In its presence we are confronted with that which we are called to be, with that which God would make us be, if we permit it. Thus the liturgy not only provides us with a moral ideal but confronts us with an ontological reality in the light of which the ambivalence of our own lives is revealed for what it is.

"Serving the Lord with Justice," in *The Liturgy and Social Justice* (Collegeville, Minn.: The Litugical Press, 1980), pp. 28-29.

17. The separation in the church which Gutiérrez criticizes in a capitalist society could be criticized in Third World totalitarian regimes as well,

> Living in a capitalist society in which one class confronts another, the Church, in the measure that its presence increases, cannot escape—nor try to ignore any longer—the profound division among its members. . . . the extreme seriousness of the situation even places some Christians among the oppressed and persecuted and others among the oppressors and persecutors, ... Under such circumstances, life in the contemporary Christian community becomes particularly difficult and conflictual. Participation in the eucharist, for example, as it is celebrated today, appears to many to be an action which, without an authentic Christian community underlying it, becomes an exercise in make-believe.

Gustavo Gutiérrez, *A Theology of Liberation,* p. 137.

In his foreword to Tissa Balasuriya's *The Eucharist and Human Liberation* (Maryknoll, N.Y.: Orbis Books, 1978), the Bishop of Badulla says, "This most liberative act [the eucharist] has been so domesticated by socioeconomic systems that it now enslaves and domesticates its participants." See also, Christopher Kiesling, "Liturgy and Social Justice," *Worship,* July, 1977.

18. As Barth says,

> In divine service there takes place that which does not take place anywhere else in the community. In divine service the sabbath intervenes between six working days on the one side and six more on the other. In it it exchanges its working clothes for its festal attire. It is now an event as community. Unpretentiously but distinctly it stands out from the secularity of its environment in which it is for the most part submerged. It now casts off the anonymity of that which is distinctive and common to it; the occasional and haphazard and private character elsewhere assumed by its manifestation. It now exists and acts in concrete actuality and visibilty as the congregation to which many individuals—each from his own human and Christian place in dispersion—come together to one place at one time in order that together, occupying the same space and time, they may realize the *communio sanctorum* in a definite form . . . in divine service it exists and acts prophetically in relation to the world to the extent that in divine service—and here alone directly—there is a serious discharge of its commission to be a provisional representation of humanity as it is sanctified in Jesus Christ. *Church Dogmatics,* vol. 4, pp. 697-98.

19. See chapter 4 of my *The Bible in Worship* on the significance of the meals with Jesus in Luke–Acts.

Chapter 7

1. Karl Rahner says that abstract preaching leads to preaching in which "abstract principles become increasingly abstract and are liable to carry within themselves the danger of a terrifying sterility." *The Shape of the Church to Come* (London: SPCK, 1974), p. 77. Liberation theology often criticizes European and North American theology for its use of metaphysics and philosophical abstraction. But theologians of liberation violate their own methodology by beginning with an abstract, generalized category like "liberation." Part of the attractiveness of metaphors like liberation is that one can assign any content one desires.

2. Richard Lischer, *A Theology of Preaching* (Nashville: Abingdon, 1981), p. 58.

3. Reinhold Niebuhr, *Leaves from the Notebook of a Tamed Cynic* (Chicago: Willett, Clark, and Colby, 1929), p. 29.

4. Albert Outler, *Psychotherapy and the Christian Message,* pp. 32-33.

5. E. P. Sanders says that we have done Paul a disservice by reading him through the eyes of Luther on this matter of law and gospel. Sanders shows that, for Paul, the problem with

Judaism is not that it is legalistic, but that it is not Christianity—it is not a new community based upon the astounding story of the person and work of Jesus. *Paul and Palestinian Judaism* (Philadelphia: Fortress Press, 1977), p. 552.

I wonder, with Stanley Hauerwas, if the rigorous application of the law-gospel typology is an admission that we no longer have a community which is capable of making sense out of our moral convictions. Once the communal linkage between our convictions and our actions is broken, no amount of conceptual clarification can restore it. Hauerwas, *A Community of Character*, pp. 98-99, 132-36.

6. David Kelsey, *The Uses of Scripture in Recent Theology* (Philadelphia: Fortress Press, 1975), pp. 208-9.

7. See my chapter on "theocentric" preaching in *The Bible in Worship*, chapter 6.

8. James A. Sanders, "Hermeneutics," *The Interpreter's Dictionary of the Bible, Supplementary Volume* (Nashville: Abingdon Press, 1976), p. 406.

9. Paul E. Dinter, "Preaching and the Inquiring of God," *Worship*, May 1978.

10. J. G. Davies, *Worship and Mission*, p. 37.

11. John Knox, *The Integrity of Preaching* (Nashville: Abingdon Press, 1957), "Effective ethical preaching . . . is confessional preaching" (p. 83).

12. Walker Percy, commenting upon the then current "secular theology," made an observation which could apply as well to any ideology without a theocentric focus.

> What is most noticeable about the new theology . . . is the triviality . . . what is served up is small potatoes indeed. What does the Christian do with his God dead and His name erased? It is proposed that he give more time to the political party of his choice or perhaps make a greater effort to be civil to salesladies and shoe clerks. . . . The positive proposals of the new theology must sound like a set of resolutions passed at the P.T.A. *The Message in the Bottle* (New York: Farrar, Straus, & Giroux, 1975), pp. 113-14.

13. Walter Burghardt, quotes an Irish layman who expresses the affectional, alluring, evocative quality of truly ethical preaching:

> Our preachers entirely ignore what we, the silent faithful, expect to hear in a sermon. . . . They address us as rebels whom they must subdue; as idlers whom they must shake up; as hardened sinners whom they must needs terrify; as the proud who require to be humiliated; as the self-satisfied who need to be disquieted. . . .

NOTES FOR PAGES 155-64

[They] are never done telling us of our duties and of our neglect of duty. . . . But if you come to examine it, there is really nothing easier than to put forward a person's duty; and to hand out reproaches costs nothing. . . . The thing which is really difficult, which is actually divine, is to give us a taste for our duties and to awaken in us a wish to do them and to be generous in the doing. And another name for a taste of duty is love. Beloved preachers, then, make us love God, or rather, help us to believe in his love for us.

Quoted in "Preaching the Just Word," in *Liturgy and Social Justice* (Collegeville, Minn.: The Liturgical Press, 1980), p. 50. This statement reminds me of Aidan Kavanaugh's remark, "The homiletical task is not to communicate the unknown to the unknowing but to rally the knowing about the known in their midst." *Proclamation 2: Pentecost 1* (Philadelphia: Fortress Press, 1981), p. 7.

14. Burghardt, *Liturgy and Social Justice*, p. 49.
15. I assume that the preacher also preaches by daring to be a doer of the truth; not merely a speaker of the truth (cf. James 1:22-23). All historic Protestant ordination rites ordain pastors to be, not merely preachers, but also pastors who are "examples to the flock." This is why the pastoral context is essential for effective preaching. See my *Integrative Preaching* (Nashville: Abingdon, 1981).

Chapter 8

1. See Rosemary Haughton, *The Theology of Marriage* (Notre Dame, Ind.: Fides Press, 1971) for a history of Christian marriage practices and theology.
2. Paul F. Palmer, S.J. has shown how the promises of Christian marriage were transformed from covenantal promises to contractual promises. The trend today, since Vatican II, is to speak of marriage as a "covenant." Palmer shows the positive significance of this change. My concern here is more basic: to show that the promises of marriage, whether we conceive of these promises as convenantal or contractual, share certain basic characteristics with other promises. "Christian Marriage: Contract or Covenant?" *Theological Studies*, December 1972.
3. Fletcher, *Situation Ethics*, p. 58.
4. J. L. Austin, *How to Do Things with Words* (Oxford: Oxford University Press, 1962).
5. In its condemnation of "secret marriages" the church tried to say that sex is a public matter. Declarations of love that cannot

go public should not be trusted. "For there is surely no area where we are more liable to self-deception than in those contexts where love is mixed with sexual desire." Hauerwas, *Community of Character,* p. 282. As Paul Ramsey says, "Since 'I love you' may simply mean, in all sorts of subtle ways, 'I love *me,* and want *you,'* . . . a person had better subject his love to this severe testing: see if he can promise permanence in love for another person precisely under those conditions, referred to in the expressions 'for worse,' 'for poorer,' and 'in sickness,' under which he will have to give rather than derive benefit from the marriage relationship." *Basic Christian Ethics* (New York: Charles Scribner's Sons, 1950), p. 330.

6. Thomas Aquinas, *Summa contra Gentiles,* 2, 25, 1023.
7. Nicolai Hartmann, *Ethics,* vol. 2, trans. by Stanton Coit (London: Allen & Unwin, 1963), p. 287. While I have argued for marriage from a linguistic view, James F. Gustafson argues for the covenant from human nature in "Nature, Sin, and Covenant: Three Bases for Sexual Ethics," *Perspectives in Biology and Medicine,* Spring 1981.

Chapter 9

1. Gary Wills, "Are Young Americans Afraid to Have Kids?" *Esquire,* March 1974, p. 170.
2. Ellen Peck, *The Baby Trap* (New York: Bernard Geis Associates, 1971).
3. *The Proposed Book of Common Prayer* (New York: Church Hymnal Corporation, 1976), p. 423.
4. *A Service of Christian Marriage: With Introduction, Commentary, and Additional Resources* (Nashville: Abingdon, 1979), p. 15. The idea that procreation was the chief end of marriage was widely debated in the medieval church. See John I. Noonan, Jr., *Contraception: A History of Its Treatment by Catholic Theologians and Canonists* (Cambridge, Mass.: Harvard University Press, 1963), pp. 300-301.
5. Bertrand Russell, *Marriage and Morals* (London: Allen & Unwin, 1929), p. 125.
6. See the argument in Richard Neuhaus, *In Defense of People* (New York: The Macmillan Co., 1971).
7. Barth, *Church Dogmatics,* III, 4, p. 269.
8. Dodds, *Pagan and Christian in an Age of Anxiety.*
9. Tertullian, *On the Soul,* chapter 30, pp. 249-50 (New York: Fathers of the Church, 1950), trans. Arbesmann, *et alia.*

10. W. H. Auden, *Epistle to a Godson and Other Poems* (New York: Random House, 1969).
11. Helmut Thielicke, *The Ethics of Sex* (New York: Harper & Row, 1964), pp. 220-21.
12. Barth, *Church Dogmatics*, III, 4, p. 272. See Hauerwas, *Truthfulness and Tragedy*, pp. 147-54 for a discussion of the limits of the language of choice when applied to having children.
13. Hauerwas, *Truthfulness and Tragedy*, pp. 147-54.
14. See Willimon and Westerhoff, III, *Liturgy and Learning Through the Life Cycle*, chapters 1, 4, and 9 for a discussion of specific ways a church might care for parents and children through its pastoral offices.
15. Hauerwas, *Truthfulness and Tragedy*, p. 143.
16. Philip Roth, *The Professor of Desire* (Des Plaines, Ill.: Bantam Books, 1978).

Chapter 10

1. From *The First Apology* of Justin Martyr, para. 65, in Bard Thompson, ed. *Liturgies of the Western Church*, p. 8.
2. From *The Apostolic Tradition* of Hippolytus, section 4, in *ibid.*
3. W. Jardine Grisbrooke, "Oblation at the Eucharist," *Studia Liturgia*, III, 4 (1964), pp. 227-39.
4. This, and the next two quotes are from "The Sacrament of the Lord's Supper or Holy Communion," *The Book of Worship* (Nashville: The Methodist Publishing House, 1964), pp. 20-22.
5. Even with all these disclaimers, Cranmer's Holy Communion is noted for its rather long post-communion prayers that stress the ethical results and benefits of our communion.
6. *We Gather Together*, pp. 9-10.
7. Gustafson, *Can Ethics Be Christian?*, pp. 102-3.

   A number of attempts have been made to develop Christian ethics from the standpoint of gratitude. Barth's final lecture fragments on ethics stress gratitude as the chief motivating factor in ethics. Karl Barth, *The Christian Life*. A. C. Cochrane's *Eating And Drinking with Jesus* is notable for its Zwinglian based move from the gratitude of the Lord's Supper to ethics. See also G. Wainwright, *Doxology*, chapter 12.
8. Thompson, ed. *Liturgies*, p. 280.
9. See the Hippolytan Anaphora on pages 20-21 in Thompson, *ibid.*

10. "We Give Thee but Thine Own," Hymn # 181, *The Book of Hymns* (Nashville: The Methodist Publishing House, 1966).
11. "When I Survey The Wondrous Cross," Hymn # 435, *Book of Hymns.*
12. Cited in Wainwright, *Doxology,* p. 423.
13. Barth, *Church Dogmatics,* III, 4, p. 13 (emphasis added).
14. From *Grooks* by Piet Hein, quoted in Charles D. Barrett, *Understanding the Christian Faith* (Englewood Cliffs, N.J.: Prentice-Hall, 1980), p. 20.
15. Augustine, Sermon 272, quoted in Melissa Kay, ed. *It Is Your Own Mystery* (Washington: The Liturgical Conference, 1977), p. 1.

Index

Second Vatican Council, 16, 23, 49, 136
Self-forgetfulness, 81-90
Sellars, J., 206 n.
Sermons. (*See* Preaching)
Service of the Word, 147
Sex, 176-85, 232 n.
Shepherd, M., 15
Sin, 82-83, 105, 107-9, 133, 223 n.
Situation Ethics, 23-27, 30, 33, 35, 162, 164, 206 n.
Stookey, L. H., 222 n., 224 n.
Story, 45, 50, 75, 87, 92, 142, 145-46, 150-51
Sweet, L. I., 221 n.
Symbols, 56-58, 102, 138, 214 n., 216 n.

Tannehill, R. C., 224 n.
Tawney, R. H., 208-9 n.
Temple, Archbishop W., 40
Teresa of Calcutta, 197
Tertullian, 74, 109, 117, 180-81
Thielicke, H., 182
Tillich, P., 27
Tradition, 69-71, 89, 219 n.
Turgenev, 221 n.

Utilitarianism, 20, 34, 42-43, 151

Virtue, 32-33, 80, 83

Vision, 34-37, 42, 53, 56, 61, 63-69, 84-85, 86, 108, 125, 128-29, 156, 210-11 n., 217-18 n.

Wainwright, G., 227 n.
Washington St. United Methodist Church, 53-56
Watts, I., 198
Webber, G., 227 n.
Weddings. (*See* Marriage)
Weil, S., 218 n.
Wesley, J., 29, 31, 40, 123-24, 126, 198
Westerhoff, J. H., 12, 233 n.
Westminster Shorter Catechism, 64
White, J. F., 212 n.
Whitehead, A. N., 66
William of Ockham, 161-62
Willimon, W. H., 219 n., 229 n., 230 n., 231 n., 233 n.
Wills, G., 171
Women, 49, 57
"World," the liturgical, 51-56
Worship, definition of, 16-17, 18

Yankelovich, D., 208 n.
Year, liturgical, 70, 89-90

Zwingli, 123, 227 n., 234 n.